WORLD WAR II
ON THE WEB

WORLD WAR II
ON THE WEB

A GUIDE TO THE VERY BEST SITES

J. DOUGLAS SMITH and RICHARD JENSEN

A Scholarly Resources Inc. Imprint
Wilmington, Delaware

Scholarly Resources Inc.
104 Greenhill Avenue
Wilmington, DE 19805-1897
www.scholarly.com

Library of Congress Cataloging-in-Publication Data

Smith, J. Douglas
    World War II on the web : a guide to the very best sites / J. Douglas Smith,
Richard Jensen.
        p. cm
    Includes bibliographical references.
    ISBN 0-8420-5020-5 (cloth : alk. paper)—ISBN 0-8420-5021-3 (paper : alk.
paper)
        1. World War, 1939–1945—Computer network resources—Directories. 2. Web
    sites—Directories. I. Title: World War 2 on the Web. II. Title: World War Two
    on the Web. III. Jensen, Richard J. IV. Title.

D743 .S55 2003
025.06'94053—dc21   2002029236

To Jo and Liz

To Katherine and Sarah

CONTENTS

PART I I

SITES WORTH A VISIT—A TOPICAL INDEX

Unit Histories   202

About the Authors   207

INTRODUCTION AND USER'S GUIDE

J. DOUGLAS SMITH

In the last decade, interest among Americans in World War II has expanded exponentially. As those men and women who lived through the war begin to age, an entire industry has turned its attention to documenting their lives. The sacrifice, heroism, and virtues of the "greatest generation" have been the subject of countless books, films such as *Saving Private Ryan,* and the HBO miniseries *Band of Brothers.* The evidence of this fascination is readily available on the World Wide Web as well. One year ago, entering "World War II" or "World War Two" into a search engine such as Google produced 1.8 million hits. Today, the same search terms prompt between 2.5 and 3 million hits.

Professional scholars, amateur historians, educators, students, genealogists, and World War II enthusiasts should delight in the accessibility of World War II–related primary documents on the World Wide Web. On the Internet, researchers can find diplomatic correspondence, government documents, official after action reports, letters and diaries from soldiers in Europe and the Pacific, a staggering array of photographs and other visual material, and oral histories from Holocaust survivors, combatants, and those who remained on the home front. These resources, however, are often difficult to find and, in fact, are becoming more difficult to locate as the number of web pages proliferates. Furthermore, the majority of World War II–related sites will not interest serious researchers. Some are no more than lists of links to other sites, while others contain little more than an announcement of an impending veterans' reunion. Researchers are likely to become frustrated as they try to identify the few sites with truly high-quality material.

Unlike search engines and links pages, this book identifies only those sites that are of value to serious researchers. Instead of a series of lists, this guide provides reviews to the 100 best World War II web pages on the World Wide Web. Some of those reviewed in *World War II on the Web* were created and are maintained by dedicated individuals who have worked for years without remuneration. At times, the navigation and web design of some of these sites reflect a lack of resources and technical expertise. Others represent the combined efforts of professional historians and archivists, graphic designers, and programmers. Each site reviewed, however, whether maintained by amateurs or professionals, contains valuable material on some aspect of World War II. Without a doubt, content was the single most important factor in determining a site's selection. Aesthetics and navigation were important criteria, and web pages hampered by poor appearance or navigational problems were generally disqualified, but no site was selected for review based on aesthetics and navigation alone.

Most of the sites included here contain rich collections of primary source material that allow students, educators, genealogists, academic scholars, and lay historians to reach their own conclusions about the most salient issues pertaining to World War II. Letters, diaries, speeches, contemporary newspaper accounts, official government documents, oral histories, and photographs dominate the best of the web sites discussed in this book. Some of the reviewed sites, on the other hand, reflect secondary treatments of key questions or individuals, but they were included because they contain information not readily available elsewhere. For instance, a site that excerpts a widely circulating biography of a well-known World War II leader would not warrant consideration for review, but several publications of the U.S. Army's Center for Military History are included because they contain secondary information on subjects such as the Army Nurse Corps and the Women's Army Corps. Furthermore, the sites reviewed in *World War II on the Web* make effective use of the medium of the Internet. The best sites reviewed here feature innovative navigation and searching techniques possible only on the web. In reviewing only 100 sites, this book emphasizes quality over quantity. Taken together, these sites offer endless opportunities for exploration and research.

The reviews are organized into ten chapters. The book opens with "A World at War," which includes reviews of web sites containing documents, maps, and timelines that provide a general overview of World War II. The remaining nine chapters, on the other hand, focus on a specific aspect of the war. Some of the sites are reviewed in multiple chapters since they contain material relevant to topics discussed in more than one chapter. The seventeen reviews in "Photographs, Posters, and Propaganda—World War II in Pictures," for instance, are all cross-listed, a clear reflection of the stunning wealth of World War II–related visual material available on the Internet. For the most part, and wherever appropriate, cross-listed reviews have been tailored to emphasize the theme of the particular chapter in which they appear.

Each chapter opens with an introduction that provides an overview of its subject and serves as a jumping off point to the reviews themselves. The reviews give a detailed description of the site's subject matter, content, and structure and provide some navigational hints. Each review ends with ratings of the site's content, aesthetics, and navigation, with five stars indicating "excellent," four stars indicating "good," and three stars indicating "average." A list of suggested readings at the end of the chapter invites the reader to explore the theme discussed in greater detail.

Although all of the sites were selected for the high quality of their content, some sites are, quite simply, better than others. In general, those sites that received only three stars for content either lack primary source material or contain less of it than those sites that received four or five stars. The ratings for aesthetics and navigation tend to be lower than those for content, a clear indication that most of the sites reviewed here were not made by professional web designers but by librarians, archivists, students, and educators. The few sites that earned five stars for navigation are those that cleanly separate historic content from other information, give researchers a clear sense of what lies behind each link, allow easy movement from section to section, and invite visitors to chart their own paths through the material. Of the three categories, aesthetics generally shows the lowest ratings, with quite a few sites earning only three stars. The pages in these sites are generally well laid out but make clumsy use of background images, colors, headings, or icons. Sites earning four stars in aesthetics have clean designs and effective graphics, and the few sites with five stars for this category warrant special mention.

The topical index in Part II provides names, addresses, and short descriptions of 250 World War II web sites. Most of them were not deemed "Best of the Web" and so are not reviewed in Part I. Although the sites in this category provide valuable historic content, they generally do not have the level of scholarly engagement, depth of analysis, or breadth of coverage exhibited by the reviewed sites. Nevertheless, they are still worth a visit. Furthermore, some very good sites were not reviewed because of a plethora of strong sites in certain categories, such as the Holocaust, Japanese American internment (see Chapter 6, "The Home Front"), and personal accounts from soldiers.

Creating a print guide to web sites is certainly a risky undertaking. Most web sites, including many of the ones reviewed and listed here, are works in progress, and the layout, navigation, and content can be altered fundamentally without notice. Readers of this book may find that some of the sites reviewed have been revised considerably since the time the review was written. Fortunately, these changes are generally for the better, providing new material, better appearance, and improved design.

Unfortunately, web sites vanish all the time—just like books go out of print. With this in mind, every effort has been made to review sites that stand a better than average chance of remaining operational (for instance, web pages maintained by government agencies or universities are less likely to disappear). Nevertheless, it is quite possible that 20 to 25 percent of the sites in this book will succumb to "link rot" and either move or disappear altogether within a year. If a site has moved, the old site will usually provide a link to the new location. If a site has disappeared, visitors should attempt to access the site via the Internet Archive, http://www.archive.org, which stores old web sites. Archived sites may prove accessible, but visitors should expect some problems. For instance, British Forces in

World War Two (http://british-forces.com/worldwar2/index.html) originally warranted a review in this book but disappeared right before publication. Its home page can still be accessed via the Internet Archive, but most of the links to individual pages are broken. If researchers are unable to find a link to a new address, and if the archived site proves unhelpful, try entering the name of a site as keywords at http://www.google.com.

The World Wide Web hosts exciting possibilities for research into all aspects of World War II. At the same time, professional scholars and lay historians must be aware of the potential for abuse. Nowhere is distortion more evident in the context of World War II than with regard to Holocaust denial. Numerous sites on the web openly deny that the Holocaust occurred. No denial site has been reviewed in this book, but Chapter 8 does include reviews of several sites specifically devoted to combating Holocaust denial. Researchers, and especially educators who encourage their students to use the web, must approach with special caution those sites that claim to be nonpolitical and not pro-Nazi but that in fact present a highly distorted view of history that serves the goals of deniers. For instance, the Hitler Museum claims not to support the views of Hitler, but its site curiously omits any mention of the Final Solution and provides links to overt denial sites.

Several people deserve special thanks for their contributions to this book. Alice E. Carter and William G. Thomas developed the very concept for *World War II on the Web* in *The Civil War on the Web: A Guide to the Very Best Sites* (Wilmington, DE, 2001). The explanation of the ratings system and the criteria for selecting sites for review, as outlined above, are drawn directly from Carter's "User's Guide" to *The Civil War on the Web*. Carter's words have been slightly modified to meet the specific needs of this volume on World War II. Courtney Spikes provided invaluable research assistance. Matt Hershey of Scholarly Resources nurtured this project from its inception and brought it to fruition. Christina Catanzarite applied her immense copyediting skills to the manuscript and, in the process, made this a better book. Richard Jensen stepped forward at a critical juncture and wrote the chapter introductions; this book would not have been completed without his substantial contributions. Most of all, many thanks to the individuals who have labored intensively to create and maintain the best World War II sites on the World Wide Web.

THE VERY BEST
WORLD WAR II
WEB SITES

REVIEWS

AND

RATINGS

CHAPTER 1

A
WORLD
AT
WAR

During World War II, every continent and every major country was involved in a total war effort for their survival and ability to shape the postwar world. The basic encyclopedias, such as *Encarta* (available online at http://encarta.msn.com/), briefly review each country's involvement in the war. Before, during, and after the war, the major and minor powers engaged in urgent diplomacy. There is no site on the web yet where these complications are unraveled; the best resource for learning about war diplomacy is the magisterial history by leading American scholar Gerhard Weinberg, *A World at Arms: A Global History of World War II* (1994).

Although America did not fully enter the war until Pearl Harbor in December 1941, the major European powers went to war in September 1939. Why the war began is a very complicated question. A solid treatise on diplomatic history, such as Weinberg's *A World at Arms* or Keith Eubank's brief *The Origins of World War II* (1990), is a good starting point for gaining a basic understanding of the causes of the war. For elaborate detail see two books by leading British scholars: Donald Cameron Watt, *How War Came: The Immediate Origins of the Second World War, 1938–1939* (1989), and Richard Overy and Andrew Wheatcroft, *The Road to War: The Origins of World War II* (1989).

After this background reading the next resource for learning about the causes of the war is the top-level documents and agreements available at Yale's Avalon Project, which is reviewed in this chapter. A recommended place to start is *The British War Blue Book* at http://www.yale.edu/lawweb/avalon/wwii/bluebook/blbkmenu.htm. (The name comes from the original blue paper cover, which indicated an official publication of the

British government.) Other countries prepared similar books; for example, *The French Yellow Book* is also on Avalon (http://www.yale.edu/lawweb/avalon/wwii/yellow/ylbkmenu.htm). The purpose of these books was to provide detailed justification for going to war in 1939 to citizens who wanted proof that the enemy was really as bad as their government claimed. The *Blue Book* contains over 140 documents, most of them previously secret, that show the diplomatic maneuvers of Britain, Poland, Germany, the Soviet Union, America, and the other powers that led to the outbreak of war. It contains a useful section entitled "List of Principal Persons Mentioned in the Documents, Showing Their Official Positions."

Europe went to war in 1939 over the German invasion of Poland. Until then the British had been "appeasing" Hitler by yielding to his demands. One of the most important of these attempts to keep Hitler contained was the Munich Conference in 1938, at which Britain, France, and Italy approved Hitler's breakup of Czechoslovakia. Key documents from Munich are included in the Avalon Project. Historians continue to debate the meaning and wisdom of the appeasement policy, and readers should be aware of three major interpretations of it. The first is that appeasement was a terrible mistake—it only rewarded and encouraged aggression. Adherents of this line of thought believe that Britain and France should have made a much stronger military stand against Germany, preferably as early as 1936, when Berlin moved its troops into the Rhineland (an area of Germany that had been demilitarized by the Treaty of Versailles in 1919). A second interpretation supports appeasement, which was promoted by British Prime Minister Neville Chamberlain. He promised it would bring "peace in our time." His position was quite popular at the time; he was supported by the pacifist movement, which was fairly strong in Britain and America in the 1930s and which recoiled at the horror of another devastating war. A third argument, propounded by the British military, is that in 1939 it was too weak to stand up to Hitler; it desperately needed more time to rearm, especially to build new warplanes that could handle the Luftwaffe, and also to finish its secret weapon, a radar system that would enable its new warplanes to oppose the much larger German bomber force. For the last sixty years the first argument has dominated American thought about war and peace. References to "appeasement" and "Munich" have been used by American policymakers to justify strong action against aggressive dictators.

The debate over America's entry into the war focuses on President Franklin Roosevelt and Pearl Harbor. All historians agree that Roosevelt strongly favored a victory by Britain and the Soviet Union over Germany and that he promised repeatedly to support them by providing munitions but not American soldiers. America should be the "Arsenal of Democracy," he proclaimed. Isolationists at the time believed that Roosevelt was secretly maneuvering the United States into the war despite the public's desire to remain uninvolved. War came at Pearl Harbor on December 7, 1941, however, and two very different interpretations of who was responsible for the attack emerged.

According to the "orthodox" view (held by Roosevelt and the great majority of poli-cymakers and historians), Japan instigated the tensions with the United States in its attempts to control China and the rest of East Asia. The United States strongly favored China and repeatedly warned Japan to stop its expansion. When Japan joined Germany and Italy in the Axis Alliance and then seized French Indonesia (Vietnam), Roosevelt cut off the sale of oil to Japan. Japan imported 90 percent of its oil and had to nego-tiate a settlement or go to war. It chose war. The "revisionist" historians (led by Charles Beard) hold that Roosevelt was as guilty as Japan for Pearl Harbor because he forced Japan into the needless war. According to this view, Roosevelt wanted to go to war with Germany, but since public opinion did not support such a move, he provoked Japan into attacking Pearl Harbor, thus producing the war he wanted. Some extreme revisionists go even further and argue that Roosevelt knew about Japan's plans but did not warn the navy because the attack would allow him to enter the war. Pearl Harbor has been investigated at length, and many of the key documents can be found online. No one has ever found a "smoking gun" that proves that Roosevelt, Churchill, or anyone else knew about Japan's planned attack.

The United States and Britain both prepared excellent multivolume official histories of the entire war, as did some smaller countries. The U.S. Navy series, by eminent historian Samuel Eliot Morison, is available in most libraries and bookstores; the one-volume abridgement, *The Two Ocean War,* is also good. The official U.S. Air Force history was edited by eminent scholars Wesley Frank Craven and James Lea Cate and published in seven large volumes as *The Army Air Forces in World War II,* now out of print but available in good libraries and online through www.abe.com, an online bookstore that specializes in used, rare, and out-of-print titles.

The U.S. Army's Center for Military History (CMH) prepared seventy-eight excellent volumes on American involvement in the war; seven can be found online at the CMH web site at http://www.army.mil/cmh-pg/catalog/WWII-Pubs.htm (see review below). Many of the volumes are also available on CD-ROM through www.wae.com, which is described as "the world's only CD ROM reseller specializing in history, military history, military interest and aviation CD ROM publications." The first volume of the excellent marine corps official history is online as well. In general, the official his-tories are recommended for specialists who have already read some of the more popular histories. Anyone who *starts* with the official histories will quickly get bogged down in minutiae.

The study of a worldwide conflict requires a good supply of maps. Many are avail-able on the web, ranging from very small-scale depictions of the entire Pacific the-ater to large-scale, highly detailed maps of a specific battle. Missing from the web are animated maps that show the movement of forces, either over hundreds of miles or on a specific battlefield. Someone with the right computer skills should try his or her hand at animated GIFs or other formats.

For daily discussions among scholars and experts on military history topics, especially regarding World War II, take a look at the daily email list H-WAR, edited by university professors, at http://www2.h-net.msu.edu/~war/. One can read the daily logs, search for a topic, or even subscribe (for free) and ask a question.

WEB SITE REVIEWS

DOCUMENTS

American War Library: World War II Files Menu
http://members.aol.com/forcountry/ww2/ww2menu.htm

The World War II Files Menu gathers together nearly fifty speeches and primary documents on various aspects of the war. This collection is a small part, and by no means the primary focus, of a site run by the American War Library, the world's oldest and largest online military and veterans registry, whose stated mission is to catalogue the name and pertinent information of every person who has served in the American military.

Researchers looking for material on the start of World War II will find speeches and proclamations from Adolf Hitler, Edouard Daladier, and Neville Chamberlain issued between September 1 and 3, 1939. All four of Franklin Roosevelt's inaugural speeches, along with his "Day of Infamy" speech, "Four Freedoms" speech, and a prayer on the occasion of D-Day, are collected on this site. An extensive list of quotations from soldiers, generals, politicians, and war correspondents is particularly interesting. Finally, the World War II Files Menu includes combat-related statistical summaries pertaining to troops as well as weapons, aircraft, submarines, and other equipment.

These materials are certainly useful to researchers, although the content is somewhat limited in terms of quantity and focus. The navigation from the American War Library's home page and registry to the World War II Files Menu is quite confusing, but the address cited above takes one straight to the relevant documents. The Files Menu itself is organized in a straightforward, easy-to-navigate manner, and the site is aesthetically attractive.

CONTENT   ★ ★ ★
AESTHETICS   ★ ★ ★ ★
NAVIGATION   ★ ★ ★

The Avalon Project: World War II Documents
http://www.yale.edu/lawweb/avalon/wwii/wwii.htm

The Avalon Project at Yale Law School has amassed a treasury of primary documents relating to law, history, and diplomacy from the second century B.C. to the present. The Avalon Project: World War II Documents does not include military planning materials and orders of battle, but the collection of legal and diplomatic documents presented here is unsurpassed by any other online source. Beautiful graphics, easy navigation, and substantive content make this site one of the very best on any aspect of World War II.

Researchers will find presidential and congressional proclamations, the full text of the Atlantic Charter, and the terms of the Lend-Lease Agreement signed in February 1942 between Churchill and Roosevelt, as well as the unabridged proceedings of every major World War II conference, including Tehran, Cairo, Casablanca, Yalta, and Potsdam. The site includes correspondence between Japanese and American officials in the days preceding Pearl Harbor, the subsequent declarations of war, and the surrender documents between the various combatants. Diplomatic materials pertaining to postwar Europe, such as the June 5, 1945, "Declaration Regarding the Defeat of Germany," can also be found on this site.

The Avalon Project: World War II Documents is not limited to American diplomatic materials. *The French Yellow Book* and *The British War Blue Book*, each of which contains hundreds, if not thousands, of documents, are posted in their entirety. In *The British War Blue Book*, researchers will find statements from Adolf Hitler beginning in the mid-1930s along with more than one hundred communiqués that detail the deterioration in relations between Britain and Germany, ending with Germany's invasion of Poland. The *Blue Book* also includes messages from Roosevelt to Hitler sent in August 1939 in a last minute attempt to prevent war.

The Avalon Project contains an entire section devoted to Nazi-Soviet relations from 1939 to 1941, as well as the complete transcripts of the Nuremberg Trials (see Chapter 8 for a separate review of Nuremberg material). Without a doubt, researchers will find the Avalon Project: World War II Documents a tremendous resource; teachers who want to expose their students to primary materials will deem this site an absolute must visit.

For a review of the materials related to the Nuremberg Trials on this site, see p. 139.

CONTENT   ★ ★ ★ ★ ★
AESTHETICS ★ ★ ★ ★ ★
NAVIGATION ★ ★ ★ ★ ★

The Center for Military History WWII Online Bookshelves
http://www.army.mil/cmh-pg/collections/USAWW2/USAWW2.htm

The resources available on the U.S. Army's CMH's web page are simply astounding. The CMH site is so extensive that it can appear daunting and at times confusing. There are, in fact, three separate sections of the site that are worth reviewing.

The seventy-eight volumes of the United States Army in World War II series, also known as the Green Books because of their green bindings, constitute the official history of the army's "organization, plans, and operations" in all theaters of operations from 1939 to 1945. At the time of this review, only seven of the volumes had been posted online; those on the Cross-Channel Attack (D-Day and the Normandy invasion), the Battle of the Bulge, Guadalcanal, Okinawa, the Persian Corridor, the employment of Black troops, and guarding the United States and its outposts are each must visits. Furthermore, researchers will be encouraged to know that the CMH continues to make additional volumes available online. A full index of the Green Books, along with a "Reader's Guide" to all seventy-eight volumes, can be found at http://www.army.mil/cmh-pg/collections/USAWW2/USAWW2.htm.

In the early and mid-1990s, the U.S. Army published the World War II Commemorative Brochures. In all, the series includes more than forty volumes covering twenty campaigns in the Asiatic-Pacific theater, fifteen battles in the European-African-Middle Eastern theater, and additional brochures on Generals Dwight Eisenhower and Omar Bradley, the Defense of the Americas, the Army Nurse Corps, and the WAC. The full text of these brochures, which run from forty to fifty pages each, can be found at http://www.army.mil/cmh-pg/collections/WW2-Broch.htm.

In addition to the Green Books and commemorative brochures, the CMH is responsible for a number of other publications. The complete list and full text of the CMH's publications can be found at http://www.army.mil/cmh-pg/online/Bookshelves/WW2-List.htm.

For a review of the material on this site pertaining to the European/Atlantic/Mediterranean theater of operations, see p. 41, and for the Pacific theater of operations, see p. 58.

CONTENT   ★ ★ ★ ★ ★
AESTHETICS   ★ ★ ★
NAVIGATION   ★ ★ ★ ★

World War II Air Power

http://www.danshistory.com/ww2/index.shtml

Webmaster Daniel Green's site contains a wealth of information about air power in World War II, and if the answer to a question cannot be found on the site, Green offers the opportunity to ask him questions. The site is incredibly thorough, and the information is presented in a seemingly authoritative manner. The only problem, however, is that Green does not identify the sources of his information. It appears that he relied on official government and military reports, but the absence of such source information is unfortunate. Furthermore, there is an undefined commercial aspect to this site. Green's site is presented "in association" with amazon.com, and frequent advertisements for World War II–related books (which, of course, can be purchased through Amazon) appear throughout the site. Nevertheless, World War II Air Power is worth a visit.

Green's site is divided into six main sections: Campaigns, Aircraft, Weapons, Air Defense, Technology, and Resources. Campaigns includes separate chapters entitled Europe, the Pacific, the Mediterranean, the Battle of the Atlantic, Night War, and the Eastern Front. Each chapter describes the role that air power played in the major battles fought within that theater, the type of aircraft and weapons used, and the number of hits and losses sustained. In addition, the chapter on the Atlantic provides substantial data on the submarine war. Those interested in the airplanes themselves will not be disappointed. The section on aircraft covers fighters, bombers, attack aircraft, and even the Japanese kamikaze. Other sections include detailed information on bombs, incendiaries, missiles, radar, flak, anti-aircraft missiles, and rocket fuel.

Although the section entitled Resources is largely intended as a vehicle to sell books and videos, it includes a most useful collection of documents. Among the primary sources available here are the full summary reports of the Strategic Bombing Survey for both Europe and the Pacific; key diplomatic documents, such as declarations of war and articles of surrender; and numerous other materials of interest, including a 1939 letter from Albert Einstein to Franklin Roosevelt regarding the development of the atomic bomb. The Resources section also contains multiple links to other sites.

Despite the commercial status of World War II Air Power, the amount of information presented is truly impressive. It is likely to keep even the most serious researchers busy for hours.

CONTENT   ★ ★ ★ ★ ★
AESTHETICS   ★ ★ ★ ★
NAVIGATION   ★ ★ ★ ★

WWII Resources
http://ibiblio.org/pha

Without a doubt, this site is one of the most comprehensive online sources of official government and diplomatic documents relating to World War II. From the causes of the conflict in the 1920s and 1930s to the development of postwar policy, webmaster Larry Jewell continues to build and expand what is an already impressive collection.

WWII Resources includes a 400-page chronology of major international events leading up to the war as well as official American, British, French, German, and Japanese documents that address the major points of tension in the prewar years. From *The British War Bluebook* to *The French Yellow Book,* to nearly 300 documents pertaining to American foreign policy in the 1930s, this site will satisfy the cravings of even the most serious students and researchers. One section, Words of Peace, Words of War, contains hundreds of treaties, declarations, and speeches from around the world arranged chronologically. Additional sections focus on intelligence efforts, the speeches of Franklin Roosevelt, and prewar and postwar policy.

Students of Pearl Harbor will find more than five thousand pages of documents and testimony from the official Pearl Harbor Attack Hearings. Although lacking the flashy graphics found on other sites, WWII Resources is well indexed, easily navigable (with the one exception of not allowing one to return to the home page once ensconced in many of the documents), and loaded with content.

For a review of the Pearl Harbor material on this site, see p. 61.

CONTENT   ★ ★ ★ ★
AESTHETICS   ★ ★ ★
NAVIGATION   ★ ★ ★ ★

MAPS

Maps of World War II
http://www.onwar.com/maps/wwii/index.htm

Created by OnWar.com, a commercial venture, this site includes nearly ninety military maps of good quality from most of the major theaters of World War II. The maps on this site emphasize operational-level information, which the web site designers explain as "a general's or admiral's point of view." Instead of denoting the location of battalions and regiments in the Ardennes Forest, for instance, the maps document the location and movement of entire divisions and armies. Although the frequent sidebars and advertisements typical of a commercial site are annoying, this site is an invaluable resource for students of World War II's military campaigns.

Logically organized by theater of operation and in rough chronological order, Maps of World War II is divided into five sections: Blitzkrieg, Eastern Front, Normandy, Western Front, and Pacific Theater. Unfortunately for researchers interested in all theaters of combat, the site does not include any maps of the Atlantic and North African/Mediterranean/Italian theaters. Students of the American experience, however, will find useful and informative maps relating to D-Day and Operation Overlord, the Battle of the Bulge, Pearl Harbor, Midway, Guadalcanal, and other major battles and campaigns. One of the more revealing maps from the Battle of the Bulge lays bare how completely isolated and surrounded the 101st Airborne found itself at Bastogne. Each map is accompanied by a brief tagline that explains the importance of the battle.

Furthermore, Maps of World War II is a valuable site precisely because it places the American experience within the broader context of the war. Researchers will be fascinated by maps tracing the German blitzkrieg ("lightning war") across western Europe as well as the four-year battle that raged on the eastern front. Some of the most interesting maps detail the Red Army's final assault on Berlin and the encircling of Hitler's chancellery and the Reichstag.

CONTENT   ★ ★ ★ ★
AESTHETICS   ★ ★ ★ ★
NAVIGATION   ★ ★ ★ ★

World War II Maps at the University of Texas Library
http://www.lib.utexas.edu/maps/historical/history_ww2.html

The University of Texas's Perry-Castaneda Library has posted nearly fifty maps from World War II, most of them originally produced by the CMH. As one might expect from the CMH, the images are of high quality, and most are in color.

The collection includes close to thirty maps from the Pacific theater and twenty from Europe. Unfortunately, the collection is uneven in what it covers. For instance, anyone interested in the invasions of Sicily and Italy will be quite pleased; maps abound with details of the campaign at Anzio, Naples-Foggia, Rome, and Sicily. On the other hand, the collection includes only one image from the rest of Europe. Fortunately, many of the obvious omissions from this collection are available elsewhere.

Similarly, the University of Texas's collection includes valuable maps from the Aleutian Islands, the Bataan Peninsula, China, Guadalcanal, Guam, Luzon, and other critical engagements in the Pacific but nothing on Pearl Harbor, Midway, or Okinawa. The map of the Bataan Peninsula in the spring of 1942, as American forces were overrun by Japanese troops, is especially well done.

CONTENT ★ ★ ★
AESTHETICS ★ ★ ★ ★
NAVIGATION ★ ★ ★

TIMELINES

The World at War, History of WWII, 1939–1945

http://www.euronet.nl/users/wilfried/ww2/ww2.htm

Dutchman Wilfried Braakhuis has created one of the most complete World War II sites on the web. Organized chronologically, the central feature of The World at War is a detailed timeline interspersed with links that provide a plethora of information drawn from a variety of primary and secondary sources, both scholarly and general. Focusing not only on the American experience in World War II but also on that of the other major combatants, Allied and Axis, Braakhuis's site includes diplomatic communiqués, biographies of major leaders, statistics on troop strength, details of military engagements, information on the Holocaust, and more. Researchers interested in the causes of the war will be happy to find that the site includes significant information on the prewar years.

In an attempt to be as thorough as possible, The World at War succeeds, for the most part, in linking to other reputable World War II sites, such as the FDR Library and Yale's Avalon Project. Visitors should be aware, however, that The World at War also links to such sites as the Hitler Museum. While claiming to be a nonpartisan, nonpolitical site, the Hitler Museum gives away its actual predilections with links to sites that are clearly devoted to Holocaust denial (see "Introduction and User's Guide" and Chapter 8 for more on denial sites). Braakhuis himself does not appear to support Holocaust denial in the text of his timelines, but visitors should be aware that all links are not necessarily reliable. Separate from the timeline, The World at War also provides links to hundreds of sites on all aspects of World War II. Many of these links, however, are old and no longer operative, and others are not in English.

Spelling errors occasionally appear on the site, more than likely a result of translation from Dutch to English. Nevertheless, The World at War is a thorough, informative site that provides a terrific starting point for an understanding of World War II.

CONTENT ★ ★ ★ ★
AESTHETICS ★ ★ ★
NAVIGATION ★ ★ ★ ★

World War II Plus 55
http://www.usswashington.com/dl_index.htm

U.S. Navy public affairs officer David Lippman has created a site that provides a comprehensive account of world events as they occurred on a daily basis during World War II. Three years after its launch, Lippman's site is only complete through November 1942, but no wonder. The amount of information gathered here is staggering. Military events dominate the daily logs, but diplomatic and scientific developments receive attention as well. A look at just one day should suffice as a review of World War II Plus 55.

November 7, 1942, the final log, begins with Vichy French officials offering support to Germany in the event of an Allied attack in North Africa. Adolf Hitler prepares for a briefing. Australian troops in the South Pacific spot a Japanese convey headed to Guadalcanal with reinforcements. General Dwight Eisenhower and British allies plan their invasion of North Africa, but General Henri-Honoré Giraud, now of the French resistance, withholds his support and demands a simultaneous landing in southwest France. Meanwhile, U-505 sinks another Allied ship in the Atlantic. The invasion of North Africa gets under way as George Patton expresses hope that God will remain on the side of the Allies. British General Bernard Montgomery and German Field Marshall Erwin Rommel try to outfox one another in the desert. On the eastern front, Joseph Stalin delivers a speech in honor of the anniversary of the Russian revolution. Finally, in Chicago, Enrico Fermi and other scientists work toward the first nuclear chain reaction.

Lippman does not identify his sources, but he appears to draw upon a plethora of primary materials—diary and journal entries, official logs, and other reports. No photographs or supporting documents are included on this site. Nevertheless, the wealth of synthesized information, presented in a form not found elsewhere on the web, makes this site well worth a visit for those seeking a greater understanding of the interconnectedness of the various facets of World War II. Well indexed by month and date, Lippman's site is easy to navigate.

CONTENT   ★ ★ ★ ★
AESTHETICS   ★ ★ ★
NAVIGATION   ★ ★ ★ ★

World War II Timeline
http://ac.acusd.edu/History/WW2Timeline/start.html

Originally conceived as a student project at the University of San Diego, World War II Timeline has grown over the years into a useful general resource. Organized by date and topic, the timeline provides a detailed chronology and includes separate pages on the people and events most important to an understanding of the conflict. The separate entries, however, are inconsistent, more than likely a reflection of the commitment of the individual students who built each page. Some pages, such as those on the atomic bomb and the German Anschluss, provide a wealth of information, while others, such as the entry on Midway, have little to offer. All entries include a list of sources, and most provide links to other sites on the same subject.

The section entitled Pictures provides a number of wonderful images of leaders, battles, and even postwar events such as the Nuremberg Trials. Most of these pictures come from the National Archives. The section on maps also includes some terrific images. Unfortunately, the chapter entitled Documents is no longer active. A few primary documents, such as the full text of the Treaty of Versailles, appear elsewhere in the timeline, but the overall value of the site would be enhanced with an active selection of documents. Finally, World War II Timeline provides an extensive bibliography of war-related books, as well as multiple links to other sites.

CONTENT   ★ ★ ★
AESTHETICS   ★ ★ ★ ★
NAVIGATION   ★ ★ ★ ★

SUGGESTED READINGS

Ambrose, Stephen E. *The Good Fight: How World War II Was Won* (New York, 2001), for young readers.

Cowley, Robert, ed. *No End Save Victory: Perspectives on World War II* (New York, 2001).

Dear, I. C. B., and M. R. D. Foot, eds. *The Oxford Companion to the Second World War* (New York, 1995).

Craven, Wesley Frank, and James Lea Cate. *The Army Air Forces in World War II,* 7 vols. (Washington, DC, 1983).

Eubank, Keith. *The Origins of World War II,* 2d ed. (Arlington Heights, IL, 1990).

Keegan, John. *The Second World War* (New York, 1989).

Keegan, John, ed. *The Times Atlas of the Second World War* (New York, 1989).

Lee, Loyd E., ed. *World War II in Europe, Africa, and the Americas, with General Sources* (Westport, CT, 1997).

Morison, Samuel Eliot. *History of U.S. Naval Operations in World War II* (Boston, 1947–1962).

———. *The Two Ocean War: A Short History of the United States Navy in the Second World War* (Boston, 1963).

Murray, Williamson, and Allen R. Millett. *A War to Be Won: Fighting the Second World War* (Cambridge, MA, 2000).

Overy, Richard, and Andrew Wheatcroft. *The Road to War: The Origins of World War II* (New York, 1989).

Prange, Gordon. *Pearl Harbor: The Verdict of History* (New York, 2001).

Sherry, Michael. *The Rise of American Air Power: The Creation of Armageddon* (New Haven, CT, 1987).

Watt, Donald Cameron. *How War Came: The Immediate Origins of the Second World War, 1938–1939* (New York, 1989).

Weinberg, Gerhard. *A World at Arms: A Global History of World War II* (New York, 1994).

Wilmott, H. P. *The Great Crusade: A New Complete History of the Second World War* (New York, 1989).

Young, Peter, ed. *The Cassell Atlas of the Second World War* (London, 2000).

CHAPTER 2

POLITICAL AND MILITARY LEADERS

The eight outstanding leaders featured in this chapter played central roles in shaping the military history of World War II. Four were national political leaders of global significance—Winston Churchill, Adolf Hitler, Franklin Roosevelt, and Harry Truman. Three were top commanders of the American armies—Omar Bradley, Dwight Eisenhower, and Douglas MacArthur.

Omar Bradley (1893–1981) was representative of the hundreds of quiet, efficient generals who led the American armies. He was the most meticulous, least flamboyant of the great military leaders of the war. Like Eisenhower he was an organization man—he did everything by the book and on schedule. He graduated from West Point in the famous class of 1915—"the class the stars fell on"—but spent World War I stateside. In the 1920s and 1930s, he excelled in the army's advanced training schools, especially the Infantry School, where he attracted the attention of Colonel George Marshall. When Marshall became chief of staff in 1939, he moved the best students into top commands. As a two-star general Bradley turned the lackluster 28th Division into a spit-and-polish unit. He was second in command behind George Patton in North Africa and Sicily in 1942–43. After Patton was benched for slapping a hospitalized soldier, Bradley moved up to command the First Army in the invasion of Normandy and then commanded the Twelfth Army Group, with Patton as his subordinate. He gained his fifth star as chairman of the Joint Chiefs of Staff during the Korean War, during which he had trouble keeping MacArthur under control. Evaluations of Bradley's performance as a combat commander in 1944–45 vary. The GIs loved him, and Eisenhower called him "America's foremost battle leader." The 1970 movie *Patton* shows Bradley (played by Karl Malden) making the wise decisions while Patton was too impulsive. (Bradley himself was the chief consultant on the film and wrote two autobiographies justifying his actions.) For his handling of the offensive at St. Lo in July 1944, see http://www.army.mil/cmh-pg/books/wwii/100-13/st-lo_0.htm. Critics, however, question his failure to close the Falaise Gap in August 1944, which allowed the escape of most of the German soldiers who nearly had been surrounded in northern France (for a good analysis see http://www.army.mil/cmh-pg/books/70-7_17.htm).

Supporters of British Field Marshall Montgomery carped about Bradley's insistence on a broad front attack on Germany in 1945 (as opposed to a narrow thrust that would have been led by Montgomery) and argue it was very wise of Eisenhower to put Montgomery in charge of defending the Battle of the Bulge instead of Bradley. (On the Bulge see the excellent official history by Hugh Cole online at http://www.army.mil/cmh-pg/books/wwii/7-8/7-8_CONT.HTM.)

When Winston Churchill was born in 1874, the British Empire dominated the globe, with unrivalled sea power and colonies on every continent. At his passing in 1965, the empire had shrunk away, with Hong Kong the only remaining important possession (and it too was lost in 1997). Churchill fervently believed in the empire, which was built in good part by his ancestors, such as the great eighteenth-century general, the Duke of Marlborough. A graduate of the military academy at Sandhurst, young Churchill quickly became famous for his exploits in the Boer War (1899). A leading politician, he was responsible for modernizing the navy and supervising it in World War I. Despite his civilian status, he largely shaped naval strategy; however, his decision to land at Gallipoli led to disaster and his resignation. He then served as an army colonel on the western front. In the 1920s, Churchill was again a senior cabinet officer, but the pendulum of politics swung against him in the 1930s. Holding no major office, he devoted himself to writing military and political history and warning against the dangers of Hitler, the folly of appeasement, and the stupidity of loosening the grip on India. When war broke out, Churchill returned to the Admiralty. When Germany moved west in April 1940, Churchill became prime minister and defense minister, running the government until his party was defeated in the 1945 elections. Churchill's major achievements were forging close alliances with the United States (Roosevelt was a personal friend) and the USSR (a deal with the devil is sometimes necessary, he explained), overseeing the full mobilization of British manpower and munitions, and, above all, sustaining the morale of a small nation confronted with an arch foe who controlled most of Europe. Churchill made time every day to provide strategic and even tactical guidance to his admirals and generals, much to their annoyance. Having suffered horrible losses in World War I, the British were reluctant to risk everything again in a great land war with Germany. Therefore, Churchill proposed any number of side attacks, especially operations against Germany's "soft underbelly," the Mediterranean. By 1944 the sheer weight of the American war effort so dwarfed the British that the Americans determined strategy, and Churchill perforce followed along. His masterful dealings with Roosevelt and Eisenhower guaranteed the British would at least have a voice in all decisions, though he failed to soften Roosevelt's hostility toward the British Empire. Keenly sensitive to American public opinion, he shifted the Royal Navy to the Pacific in 1945 to help defeat Japan. Upon leaving office after the war, he warned about the Iron Curtain and wrote a superb multivolume history of the war. Churchill's popularity as the greatest Brit of the century was never doubted by Americans.

Although he never saw combat in his life, Dwight Eisenhower (1890–1969) was the biggest hero of World War II, moving from an obscure lieutenant colonel in 1941 to the best-known, best-liked man in the world four years later. A graduate of West Point in the famous class of 1915, Ike rose swiftly in World War I, becoming the third ranking officer of the new Tank Corps (George Patton was the second ranking officer). He stayed in the army in a series of staff jobs after the war when most of his friends began civilian careers. His army superiors disbanded the tank unit and warned Ike that he would damage his career if he kept writing about the versatility of the tanks. Ike dutifully went into the infantry, and Patton, after receiving the same warning, gave up tanks for the horse cavalry. Eisenhower was the best committee man and planner in the army. When war broke out in 1941, General Marshall tasked him with planning how to defeat the Germans and then promoted him to command of that operation. Eisenhower had command in the Mediterranean in 1942–43. His military decisions were too cautious, however; the Germans repeatedly gained the jump on him (for example, seizing Tunisia, beating the Americans at Kassarine Pass, withdrawing from Sicily with minor losses). No matter, for overwhelming air and naval power guaranteed Allied victories until the land war bogged down in the Italian mountains. Eisenhower learned how to relate large plans to real combat, and he also learned how to manage a multinational force, showing remarkable diplomatic skills with the British, French, and even U.S. navies. Named supreme commander for the invasion of Europe in 1944, Ike planned brilliantly. He planned the massive logistics buildup and coordination and the critical use of air power to destroy German logistics (over the opposition of the American and British air forces). The actual invasion, commanded by British Field Marshall Montgomery, worked like clockwork. Ike later assumed direct command of the Allied forces and led the counterattack at the Battle of the Bulge and the invasion of Germany. Fearing excessive casualties, he decided not to race the Russians to capture Berlin. On Eisenhower's planning for Normandy see the CMH's excellent official history at http://www.army.mil/cmh-pg/books/wwii/7-4/7-4_cont.htm.

Adolf Hitler (1889–1945) goes down in history as the man who nearly conquered the world and destroyed the Jews but in the end destroyed Germany. He was a fanatic with a mesmerizing voice, a criminal dictator, and the leading anti-Semite, and yet to this day he is a hero to a few neo-Nazis and skinheads. As a military leader, Hitler's reputation is mixed. He succeeded in rearming Germany in the late 1930s before anyone else, building an unusually powerful army and air force from nothing. His bluffs and threats secured control of Austria and Czechoslovakia without war. Through a timely alliance with Stalin in 1939, he was able to isolate and crush Poland in a matter of weeks and then divide up control of eastern Europe with the Soviets. The alliance not only guaranteed against a second front, it also allowed access to oil and food from Russia and caused the Communist left in Europe and America to silently accept Hitler's victories without protest. The "phony" war without battles in western Europet suddenly ended in the spring of 1940 as Hitler blitzkrieged against the dazed and confused Allies, decisively defeating them in six weeks. In summer of 1940, Hitler was master of Europe, with Stalin his ally in the east, the United States neutral, and Britain the only remaining foe. After Hitler's Luftwaffe was defeated in the Battle of Britain, however, he turned his attention east, realizing that ultimately only one dictatorship was possible in Europe—his or Stalin's. Hitler believed in lightning war (blitzkrieg) with sudden victories. He therefore postponed full economic mobilization and discouraged long-range planning or development of weapons systems that would take more than a couple years to make operational. Experimental jet planes were flying in 1942, but Hitler repeatedly delayed and modified them until they arrived too late and in too few numbers to challenge Allied air power. In a more general sense, Hitler delayed the full mobilization of the German economy until 1943. Perhaps fearful of the collapse of home front morale, as happened in 1918, he deceived the German people into thinking the war was going well and that extreme sacrifices were not necessary. By 1939, Hitler had seized personal command of the military and made every major decision himself. The lightning successes of 1939–40 silenced most of his military critics, though a few upper-class officers plotted assassination. In 1942–1945, even as his military intuition failed, Hitler routinely reversed the advice of his senior generals. When army leaders tried to assassinate him in 1944, he began to rely more on Himmler's notorious SS for its blind loyalty and ferocious fighting. Hitler refused to allow his forces to retreat, regroup, or maneuver. Increasingly outnumbered and outgunned, they were systematically defeated east and west until Hitler finally realized his defeat and committed suicide in his bunker in April 1945. Hitler figures in the background of many web sites; a few are devoted to glamorizing him, usually with no mention of his military follies or his merciless attacks on the Jews.

Douglas MacArthur (1880–1964), George Patton, and George Custer have been the most controversial generals in American military history among the public, the military, and historians—they love them or hate them, with no middle ground. MacArthur's father Arthur was a hero in the Civil War, an officer in the Indian wars, and the American commander who suppressed the Philippine insurrection. His son Douglas became a close student of Far Eastern affairs and emerged from World War I as one of the country's youngest and most famous generals. As army chief of staff

from 1930 to 1935, he routed the Bonus Army from Washington and criticized paci-
fists, thereby earning the permanent hatred of the left. In the late 1930s, he commanded the Philippines army in preparation for the independence of the islands,
which was scheduled for 1946. When the attack on Pearl Harbor was announced
in the Philippines, MacArthur sent his bombers to attack, but when they returned
they were caught on the ground and destroyed. The Japanese Army landed in the
Philippines in December and soon forced the poorly equipped Filipino-American
forces to retreat to Bataan, where they surrendered. MacArthur, ordered out by
Roosevelt, swore, "I shall return." Despite the humiliating defeats, MacArthur's reputation soared: America needed a fighting hero. An excellent online source for this
period is the official army history for 1941–42 by Louis Morton, available at
http://www.ibiblio.org/hyperwar/USA/USA-P-Strategy/ (see review in Chapter 1).

In Australia, MacArthur rallied a psychologically downcast ally and led a long campaign to reconquer New Guinea (1942–1944). After taking command of the Southwest
Pacific Area (SWPA), MacArthur leapfrogged over most of the Japanese strongholds
with "Operation Cartwheel," jumping just as far as his aircraft could provide tactical
air cover (see http://www.army.mil/cmh-pg/brochures/northsol/northsol.htm). The Pentagon wanted to bypass the Philippines in 1944–45, but MacArthur was adamant that
America had a duty to liberate its colony. He did return—landing on Luzon in October 1944—and was immediately threatened with annihilation by a Japanese fleet
that had deceived the American navy. It was a close call, but MacArthur's own fleet
and Admiral Halsey's separate fleet destroyed the Japanese in the largest naval battle of all time, Leyte Gulf. The reconquest of the Philippines was grueling, although
it is far less well known than the Iwo Jima and Okinawa campaigns. MacArthur was
planning an invasion of Japan scheduled for October 1945 when Japan surrendered.
He became the dictatorial head of American occupational forces and succeeded in
converting the Japanese to democracy and pacifism. His last military challenge—
and the most controversial—came in 1950, when North Korea invaded the South.
MacArthur's forces had been driven into a small pocket at Pusan when he leapfrogged
behind the enemy, landed at Inchon, and destroyed the invaders. MacArthur then
turned the tables and invaded North Korea. Late in 1950, China unexpectedly sent
a million soldiers into North Korea, thereby rolling MacArthur back. When he called
for more support he discovered that Washington preferred a stalemate rather than
fighting what Bradley called "the wrong war in the wrong place at the wrong time."
MacArthur was fired; the Old Soldier returned home to a hero's welcome in 1951.

Franklin Delano Roosevelt (1882–1945) had many roles as president from 1933 to
1945; the one he enjoyed most was commander in chief, especially the command
of his beloved navy. He had been the civilian in actual charge of the navy during
World War I and personally knew many of the senior officers. He especially trusted
Admiral William Leahy, whom he installed as his personal military adviser and chairman of the new Joint Chiefs of Staff in 1942. For command of the army, Roosevelt

selected George Marshall, a highly efficient and high-minded staff officer who was trusted by everyone in Washington. He passed over Marshall in favor of Eisenhower to be supreme commander in Europe. Although Ike was nonpolitical at the time, he was the favorite of the New Dealers (indeed, his brother was a senior New Deal official). Roosevelt promoted the air force even more vigorously than the fly-boys themselves, demanding and getting an astonishing 300,000 warplanes to destroy Germany and Japan. For civilian control of the Pentagon, he selected a conservative Republican, Henry Stimson, to run the War Department. Frank Knox, another prominent Republican, was the nominal secretary of the navy, but the real power was held by Roosevelt's former assistant, James Forrestal. Ignoring the State Department, Roosevelt handled all major diplomatic issues personally or with the aide of his assistant, Harry Hopkins. His administrative style involved giving overlapping responsibility to two or three agencies, knowing they would fight and bring their disputes to him and he would make the final decision. This technique centralized power in the White House and destroyed potential opponents, but it proved highly wasteful in wartime. After 1942, therefore, Roosevelt let his senior people make the decisions so he could focus mostly on diplomacy. He was not a hands-on military leader like Stalin, Hitler, and Churchill, but he did build a very successful team that got the job done.

Joseph Stalin (1879–1953) was one of the greatest tyrants and mass murderers of the twentieth century, and he was also the generalissimo most responsible for the defeat of Germany. His relationship with Germany was based on extremes. In 1917–18 the Germans helped bring the Bolsheviks to power in Russia; in the 1920s, Germany secretly used Soviet bases to build up the air force it was forbidden to have; in the 1930s, Fascist and Communist supporters battled it out in the streets of cities across the world, hurling the most horrid epithets at each other and actually engaging in combat with each other in the Spanish Civil War. In the late 1930s, Stalin shot most of his generals and colonels, leaving a very young and untested, but talented, group of survivors. In 1939, in the most unexpected turnaround in diplomatic history, Hitler and Stalin came to terms, divided Poland and eastern Europe, and opened the door for the Nazi invasion of western Europe. Stalin fooled himself, refusing to accept repeated urgent warnings that his ally was about to attack. For a few weeks after the invasion in June 1941, Stalin was paralyzed as the German armies made massive advances and captured hundreds of thousands of prisoners. Then Stalin suddenly stiffened, called upon the traditions of the Russian spirit to resist a Germanic threat, moved thousands of factories back to the Urals, and took day-to-day command of his armies. The Soviet lines held at the gates of Moscow and Leningrad (St. Petersburg). At Stalingrad (1942–43) the Germans, far too overextended, suffered a decisive defeat. The next two years saw the Soviets build up strength as they relentlessly pushed the weakening German armies back mile by mile. The Battle for Berlin in 1945 was one of the largest battles in world history and certainly the most decisive. Stalin successfully negotiated with Churchill and Roosevelt at a series of conferences, and at Yalta he seemed to agree to a democratic regime in Poland. He reneged on this agreement, however, and ordered his Red Army to force each of the East European nations into a Communist camp tightly controlled by Moscow. Thus began the Cold War. Historians continue to debate whether Stalin's motivation was to expand Communism, to achieve old traditional Russian goals, or was just a result of his paranoid personality, which prompted the execution of all real or imagined enemies. (For web sites on Stalin, see Part II.)

Harry Truman (1884–1972) was the little man who had greatness thrust upon him. As a senator his main concern had been domestic affairs and the budget. He was ill prepared to assume Roosevelt's mantle, having little understanding of military strategy or diplomatic events and knowing few of the senior leaders of his own government. News that the top secret atomic bomb was almost ready made little impact on Truman; he asked few questions and received little advice from his aides. Although in his memoirs he claims he thought long and hard about using the bomb, in actuality he asked few questions and let Secretary of War Stimson make all the major decisions. The Truman Library has a good web site (see review below, http://www.trumanlibrary.org/whistlestop). Curiously, it slights Truman's important role as senate watchdog of government spending during the war.

WEB SITE REVIEWS

BRADLEY, OMAR NELSON

Omar Nelson Bradley
http://www.army.mil/cmh-pg/brochures/bradley/bradley.htm

After leading American troops in the successful invasions of North Africa and Sicily, Omar Bradley was selected by Dwight Eisenhower to command the First U.S. Army during Operation Overlord, the D-Day invasion of Normandy. Troops under Bradley's command then liberated Paris, fought off a German counteroffensive at the Battle of the Bulge, and ultimately linked up with Soviet forces in the final stages of the war. By the end of the war, Bradley commanded the Twelfth U.S. Army Group, "the largest body of American soldiers ever to serve under one field commander." Less flamboyant than fellow generals George Patton and Douglas MacArthur, Bradley nevertheless earned a reputation as a "soldiers' general" and enjoyed the complete confidence of his superiors. After

World War II, Bradley was appointed chief of staff of the army, followed by two terms as the first chairman of the Joint Chiefs of Staff. While chairman of the Joint Chiefs, he was promoted to the rank of five-star general. He was the last five-star general at the time of his death in 1981, and no other American has held that rank since.

In commemoration of the centennial of Bradley's birth, the CMH published a lengthy brochure that has been posted online at this site. Although the site includes no documents or other primary sources, it does provide a comprehensive biography of one the most important American generals of World War II. Beginning with Bradley's early years and continuing through his service in World War I (a disappointed Bradley never made it overseas), the interwar years, and finally World War II, the brochure concludes with a look at the general's postwar service. Given Bradley's rank and importance, the brochure will prove informative to those interested in American military command during World War II.

CONTENT   ★ ★ ★
AESTHETICS   ★ ★ ★
NAVIGATION   ★ ★ ★ ★

CHURCHILL, WINSTON SPENCER

Churchill: The Evidence
http://www.churchill.nls.ac.uk/main.html

Created by the National Library of Scotland and the Churchill Archives Center at Cambridge University, Churchill: The Evidence is based on a major exhibition of Winston Churchill's life developed by the National Library of Scotland in the summer of 1999. Based upon primary documents and photographs from the Churchill Archives, an invaluable collection not yet available online, the exhibition chronicles the full scope of Churchill's life. Teachers and educators will find this site particularly valuable and quite accessible to their students, while researchers will have to be satisfied with but a taste of what awaits them in the full holdings of the Churchill Archives.

The major part of Churchill: The Evidence is entitled Life and Times: 1874–1965 and is divided into ten chapters: Early Life, The Roving Commission, A Young Radical, A Frank and Clear-eyed Friendship, The World Crisis, The Member for Dundee, From War to War, The Finest Hour, The Tide of Victory, and The Final Days. Each chapter includes a brief biographical sketch and seven to ten primary documents, including posters, letters, diary entries, maps, newspaper articles, and photographs. Taken together, these documents will provide students a sense of the full scope of Churchill's remarkable life.

The second part of the site, entitled Resources for Schools, offers tantalizing possibilities for middle and high school teachers. Consisting of additional primary materials that relate to Churchill's political life, the documents are accompanied by a series of instructional questions. For instance, students can read Churchill's early thoughts on Benito Mussolini and Adolf Hitler and discuss the implications of his analysis. Designed for use in the Scottish curriculum, the arrangement of the materials may be confusing to American teachers. At the very least, however, Resources for Schools offers a unique opportunity for students to engage directly with primary documents.

CONTENT   ★ ★ ★ ★
AESTHETICS   ★ ★ ★ ★
NAVIGATION   ★ ★ ★ ★

Life and Times of Winston S. Churchill
http://www.winstonchurchill.org

Unless and until Winston Churchill's official papers, housed at the Churchill Archives Center at Cambridge University, are made available online, Life and Times of Winston S. Churchill is likely to remain a critical online source of information on Great Britain's wartime prime minister. Maintained by the Churchill Center of Washington, D.C., this site contains some primary documents along with extensive secondary materials that detail the full scope of Churchill's life. Since Churchill was already well into his sixties at the start of World War II, much of the information obviously predates that conflict. Nevertheless, researchers and students of World War II will not want to miss this web page.

The section entitled Spoken Words includes numerous quotations (it is hard to imagine a World War II figure more frequently quoted than Churchill) as well as several famous utterances falsely attributed to Churchill. In addition, Spoken Words includes fifteen of Churchill's most important wartime speeches. Researchers will find the full text of "Blood, Toil, Tears, and Sweat," his first speech as prime minister; "Their Finest Hour"; "Sinews of Peace," in which he warned in March 1946 of an "Iron Curtain" descending over Central and Eastern Europe; and other notable orations. A link to a commercial site allows visitors to listen to many of these same speeches.

The Churchill Center makes an honest effort to provide a balanced, scholarly appraisal of Churchill's life. The site includes current and past issues of the center's journal, *The Finest Hour*, as well as the official proceedings of the International Churchill Society. Although published for Churchill enthusiasts, both forums present a variety of scholarly points of view. In addition, one of the more unique and fascinating aspects of this site is a section entitled Debates about Churchill. Researchers will benefit from an exposure to historiographical points of contention that have suffused interpretations of Churchill's public life.

A brief look at the comprehensive index will be enough to give visitors a sense of the scope of the materials available. Dozens of articles and reviews of books, both by and about Churchill, address his early life and adulthood, the England in which he came of age as well as the England he led during the war, and his relationships with other world leaders and his own generals. The index is organized by subject—by persons as well as significant events, such as World War II— and easily searchable. Visitors to this site should set aside ample time, or plan on numerous visits in order to sift through the available materials.

CONTENT   ★ ★ ★ ★
AESTHETICS   ★ ★ ★ ★
NAVIGATION   ★ ★ ★ ★

EISENHOWER, DWIGHT DAVID

Dwight David Eisenhower
http://www.army.mil/cmh-pg/brochures/ike/ike.htm

Untested in combat and lacking significant experience with troops when the United States entered World War II, Dwight David Eisenhower nevertheless rose to become the supreme commander of the Allied Expeditionary Forces and thus militarily responsible for all aspects of the Allied invasion of Europe. Eisenhower's rise to the top post was no accident; Army Chief of Staff George Marshall had recognized Eisenhower's abilities early in the war and steadily promoted him up the chain of command. Eisenhower, of course, parlayed his leadership of Allied forces into two terms as president of the United States.

Considering Eisenhower's stature and importance, it is surprising and unfortunate that more comprehensive materials on his life, and especially his military career, are not available on the web. The most likely repository for such material, the Eisenhower Presidential Library (see review in Part II), focuses on his presidential administration. The library's web page includes little of relevance to World War II; the few documents available on D-Day and Operation Overlord are terribly slow to load and much more effectively viewed elsewhere.

Given the relative dearth of adequate online source material, the brochure posted here provides welcome biographical information on Eisenhower's army years. Prepared by the CMH in 1990 to commemorate the centennial of the general's birth, the brochure focuses on Eisenhower's rise through the ranks, his apprenticeship under George Marshall, and his command of Allied forces. Although researchers and educators will not find primary source materials on this site, the biographical information is comprehensive and sheds light on the life and military career of one of the war's most important personalities. One primary document, however, is included in full: Eisenhower's often quoted letter to the "Soldiers, Sailors, and Airmen of the Allied Expeditionary Forces." Issued on the eve of the invasion of Normandy, Eisenhower reminded his troops that "you are about to embark upon the Great Crusade. . . . The eyes of the world are upon you. The hopes and prayers of liberty loving people everywhere march with you." Fully aware of the struggle that lay ahead, the Allied commander warned that "your task will not be an easy one. Your enemy is well trained, well equipped and battle-hardened. He will fight savagely." Nevertheless, Eisenhower asked for and expected "nothing less than full Victory."

CONTENT   ★ ★ ★
AESTHETICS   ★ ★ ★
NAVIGATION   ★ ★ ★ ★

HITLER, ADOLF

Adolf Hitler
http://www.us-israel.org/jsource/Holocaust/hitlertoc.html

The Jewish Virtual Library (see also Chapter 8, http://www.us-israel.org/jsource/index.html), a division of the Jewish-American Cooperative Enterprise, has built an impressive digital collection of primary and secondary source material on all aspects of Jewish life. As part of an extensive chapter on the Holocaust, the section on Adolf Hitler is by no means exhaustive but certainly instructive.

The material on Hitler includes an informative biography with links to biographies of other important Nazi leaders such as Joseph Goebbels, Heinrich Himmler, Hermann Göring, Reinhard Heydrich, and Rudolf Hess. In addition, the biography of Hitler links to important primary documents such as the Nuremberg Laws and the Final Solution. The bulk of the site consists of excerpts from Hitler's letters, speeches, and writings on such topics as the Jewish Question, propaganda, and cruelty. Visitors will find Hitler's last will and testament as well as a political statement dictated hours before his suicide, in which he continued to blame Jews for all of Europe's problems.

One of the more detailed and interesting documents is a letter that Hitler wrote to Benito Mussolini on June 21, 1941. Explaining the need for and timing of Germany's imminent invasion of the Soviet Union, Hitler told his Italian counterpart that England had lost the war and that any remaining hope among the English rested on the United States and Russia. Acknowledging "no chance of eliminating America," Hitler simultaneously claimed that "whether or not America enters the war is a matter of indifference, inasmuch as she supports our opponent with all the power she is able to mobilize." Hitler expressed no such reservations about his capacity to destroy the Soviet Union, which, he argued, would have the added benefit of taking pressure off of Japan in the event of American involvement.

CONTENT   ★ ★ ★ ★
AESTHETICS   ★ ★ ★ ★
NAVIGATION   ★ ★ ★ ★

The History Place: Adolf Hitler

http://www.historyplace.com/worldwar2

Philip Gavin, the founder and publisher of The History Place, has written a biography of Hitler specifically for this web page. An amateur historian, Gavin cites as sources for his online biography the most well-known scholarly works on Hitler, including William Shirer's *The Rise and Fall of the Third Reich*, Alan Bullock's *Hitler: A Study in Tyranny*, and Ian Kershaw's recently published, two-volume study, *Hitler: 1889–1936, Hubris* and *Hitler: 1936–1945, Nemesis*.

Drawing material from these scholars and others, Gavin has produced a two-part, 42-chapter biography. The first twenty-four chapters comprise part one, The Rise of Hitler, and cover the years from his birth to his appointment as chancellor in 1933. Part two, The Triumph of Hitler, extends the story from 1933 to 1939 and focuses on Hitler's consolidation of power, his persecution of German and European Jews, and his territorial ambitions. Presumably a third part, something along the lines of The Fall of Hitler, is being developed.

Each chapter focuses on a central theme or event, such as The Night of the Long Knives, The Nuremberg Laws, The Conquest at Munich, The Night of Broken Glass (Kristallnacht), and The Nazi-Soviet Pact. Some, but not all, of the chapters are accompanied by photographs. Gavin's biography of Hitler is essentially a tertiary source (drawn almost entirely from secondary accounts) and includes no primary documents. Nevertheless, it is as comprehensive a biography of the German leader as one will find on the web and will certainly prove interesting and useful to anyone looking for general information on Hitler's life and rise to power.

CONTENT   ★ ★ ★
AESTHETICS   ★ ★ ★
NAVIGATION   ★ ★ ★

MACARTHUR, DOUGLAS

Douglas MacArthur: The American Experience
http://www.pbs.org/wgbh/amex/macarthur/index.html

Simultaneously admired and reviled, Douglas MacArthur served as army chief of staff during the Great Depression, commanded American forces in the Pacific during World War II, served as the supreme Allied commander of occupied Japan from the end of World War II until 1950, and commanded an American-led coalition of United Nations forces in the Korean War until relieved by President Harry S. Truman. Created in conjunction with a PBS American Experience documentary, this site contains a variety of primary source material on the life of a man whom narrator David McCullough describes "as a glamorous, patriotic, often brilliant, sometimes not so brilliant, infinitely interesting American leader, who was as gifted at holding center stage as any of the other great actors of his time."

The web page is divided into six sections, several of which merit mention. The Film and More section contains a complete transcript of the documentary, plus extended transcripts with some of the historians interviewed for the film. Most important and of greatest interest to researchers and educators, The Film and More contains a host of primary source documents, including letters from MacArthur's mother (in 1924 she wrote General John Pershing and asked that her son be promoted to major general—MacArthur received the promotion), letters from MacArthur to his wife during World War II, the general's most famous speeches, and a number of documents relating to Truman's dismissal of MacArthur.

Special Features includes interviews with American and Filipino soldiers who were captured at Bataan in 1942 and forced on the infamous Bataan Death March. Several of those interviewed escaped from the march and fought the Japanese with guerilla units for three years until MacArthur's triumphal return to liberate the island in 1945. A section entitled Maps has a small selection, but students will enjoy an interactive map that allows them to follow MacArthur around the world. In addition, a series of four maps details MacArthur's invasion of the Philippines in 1945.

People and Events contains useful descriptions of key events such as the Battle for Manila and the Tokyo War Crimes Trial, as well as biographies of MacArthur, several of his relatives, and key political and military officials such as Army Chief of Staff George Marshall; Admiral Chester Nimitz, commander of the Pacific Fleet; and Japanese emperor Hirohito. Although none of these biographies is extensive, each is informative and helps to put MacArthur's life and military career in perspective.

CONTENT   ★ ★ ★ ★
AESTHETICS   ★ ★ ★ ★
NAVIGATION   ★ ★ ★ ★

ROOSEVELT, FRANKLIN DELANO

Fireside Chats of Franklin D. Roosevelt
http://www.mhric.org/fdr/fdr.html

More so than in response to any one idea or set of beliefs, a majority of the American public embraced Roosevelt because of his ability to connect with them emotionally at a time of great economic and personal distress. Central to his rapport with the public was his mastery of the radio as a means of communication, conveyed most effectively through his Fireside Chats. On March 12, 1933, just a week after his inauguration, Roosevelt spoke to the nation in a speech entitled "On the Bank Crisis" in an effort to assure nervous depositors that their money was safe. He succeeded.

Roosevelt's address that night was the first of thirty-one Fireside Chats that he delivered throughout his presidency, more than half of which pertain to World War II. On September 3, 1939, after years of using the Fireside Chats to discuss the Great Depression and New Deal, he turned his attention to the conflict that would consume the remainder of his presidency and life. On January 6, 1945, he delivered the last of his Fireside Chats, when he spoke to the American people in an address entitled "Work or Fight." In between he used the chats to talk about the declaration of war against Japan, the Teheran and Cairo conferences, and the fall of Rome.

This site has gathered together the full text of each of Roosevelt's Fireside Chats. Given his command of the radio as a medium of communication, students of the war and fans of Roosevelt can only hope that Fireside Chats of Franklin D. Roosevelt will eventually include audio versions of his radio addresses. Nonetheless, this site is an important source for an understanding of Roosevelt and World War II.

CONTENT   ★ ★ ★ ★
AESTHETICS   ★ ★ ★ ★
NAVIGATION   ★ ★ ★ ★

Franklin Delano Roosevelt Library and Digital Archive
http://www.fdrlibrary.marist.edu

Without a doubt, the Franklin Delano Roosevelt Digital Archive is the single most comprehensive and important online resource for understanding Roosevelt's leadership throughout World War II. Although the library has to date placed only a fraction of its holdings online (new material is added regularly), researchers, educators, and students can peruse more than 13,000 primary documents and thousands of photographs.

The documents that have been digitized so far all come from the collection known as the President's Secretary's File (PSF). Half of the documents come from that portion of the PSF known as the Safe Files, so named because they were literally kept in a locked safe in the White House. Covering Roosevelt's entire presidency, 1933 to 1945, but concentrated on the war years, the Safe Files consist primarily of declassified national security material. Researchers will find correspondence, memoranda, and reports relating to the Manhattan Project, the Atlantic Charter, the United Nations, the War and State Departments, and various Allied and Axis leaders.

The other 6,500 documents are from the PSF's Diplomatic Files and detail relations between the United States and Britain, Germany, and the Vatican. The wealth of material available here is staggering; researchers and students can trace the relationship forged between Roosevelt and Churchill throughout the late 1930s and read the two leaders' discussions about the deteriorating military situation. The German Diplomatic Files are equally fascinating and include intelligence reports on Hitler and other Nazi leaders; reports filed in the later stages of the war discuss the postwar treatment of Germany. The Vatican Files include wartime correspondence between Roosevelt, Pope Pius XII—whose role in the war has come under sharp criticism in recent years—and the American ambassador to the Vatican (the United States had not appointed a representative to the Vatican in seventy years, but Roosevelt thought it important to do so in 1939 as war threatened Europe).

In addition to the wealth of documents Franklin Delano Roosevelt Library and Digital Archive includes thousands of photographs divided into three sections: Franklin and Eleanor Roosevelt, The Great Depression and the New Deal, and World War II. Shot by photographers hired by the federal government, the photographs are in the public domain and thus available to the public without copyright restrictions. Images from World War II run the gamut from the ceremonial to the horrific. Visitors will find images of female welders on the home front, commando training, soldiers in combat, leaders such as Roosevelt and Churchill, and the gruesome juxtaposition of Christmas wreaths and a pile of dead bodies at Buchenwald.

While the documents and photographs are undoubtedly the most important holdings of the Franklin Delano Roosevelt Digital Archive, researchers will also be interested in a handful of sound clips from some of Roosevelt's most famous speeches. Despite the size of the archive, the materials are well indexed by category and thus easily navigable.

CONTENT   ★ ★ ★ ★ ★
AESTHETICS   ★ ★ ★ ★
NAVIGATION   ★ ★ ★ ★ ★

TRUMAN, HARRY S.

Project Whistlestop: Harry S. Truman Digital Archive
http://www.trumanlibrary.org/whistlestop

Originally conceived as a joint venture of the Truman Presidential Library, the University of Missouri, and public school teachers and administrators throughout Missouri, Project Whistlestop will interest educators intent on introducing technology and primary source material in the classroom, as well as researchers hoping to access a portion of the vast holdings of the Truman Library. While the Truman digital archive contains but a fraction of the materials held by the Truman Library, this site does include a wealth of letters, diary entries, speeches, cartoons, photographs, and official documents that tell the story of Harry Truman's involvement in some of the twentieth century's most pivotal events.

Until the fall of 2001, Project Whistlestop existed as its own well-organized, easy-to-navigate site. More recently, however, Project Whistlestop has merged with the Truman Library's web site. Researchers who go directly to the library's home page will discover that the merger has made it more difficult to navigate the rich offerings in the Whistlestop archive. A link from the home page to Project Whistlestop does exist, but it does not make the researcher's job much easier. Fortunately, the above URL allows visitors to bypass the Truman Library home page and directly access the Site Integration Map, which pairs the old table of contents (which corresponds with the following review) with links to the same materials on the new site. Therefore, visitors are advised to navigate the site via the Site Integration Map.

Project Whistlestop's research materials are divided into six main sections: Truman: Life and Times, Photos, Cartoons, Letters, Speeches, and Official Documents. Truman: Life and Times provides comprehensive biographical information on the life of the nation's thirty-third president. Dozens of photographs from all periods of Truman's life show him in the company of family and friends as well as other prominent Americans and world leaders. Although the editorial cartoons posted on Project Whistlestop pertain specifically to post–World War II events, the creators of the site have included a helpful guide for teachers called Teaching with Cartoons, which offers suggestions for incorporating editorial and political cartoons into the curriculum. Both audio and textual versions of significant Truman speeches are available.

Project Whistlestop includes more than twenty letters that Truman wrote to his wife Bess between 1911 and 1943, plus two dozen additional letters written to Bess while he was serving as an infantry officer in World War I. In addition, visitors will find close to a dozen letters that Truman wrote to his daughter Margaret. The site contains the full text of each of these letters as well as scanned versions of many of the original handwritten letters to Bess.

The Official Documents section alone makes Project Whistlestop a must visit for educators, students, and researchers. Drawing on an array of primary materials from the holdings of the Truman Library, the site's designers have created study collections on ten major events of Truman's presidency: the decision to drop the atomic bomb, the Marshall Plan, the Truman Doctrine, the desegregation of the armed forces, the recognition of Israel as a state, the 1948 campaign, the Korean War, the Berlin Airlift, NATO, and the United Nations. To provide just one example of the value of these materials, the documents on the decision to drop the atomic bomb include minutes from internal White House meetings, commission reports, letters to and from various military officials with regard to testing and targeting, official press releases, and more. In addition, each study collection comes with suggested teaching units, lesson plans, and classroom activities.

In fact, the emphasis on students, teachers, and interactive learning is one of the truly unique aspects of Project Whistlestop. Separate sections entitled Teacher Resources and Student Guide offer creative suggestions for lesson plans, student projects, and other curricular activities based on the Truman digital archive. For example, students who select Student Guide and scroll down to Games will discover "A Spy's Dilemma: A Problem in Intelligent Choice and a Matter of Life and Death," in which they must imagine themselves as a Soviet spy who has slipped into Truman's office and broken into his files. The students are then presented with an array of secret documents, and as a result of a shortage of film, must choose five to return to Stalin. The spy's life depends upon choosing the right documents. Although students are unlikely to end up in the Gulag for making the wrong decision, they will find such exercises a stimulating way to engage the rich primary resources available on Project Whistlestop.

With the exception of the invaluable section on the decision to drop the atomic bomb, the content of Project Whistlestop, like Truman's presidency, is focused on the postwar period. Nevertheless, researchers, students, and teachers interested in the affect of World War II on Cold War politics, diplomacy, and national security will not want to miss this site. For those interested specifically in the war years, the Truman Library home page, accessible from the Project Whistlestop Site Integration Map, does provide a link to an interesting collection of Pearl Harbor radio newscasts that the library comaintains with the University of Missouri at Kansas City.

CONTENT   ★ ★ ★ ★ ★
AESTHETICS   ★ ★ ★ ★
NAVIGATION   ★ ★ ★

SUGGESTED READINGS

Ambrose, Stephen E. *The Supreme Commander: The War Years of General Dwight D. Eisenhower* (Garden City, NY, 1970).

Bix, Herbert P. *Hirohito and the Making of Modern Japan* (New York, 2000).

Berthon, Simon. *Allies at War: The Bitter Rivalry among Churchill, Roosevelt, and DeGaulle* (New York, 2001).

Best, Geoffrey. *Churchill: A Study in Greatness* (London, 2001).

Blumenson, Martin. *Patton* (New York, 1985).

Bradley, Omar, with Clay Blair. *A General's Life* (New York, 1983).

Bullock, Alan. *Hitler and Stalin: Parallel Lives* (New York, 1992).

———. *Hitler: A Study in Tyranny* (New York, 1999).

Burns, James MacGregor. *Roosevelt: The Soldier of Freedom* (New York, 1970).

Cornwell, John. *Hitler's Pope: The Secret History of Pius XII* (New York, 2000).

Dallek, Robert. *Franklin D. Roosevelt and American Foreign Policy, 1932–1945* (New York, 1995).

———. "Franklin Roosevelt as World Leader," *American Historical Review* 75, no. 5 (1971): 1503–13 (also available online at JSTOR; requires paid subscription).

Daso, Dik Alan. *Hap Arnold and the Evolution of American Airpower* (Washington, DC, 2000).

Davis, Kenneth S. *FDR: Into the Storm, 1937–1940* (New York, 1993).

———. *FDR: The War President, 1940–1943* (New York, 2001).

Deutscher, Isaac. *Stalin* (New York, 1967).

Eisenhower, David. *Eisenhower at War* (New York, 1986).

Emerson, William. "Franklin Roosevelt as Commander-in-Chief in World War II," *Military Affairs* 22, no. 4 (1958): 181–207 (also available online at JSTOR; requires paid subscription).

Erickson, John. *Stalin's War with Germany*, 2 vols. (New York, 1975).

Gilbert, Martin. *Churchill: A Life* (New York, 1991).

James, D. Clayton. *The Years of MacArthur*, 3 vols. (Boston, 1970–1985).

Jenkins, Roy. *Churchill: A Biography* (New York, 2001).

Kershaw, Ian. *Hitler: 1889–1936, Hubris* (New York, 1999).

———. *Hitler: 1936–1945, Nemesis* (New York, 2001).

Larrabee, Eric. *Commander in Chief: Franklin Delano Roosevelt, His Lieutenants, and Their War* (New York, 1987).

Lucas, James. *Hitler's Commanders: German Bravery in the Field, 1939–1945* (Dorset, U.K., 2001).

Machtan, Lothar. *The Hidden Hitler* (New York, 2001).

Manchester, William. *American Caesar: Douglas MacArthur, 1880–1964* (Boston, 1978).

McCullough, David. *Truman* (New York, 1996).

Megargee, Geoffrey P. *Inside Hitler's High Command* (Lawrence, KS, 2000).

Overy, Richard J. *Russia's War* (New York, 1998).

Perret, Geoffrey. *Old Soldiers Never Die: The Life of Douglas MacArthur* (New York, 1996).

———. *Eisenhower* (New York, 1999).

Persico, Joseph. *Roosevelt's Secret War: FDR and World War II Espionage* (New York, 2001).

Pogue, Forest C. *George C. Marshall*, 4 vols. (New York, 1963–1987).

Radzinskii, Edvard. *Stalin: The First In-Depth Biography Based on Explosive New Documents from Russia's Secret Archives*. Translated by H. T. Willets (New York, 1997).

Roskill, Stephen. *Churchill and the Admirals* (New York, 1978).

Shirer, William L. *The Rise and Fall of the Third Reich* (New York, 1998).

Stafford, David. *Roosevelt and Churchill: Men of Secrets* (Woodstock, NY, 2000).

Stewart, Graham. *Burying Caesar: The Churchill-Chamberlain Rivalry* (New York, 2001).

Weinberg, Gerhard L. *Germany, Hitler and World War II* (New York, 1995).

CHAPTER 3

EUROPEAN/ ATLANTIC/ MEDITERRANEAN THEATER OF OPERATIONS

There were six phases to the vast military actions that took place in the European/Atlantic/Mediterranean theater of war in 1939–1945: the western front (1939–1940), the Battle of the Atlantic (1939–1945), the Mediterranean theater (1940–1945), the eastern front (1939–1945), the strategic bombing of Germany (1943–1945), and the western invasion (1944–1945). The amount of coverage on the Internet (and on paper in libraries) varies greatly, with most attention by far to the last topic.

The battles of the western front began when Hitler invaded Poland in September 1939, and Britain and France immediately declared war. Although outnumbering the German forces, the French and British remained in defensive mode behind their Maginot line. This so-called phony war ended in April 1940, when one Nazi blitzkrieg overran Denmark and Norway and another entered Holland. The French and British rushed toward Holland, but their forces were cut in half by the surprise German attack through the rugged Ardennes Forrest. Miraculously, the Royal Navy managed to evacuate 340,000 British and French troops at Dunkirk and other ports; however, all the weapons, vehicles, supplies, and munitions were lost. France, badly defeated, quickly surrendered. It became "Vichy France," a supposedly neutral country that still controlled a navy and an overseas empire but was in effect a puppet controlled by Berlin. Britain was now defended only by the Royal Navy (RN), which was still powerful, and the Royal Air Force (RAF). Hitler gambled that the Luftwaffe could defeat the RAF in the skies, and then he could neutralize the RN. The Battle of Britain in late summer 1940 saw

Churchill rally the British spirit, while the RAF shot down the Luftwaffe using its new secret weapon—radar. The Luftwaffe had the advantage until it changed strategies; instead of neutralizing the RAF and its radar, it concentrated on the "Blitz" or terror bombing of London. The British people never faltered—the Luftwaffe's air power was wasted against civilians while the RAF had a chance to rebuild its strength. Defeated, Hitler turned his ugly attentions to his ally, the Soviet Union.

The Battle of the Atlantic began in September 1939 when Britain tried to impose the same tight naval blockade that had been so effective in World War I. This time, however, the Germans were ready with a series of moves that made the North Atlantic a contested zone until the last months of the war. In 1940, Germany seized the entire European coastline from Spain to Norway. The British navy could stop most enemy coastal shipping and all trans-Atlantic shipping. Germany sent both a surface fleet and the Luftwaffe to Norway to hunt down British convoys bound for the Soviet Union, leading to a spectacular series of battles. Along the French coastline, the Germans built U-boat (submarine) bases that could intercept Allied shipping. Again the Allied convoy system defeated the submarines. The British, Americans, and Canadians used naval surface and air power to stop the subs. They also developed sophisticated new technologies, including sonar, statistical methods (operations research) to maximize the distribution of assets (see http://www.math.purdue.edu/~eremenko/submarine.html), and analog computers to break the German Enigma codes.

The Allies defeated the U-boats by 1943 and were able to deliver the vast supplies Eisenhower wanted for his invasion. Germany responded with the Schnorchel breathing tubes, which allowed the U-boats to run the diesels and recharge their electrical batteries while still submerged (see http://uboat.net/technical/schnorchel.htm, part of www.uboat.net, an outstanding site reviewed below). They also invented a series of advanced submarines that could run much faster underwater and stay submerged longer to avoid circling aircraft; however, the new boats became operational too late and there were too few to make a difference. (During the Cold War, the Soviet and American navies both copied the new designs.)

In the Mediterranean theater a number of small countries formed alliances with one or the other major powers, tried to stay neutral, and then switched sides, thereby suffering invasion first by one side then the other. In the end, the Mediterranean was a stalemate and sideshow for the main stage further north, though it did provide essential training for Eisenhower, Bradley, Patton, and their inexperienced forces. This, of course, is the American perspective. British historians insist the Mediterranean was the site of heroic episodes in which British forces not only muddled through but outsmarted and outmaneuvered the devilishly clever Germans. Both the American and British historians stage this theater with the Italians playing a comic role of gross stupidity. (Bombing their own fleet, for example, or sending wood-burning stoves to the treeless desert, or being too eager to surrender, and then even botching that.) The main stories involve North Africa and Italy, though Yugoslavia, Greece, and numerous islands played important roles. After the Italians made fools of themselves trying to invade Egypt from their colony in Libya, Hitler sent in Erwin Rommel and the Afrika Corps (see http://www.spartacus.schoolnet.co.uk/GERrommel.htm), who pushed back the British lines. Finally, the British found Rommel's equal in General Bernard Montgomery (see http://www.spartacus.schoolnet.co.uk/2WWmontgomery.htm), and the Germans were rolled back and finally surrendered in spring 1943. In recent years, historians have downplayed the heroes and emphasized logistics and code breaking as the keys to victory. Rommel ran out of fuel because the British had broken the German and Italian codes and were able to sink his tankers.

Using North Africa as a base, Eisenhower led the invasion of Sicily in July 1943 (but allowed the Germans and Italians to escape). The Allies then invaded mainland Italy, which deposed Mussolini and switched sides. Italy was too late, however; its delays allowed the Germans to seize nearly all of the boot and capture the hapless Italian armies. They rescued Mussolini from jail (he had been imprisoned in 1943 and was later killed in 1945 by partisans) and set up a series of strong defensive lines. Although the Germans gradually were pushed back, they did succeed in tying down major Allied forces.

On the eastern front, vast armies moved rapidly over thousands of miles, and millions of soldiers were killed in combat and as many killed as prisoners or civilians. It was a theater of movement and decisive results. Curiously, only one "hero" stands out, Soviet general Georgi Zhukov, on whom web sources are scarce. The Russians have a great deal of interest in Zhukov and the eastern front, but they have limited access to the web. For that matter, historians there still have little access to the basic paper archives. The Germans have good web access but avoid the topic of the eastern front because of all the atrocities and guilt involved. When the war ended, American intelligence interviewed German officers, and some of the reports are online from the CMH's web page at http://www.army.mil/cmh-pg/online/per-ger.htm. Hollywood dealt with the great battle of Stalingrad in *Enemy at the Gates* (2001).

The bombing of Germany was a result of the British and American belief in the doctrine of strategic bombing—the enemy could be defeated by destroying its industrial base far behind the front lines. No other country adopted this doctrine, so no one else had the huge bombers that were needed. Raids began on a large scale in 1943 but were ineffective because only a small fraction of the bombs hit their targets. The solution was more bombs—and more bombers. The main targets were munitions factories and railroad yards in the large cities, along with oil refineries and V-2 sites. The Germans responded by evacuating nonessential civilians from the cities, beefing up civil defense, building bomb shelters, and moving prisoners of war into their factories. As the air war escalated, the Germans spent a larger and larger fraction of their defense budget on interceptor aircraft and anti-aircraft guns and assigned women to combat duty on the gun crews. For the history of these women in combat, see D'Ann Campbell's "Women in Combat: The World War Two Experience in the United States, Great Britain, Germany, and the Soviet Union" (*Journal of Military History* 57 [April 1993]: 301–23; online at http://members.aol.com/DAnno1/combat.html). The effect of the air war remains highly controversial. The German oil system was destroyed, its transportation crippled, and troop movement drastically slowed. Even so the Germans had to be overrun by infantry before they were defeated. After the war the American Strategic Bombing Survey evaluated the impact in great detail (see the summary report at http://www.anesi.com/ussbs02.htm).

The western invasion, launched at Normandy on June 6, 1944, represented the triumph of Allied planning and logistics buildup. The Allied forces did not outnumber the Germans, but with complete command of the air they had mobility; the Germans could only move at night and were desperately short of fuel. In mid-August the German lines suddenly cracked, and they were almost encircled but managed to escape through the Falaise Gap. The Germans abandoned France and found safety behind the Rhine. Hitler gambled his last reserves in the surprise attack known as the Battle of the Bulge in December 1944, but the Germans were decisively defeated. In March the Allies crossed the Rhine (using the Remagen Bridge the Germans had neglected to destroy). Eisenhower's forces met fading resistance as they roared through the industrial heartland and headed toward Berlin. Normandy and its aftermath have been favorite subjects for filmmakers, popular historians and scholars, and now for web builders. The major controversy has been the debate between advocates of the rejected British strategy (calling for a narrow knife thrust forward) and the American strategy of a broad-based advance.

WEB SITE REVIEWS

GENERAL

Band of Brothers
http://www.hbo.com/band

Created in conjunction with the ten-part HBO miniseries of the same name, which chronicles the exploits of the 101st Airborne's 506th Regiment's "Easy" Company from D-Day to the end of the war, the Band of Brothers web site devotes considerable attention to the series and the adventures of its major characters. The most interesting features of this site, however, do not focus exclusively on D-Day or the 101st Airborne. Most notably, viewers will discover six World

War II Experiences, short films of original footage plus related content, entitled Battle of Britain, Combat Training, Occupation of Holland, Invasion of Sicily, The Home Front, and Paratrooper–D-Day.

Furthermore, the creators of Band of Brothers clearly intended that their efforts would remain relevant after the airing of the miniseries. To this end, they have established a continuously expanding Living Memorial of short biographies and anecdotes that can be searched in a variety of ways, including state of residence and branch of service. In addition to the Living Memorial, Band of Brothers includes a section entitled Related Exhibits, which provides an encyclopedic snapshot of a variety of war-related topics, from African Americans in combat, to rationing at home, to the history of the jeep. Finally, the site invites viewers to explore a section entitled Revisit the Home Front, a unique feature that provides factual information of domestic events arranged by zip code.

Although not likely to be of great interest to specialists looking for primary documentation, Band of Brothers hosts an array of basic but useful information. The graphics are excellent, even stunning, but the navigation is at times unnecessarily clumsy. In particular, the main menu lacks direct links to World War II Experiences and Related Exhibits. And although the exhibits can be searched by category, no comprehensive index is available.

CONTENT ★ ★ ★
AESTHETICS ★ ★ ★ ★ ★
NAVIGATION ★ ★ ★

The Center for Military History
WWII Online Bookshelves

http://www.army.mil/cmh-pg/collections/USAWW2/USAWW2.htm

For a full review of this site, see p. 8, and for a review of the material pertaining to the Pacific theater of operations, see p. 58.

Of the seventy-eight-volume official history of the United States Army during World War II, fourteen pertain specifically to the European and Mediterranean theaters. Although only two of these Green Books are currently posted online by the CMH, the volumes on the Cross-Channel Attack (D-Day and Normandy invasion) and the Battle of the Bulge will keep researchers busy for days. The Green Book on the Battle of the Bulge, also known as the Ardennes Offensive, runs nearly seven hundred pages, and the volume on the Cross-Channel Attack contains extensive documentation, including a list of code names and directives from Hitler.

Researchers interested in the European and Mediterranean theaters of operation will also want to peruse fifteen commemorative brochures that cover various battles and campaigns. Published by the CMH in the early 1990s, the full text of these brochures cans be found at http://www.army.mil/cmh-pg/collections/ WW2-Broch.htm. Twenty additional publications from the CMH relating to the war in Europe and the Mediterranean are available at http://www.army.mil/ cmh-pg/online/Bookshelves/WW2-List.htm.

CONTENT   ★ ★ ★ ★ ★
AESTHETICS   ★ ★ ★
NAVIGATION   ★ ★ ★ ★

ATLANTIC/MEDITERRANEAN THEATER

The Merchant Marine in World War II
http://usmm.org/index.html#anchor252856

Often overlooked in histories of World War II, the U.S. Merchant Marine played a crucial role in supplying Allied forces in Europe and the Pacific. In fact, according to this site, the official web page of the merchant marine, it took seven to fifteen tons of equipment to supply each soldier for one year. Involved in every major invasion of World War II, merchant mariners died in the line of duty at a higher rate than troops in all other branches of the military.

Although not solely limited to World War II, this site does a nice job of explaining the importance of the merchant marine to overall Allied strategy. Separate internal links connect visitors to chapters entitled Merchant Marine in WWII, Men and Ships in WWII, Ships Sunk and Damaged, African American Mariners, Women Mariners, POWs, and Names of WWII Mariners Killed. Visitors can read about what the Germans termed "the greatest convoy battle of all time," an engagement in the North Atlantic in March 1943 that pitted eighty-eight merchant ships and their fifteen escorts against forty-five U-boats. Given the constant threat posed to the merchant marine by German U-boats, researchers will find this site useful in conjunction with uboat.net (see review below).

As a whole, this site provides helpful information on a number of merchant marine activities in the Atlantic, including the invasion of Normandy. Furthermore, the section on African American mariners is particularly illuminating. While the rest of the U.S. armed forces remained segregated, the merchant marine integrated its ranks. In 1942, Captain Hugh Malzac became the first black officer to lead an integrated crew when he took command of the SS *Booker T. Washington*.

For a review of the material on this site pertaining to the Pacific theater of operations, *see p. 63.*

CONTENT   ★ ★ ★ ★
AESTHETICS   ★ ★ ★
NAVIGATION   ★ ★ ★ ★

The U-boat War, 1939–1945

http://www.uboat.net

Created by Gudmundur Helgason, The U-boat War, 1939–1945 contains a rich collection of materials on the German U-boats (submarines) and the critical role they played in Germany's overall war strategy. Nearly 13,000 pages contain information on every one of the more than 1,150 commissioned U-boats and the more than 1,400 men who commanded them. Visitors can search the site by boat, simply typing in the number of any vessel, and discover the history of each one: date of commission, commander, number of ships sunk, and even its ultimate fate. A series of maps, divided by regions of the Atlantic and Mediterranean, reveal where each boat engaged its enemy and, in many cases, met its demise. A link allows viewers to move from the map to the individual page of the vessel.

For those less interested in the fate of each German U-boat, this site provides ample information on the commanders and crews. Discover the records of the most successful commanders, or "listen to the commanders in their own words." Separate pages contain biographical information on every commander.

Helgason's interest in the U-boat war extends beyond the German perspective. In a section entitled Fighting the U-boats, visitors will find biographies of many of the American and British submariners who waged the naval war, including Royal Navy captain Johnny Walker, who is considered the "most successful hunter." In addition to the individuals involved in the Allied effort, Helgason provides ample information on the aircraft, ships, and technologies used to find and disable the U-boats.

Furthermore, this site includes more than 1,100 photographs of the boats and men, songs sung on the boats, and models of the various vessels. Ever wonder how many pounds of meat or potatoes a submarine must stock? This site includes a complete list of the food rations carried on board a typical U-boat.

CONTENT ★ ★ ★ ★ ★
AESTHETICS ★ ★ ★
NAVIGATION ★ ★ ★ ★

USS Savannah (CL-42)

http://www.concentric.net/~drake725

Known as the "Streetwalker of the Atlantic," this Brooklyn-class cruiser saw significant action in the Mediterranean. After taking part in the assault on French Morocco in November 1942, the Savannah and her crew played a pivotal role in the invasion of Sicily in July 1943 and the invasion of Italy in September 1943. More than 200 men on the Savannah died during the invasion of Italy and the ship itself was put out of commission, but Winston Churchill's plan to establish a southern front in Europe proved a success and major turning point in the war. In part, the value of this site, which is maintained by the child of a former quartermaster on the *Savannah*, lies precisely in the relative anonymity of the ship. Visitors will come to recognize that hundreds of other such ships and crews contributed mightily to the Allied effort.

Visitors will take particular interest in The Sharon Chronicle, diary and log entries kept by Richard O. Sharon from June 28, 1943, until the invasion of Italy in September. Unfortunately, the navigation is quite clunky; viewers can only move forward or backward one entry at a time rather than skip around at will. Nonetheless, Sharon's words provide a fascinating look at the thoughts, fears, excitements, and even the mundane concerns of at least one enlisted man. On June 28, 1943, for instance, Sharon remarked, "We are still in Algiers and waiting impatiently for the invasion to start." Before long, the invasion had indeed begun, and viewers can sense the pulse of battle as Sharon writes, "heavy bombing attack in progress and we are really pouring lead into the heavens." The log entries are enhanced by photographs with accompanying audio of ships slicing through the water and fending off German dive bombers.

The *Savannah* suffered no deaths in the invasion of Sicily but was not so lucky in the September invasion of Italy. On September 8, Richard Sharon anticipated a tough fight in Italy and expressed hope that he would "still be around after it's all over." Although the creator of this web site provides no information concerning Sharon's fate, that entry proved to be his last.

CONTENT   ★ ★ ★ ★
AESTHETICS   ★ ★ ★
NAVIGATION   ★ ★ ★

EUROPEAN THEATER

Battle of the Bulge
http://users.skynet.be/bulgecriba/battlebul.htm

The official web page of the Belgian-based Center of Research and Information on the Battle of the Bulge (CRIBA), this site provides the most comprehensive collection of online resources for anyone interested in the Battle of the Bulge. Fought between December 16, 1944, and January 28, 1945, in the towns, villages, and woods in and around Belgium's Ardennes Forest, the campaign proved to be the last great German offensive of World War II.

Battle of the Bulge includes an historical overview that sets the battle within the broader context of the Allied offensive that began with D-Day in June 1944. A quick glance at the accessible and comprehensive index reveals the multiplicity of sources that make this site an essential visit: after action reports, combat interviews, maps, letters from the front and hospital, memoirs penned a half century later, battle orders, and accounts of specific engagements. The site contains some information on the role played by British forces during the Battle of the Bulge, although most of the material pertains to their American Allies.

A list of American units that participated in the battle is so extensive that one cannot help but recognize the enormity of the offensive. Detailed accounts of the involvement of several of these units, including the graves registration service, enhance the value of this site.

CONTENT ★ ★ ★ ★ ★
AESTHETICS ★ ★ ★
NAVIGATION ★ ★ ★ ★

Normandy 1944

http://www.normandy.eb.com

The brainchild of the creators of *Encyclopedia Brittanica,* Normandy 1944 provides a thorough and easily navigable analysis of D-Day and the Normandy invasion from a multiplicity of perspectives. The site is centered on five chapters of text authored by famed military historian John Keegan. Entitled Buildup, Invasion, Fighting Inland, Breakout, and Normandy in Memory, the chapters provide an informative history of the invasion that will prove more interesting to generalists than scholars. Nevertheless, the site contains additional information that should attract even the most serious researchers.

Each of Keegan's chapters contains a host of links to biographies of key political and military leaders, many of them well known but others less likely to be recognized. Other links provide information on places and events that figured prominently in the Normandy invasion. In addition, sidebars to each chapter connect viewers to news stories, radio broadcasts, personal histories, maps, and significant war documents. At the foot of each chapter, an easy-to-navigate table of contents allows visitors to view a series of indexes, each of which catalogues the people, places, maps, documents, and weapons and tactics mentioned throughout the site.

Normandy 1944 is particularly valuable because of its attention to both sides of the invasion. Although relatively short and somewhat encyclopedic, Allied and Axis oral histories appear alongside one another. The assembled documents include not only the Allied "Joint Operation Plan" for Operation Overlord but also the November 1943 "Directive Number 51," in which Hitler anticipated the likely Allied invasion.

CONTENT ★ ★ ★
AESTHETICS ★ ★ ★
NAVIGATION ★ ★ ★ ★

World War Two in Europe
http://www.historyplace.com/worldwar2/timeline/ww2time.htm

Maintained by The History Place, a commercial venture, World War Two in Europe provides a timeline of major events from Germany's defeat in World War I through the end of World War II and the Nuremberg Trials. Although the chronology itself will be of general interest to students of the war, the accompanying photographs and text earned this site its review. The majority of events noted in the chronology do not link to extended text, but enough do to make this site worth a visit.

The History Place's timeline is strongest in its treatment of Hitler and the Third Reich. Significant attention is paid to the pre-1939 history of the Nazi Party and its key figures. The site includes a substantial biography of Hitler (in the form of forty-two short chapters, which are reviewed in Chapter 2), along with shorter treatments of Reinhard Heydrich and Rudolf Hess. A number of speeches, including an audio version of one Hitler diatribe, and primary documents, such as the Nazi-Soviet Pact, are available. Perhaps most chilling is the plan for the Final Solution, which itemizes the homelands of more than 11 million European Jews targeted for destruction. In addition to Hitler's rise to power, World War II in Europe devotes significant space to his fall. Visitors will find a detailed account of the führer's final days and suicide.

Wonderful photographs, most of them from the National Archives, enhance the value of this site. In addition to pictures of war-related destruction, particularly moving and memorable images include a tearful Frenchman watching as the Germans occupy Paris and Japanese American children on their way to internment camps.

CONTENT   ★ ★ ★ ★
AESTHETICS   ★ ★ ★
NAVIGATION   ★ ★ ★

CODE BREAKING

Codes and Ciphers in the Second World War
http://www.codesandciphers.org.uk

Those interested in the importance of code breaking to overall Allied strategy in World War II will not find a more interesting or important web site than Codes and Ciphers in the Second World War. Tony Sale, who began his career at Bletchley Park, the famed World War II home of Britain's top secret program, and later became the first curator of the Bletchley Park Museum, is the inspiration behind Codes and Ciphers. Although not particularly well designed, this site combines a remarkable wealth of information with an exceptional interactive learning experience.

Codes and Ciphers is divided into four main sections entitled The Enigma, The Lorenz Cipher and the Colossus, Original World War II Documents, and *Enigma* (the motion picture, 2002). Sale's pages on the Enigma offer an exceptionally detailed, step-by-step explanation of the principle behind cipher systems in general and the Enigma in particular, how the machine was built and operated, how it was adapted for military use, the problems that confronted code breakers, and the ultimate weaknesses in the system that allowed its penetration. In addition to providing a thorough course on the nuances of code breaking, Codes and Ciphers comes loaded with a terrific Enigma simulator; Sale actually walks visitors through the steps that an operator of the machine would have followed before encoding a message. Hired as the technical adviser for *Enigma*, Sale has posted a series of messages that he encoded and then deciphered for the film.

Like its counterpart the Enigma, the Lorenz Cipher occupied the attention of those employed at Bletchley Park. Even when code breakers succeeded in decoding and deciphering messages, the process often took so long that the information was useless by the time of its discovery. Consequently, cryptanalysts began looking for a way to automate the process. Eventually, just in time to prove crucial for final D-Day preparations, the creation of the Colossus reduced the time needed to break messages from weeks to hours. Sale's pages on the Colossus are as informative as those on the Enigma. And, once again, visitors have a rare opportunity for true interactive learning with a Virtual Colossus. The section entitled Original World War II Documents includes such fascinating source material as the German manual for the naval use of the Enigma, instructions for the double encryption of naval messages, the Bletchley Park Cryptographic Dictionary, and several documents on the breaking of the Lorenz Cipher, including one that was kept secret until 2000.

CONTENT   ★ ★ ★ ★
AESTHETICS   ★ ★ ★
NAVIGATION   ★ ★ ★

Decoding Nazi Secrets
http://www.pbs.org/wgbh/nova/decoding

Similar to a typewriter in appearance, the German Enigma contained 159,000,000,000,000,000,000 possible settings for enciphering and deciphering messages. From the start of World War II, British intelligence devoted vast resources to breaking the Enigma code. British and American mathematicians, scientists, crossword fanatics, and chess masters, most with little or no experience in code breaking, were brought together at England's Bletchley Park to solve the riddle of the Enigma. According to many historians, the success of this most top secret of Allied efforts may have shortened the war by as much as two or three years.

A companion web site to a PBS Nova documentary of the same name, Decoding Nazi Secrets presents a fascinating look at the Enigma and the efforts of those at Bletchley Park to break the code. Given the incredibly complex permutations of the Enigma, visitors to Decoding the Nazi Secrets may want to begin with the sections entitled How the Enigma Works and Mind of a Codebreaker. Both are excerpted from scholarly books and provide a necessary introduction to a subject that might easily appear beyond comprehension. The site also includes an unabridged transcript, complete with interviews of key participants, of the two-hour television broadcast that originally aired in 1999. The transcript provides a detailed look at the contributions of various individuals, including a lesser-known group of Polish cryptologists who cracked an earlier version of the Enigma at a time when their British and French counterparts showed little interest. A tale of genius, luck, and human error, the decoding of the Enigma is a riveting story.

To their credit, the creators of Decoding Nazi Secrets chose not to turn this web site into a mere online version of their documentary film. Instead the site allows visitors the opportunity for interaction in the sections entitled Solve the Cipher and Send a Coded Message. Computer scientists have created a series of increasingly difficult exercises that put participants in the shoes of the original code breakers at Bletchley Park.

CONTENT ★ ★ ★ ★
AESTHETICS ★ ★ ★ ★
NAVIGATION ★ ★ ★ ★

GERMAN WAR EFFORT

Feldgrau.com
http://www.feldgrau.com

Created in 1996 by Californian Jason Pipes, Feldgrau.com is the most comprehensive online resource on the history of the German military from 1919 to 1945. Although the site is still a work in progress, Pipes and his assistants have already produced more than 1,800 pages on the units, formations, and organizations of all branches of the German armed forces. An amateur historian whose interest in military history began in high school, Pipes has drawn his information from an extensive list of primary and secondary sources as well as thousands of photographs, a number of which are included on this site.

Feldgrau.com is divided into separate sections on the Reichswehr (the German armed forces prior to 1935), Heer (army), Luftwaffe (air force), Kriegsmarine (navy), Waffen SS, and auxiliary units. In addition, Feldgrau.com includes useful histories of the units and organization of other European Axis forces, a section on the major campaigns of World War II, and several other features. Well indexed and organized, the site allows visitors to move easily from deep within one section to another without backtracking to the home page. A site-specific search engine aids the navigation. Unit names appear in German, often but not always with English translations. Although a comprehensive glossary provides such translations, those who do not read German may find some aspects of the site confusing.

Without a doubt, Feldgrau.com is for those specifically interested in the organization of the German military. It is highly specialized and full of orders of battle for a given campaign or unit, but researchers should not expect to find after action reports or biographies of major commanders. For instance, a search for Erwin Rommel produces numerous references and citations but no biography of one of the German military's most important figures.

CONTENT   ★ ★ ★ ★
AESTHETICS   ★ ★ ★ ★
NAVIGATION   ★ ★ ★ ★

German Propaganda Archive
http://www.calvin.edu/academic/cas/gpa

The German Propaganda Archive contains a rich collection of primary source materials on Nazi propaganda. Part of a larger site devoted to exposing the use of propaganda in both Nazi Germany and the German Democratic Republic (East Germany), the archive is maintained by Randall Bytwerk, a professor of Communication Arts and Sciences at Calvin College in Michigan. Pre-1933 Nazi Propaganda includes numerous speeches, pamphlets, and essays, most of them authored by Joseph Goebbels, the future minister of propaganda for the Third Reich. Cartoons from a Nazi magazine as well as more than forty color posters provide visual imagery of Nazi election slogans and attacks on Jews and communists.

The bulk of the archive can be found in the six main sections organized collectively under the heading 1933–1945 Material. More than seventy speeches and essays by Goebbels, including his annual New Year's Eve addresses and tributes to Hitler's birthday, plus assorted speeches from other Nazi leaders, are gathered together in Speeches and Writings by Nazi Leaders. A section entitled Anti-Semitic Material contains speeches and essays outlining Nazi racial policies and theory as well as selections from Julius Streicher's fiercely anti-Semitic newspaper, *Der Stürmer*. One Streicher article called for the extermination of the Jews as early as 1933.

Visual Material contains a fascinating array of photographs, postcards, art, cartoons, posters, and even postage stamps. Photographs document Hitler's seizure of power in 1933 and a subsequent rally in Nuremberg. Booklets celebrate Hitler's "achievements." Nearly four dozen posters document important events from the election of 1933 to World War II.

The remaining sections—War Propaganda, 1939–1945, Miscellaneous Propaganda, and Material from Nazi Periodicals for Propagandists—are equally rich. A pamphlet entitled "Europe and America," one of the many items of Miscellaneous Propaganda, offers an analysis of America's racial makeup from the Nazi perspective. A collection of leaflets from D-Day, found amidst the collection in War Propaganda, 1939–1945, attempts to demoralize American troops and lead them to question their participation in the war. One asks if the American GI can be sure of getting a job if he is lucky enough to make it home alive. Another reads: "A gravestone somewhere in France or somewhere in Europe. He was rather a nice boy, was Sam Doodle, his parents joy, beloved of all who used to know him. But he lost, first his head and then his life and became an ass and then a stiff."

The primary source materials available on the German Propaganda Archive are staggering in their richness and scope. Serious researchers will not want to miss this well-indexed and easily navigable site.

CONTENT	★ ★ ★ ★
AESTHETICS	★ ★ ★
NAVIGATION	★ ★ ★

POWs

A Raid on Munich
http://camomilesworld.com/raid/index.html

On December 21, 1942, Canadian Harry Sanders and the rest of his Royal Air Force flight crew were shot down after a bombing run on Nazi headquarters in Munich. Sanders was one of only two survivors. Captured within fifteen minutes, Sanders spent more than two years in Stalag VIIIB, the largest prisoner of war (POW) camp in Germany. The camp was located in the remote region of Upper Silesia in eastern Germany, making escape difficult. Furthermore, the camp had, as Sanders points out, a notorious reputation among prisoners. Sanders, for instance, was forced to wear a body harness and iron ball for more than a year of his confinement. A Raid on Munich is maintained by Sanders's daughter as a tribute to her father and includes brief first-person accounts of the crash and imprisonment, as well as an excellent map that delineates the distance between the crash site and POW camp.

While Sanders's accounts of the crash and imprisonment are interesting, his much more detailed log of the infamous, and inhumane, Lamsdorf Death March makes this site a must visit. On January 22, 1945, as the German army crumbled in the east and west, Sanders and other prisoners—poorly clothed and fed—began a forced march through the dead of winter, much of it by foot and some by train, that lasted three months. Sanders kept a log of this ordeal, as his captors forced the POWs to march across eastern Germany into Poland, back west toward Bavaria, and then southeast toward the Czech border. Finally, on April 22, 1945, the German guards abandoned their prisoners, who were then found by an advance guard of American troops. An excellent map traces the entire route of the march.

The details of Sanders's log are horrifying. On only the third day, he wrote, "marched again well into the night, numerous fellows falling out only to die by the wayside. Germans just leaving tags on them. No rest halts." The conditions did not improve. Starvation, frozen limbs, and aching joints were ever present. When allowed out of the cold, the men were crammed into jail cells or other tight spaces. As the days and weeks passed, Sanders wrote less and less, no doubt a reflection of his worsening condition. On April 22, snow and hail fell continuously. Without food or shelter, Sanders describes himself as covered in lice, too weak to go much farther. Within hours, American forces freed Sanders and those who remained alive.

CONTENT   ★ ★ ★ ★
AESTHETICS ★ ★ ★ ★
NAVIGATION ★ ★ ★ ★

Stalag Luft I Online
http://www.merkki.com

During World War II, nearly 9,000 Allied airmen, most of them Americans, were imprisoned at Stalag Luft I in Barth, Germany. Among the POWs at Stalag I was Dick Williams, a native of Alabama, who was shot down on his twenty-ninth bombing run in November 1944 (airmen were normally considered to have finished their tour of duty after thirty missions). Williams died years later without sharing his POW experience with his family, a void that led them on a journey of discovery culminating in the creation of this web site. To the credit of the Williams family, Stalag Luft I Online is not a memorial to one man but rather a comprehensive online resource that combines primary documents, oral histories, and secondary sources. Researchers will be happy to know that this site remains a work in progress and is therefore destined to offer more than it does already.

Stalag Luft I Online combines attractive graphics and a sensible index that allows for easy navigation between more than a dozen sections. The most important chapters are The POW Stories, a series of oral histories and recollections of former POWs; The Photos, a collection of images from a variety of sources, including the album of a German guard known as "Henry the Butcher" because of his prewar job in New York; The Interrogators and The Guards, a selection of biographies and photographs of German officers and guards; and The Russians, a synopsis of the Red Army's liberation of the camp on May 1, 1945.

Two other chapters deserve special mention: The Camp Newspaper and Documents. Prisoners at Stalag Luft I secretly published the *POW-WOW* (Prisoners of War—Waiting on Winning), a two-page (one sheet, front and back) daily billed as "The Only Truthful Newspaper in Germany." Gathering their news from a radio assembled from stolen parts, the prisoners smuggled the newspaper between barracks in a hollowed-out wristwatch. Prisoners were under strict instructions to read the *POW-WOW* "silently, quickly, and in groups of three." Among the issues of the *POW-WOW* available online are those announcing D-Day, the liberation of Paris, the breaking of the Siegfried Line, the liberation of the camp, and V-E Day.

The section entitled Documents contains a variety of primary and secondary sources, including official reports from military intelligence detailing conditions in the camp, instructions to airmen on what to do in the event of capture, POW bulletins from the Red Cross, and an account of a speech by Colonel Henry Spicer that led to a sentence of death for inciting a riot. The Red Army liberated Stalag Luft I the day before Spicer's scheduled execution.

CONTENT   ★ ★ ★ ★ ★
AESTHETICS   ★ ★ ★ ★
NAVIGATION   ★ ★ ★ ★

SUGGESTED READINGS

Ambrose, Stephen E. *Band of Brothers: E Company, 506th Regiment, 101st Airborne from Normandy to Hitler's Eagle Nest* (New York, 2001).

Barnett, Correlli, ed. *Hitler's Generals* (New York, 1989).

Beevor, Antony. *Stalingrad: The Fateful Siege, 1942–1943* (New York, 1998).

Bradley, John F. *The Illustrated History of the Third Reich* (New York, 1998).

Burleigh, Michael. *The Third Reich: A New History* (New York, 2000).

Carafano, James Jay. *After D-Day: Operation Cobra and the Normandy Breakout* (Boulder, CO, 2000).

Carruthers, Bob, and John Erickson. *The Russian Front, 1941–1945* (New York, 1999).

Center for Military History, *American Military History* (http://www.army.mil/cmh-pg/books/AMH/amh-toc.htm).

Chancellor, Henry. *Colditz: The Untold Story of World War II's Great Escapes* (New York, 2002).

Claasen, Adam R. A. *Hitler's Northern War: The Luftwaffe's Ill-Fated Campaign, 1940–1945* (Lawrence, KS, 2001).

Clay, Blair, Jr. *Hitler's U-Boat War: The Hunters, 1939–1942* (New York, 2000).

——. *Hitler's U-Boat War: The Hunted, 1942–1944* (New York, 2000).

Cole, Hugh. *Ardennes: Battle of the Bulge* (Washington, DC, 1965).

Craven, Wesley Frank, and J. L. Cate. *The Army Air Forces in World War II,* 7 vols. (Chicago, 1948–58).

Dear, I. C. B., and M. R. D. Foot, eds. *The Oxford Companion to the Second World War* (New York, 2000).

D'Este, Carlo. *Decision in Normandy* (New York, 1994).

——. *Patton: A Genius for War* (New York, 1996).

Dupuy, Trevor N., et al. *Hitler's Last Gamble: The Battle of the Bulge* (New York, 1994).

Durand, Arthur A. *Stalag Luft III: The Secret Story* (Baton Rouge, LA, 1999).

Glantz, David M. *When Titans Clashed: How the Red Army Stopped Hitler* (Lawrence, KS, 1998).

Hamilton, Nigel. *Monty: The Battles of Field Marshal Bernard Montgomery* (New York, 1994).

Keegan, John. *Six Armies in Normandy: From D-Day to the Liberation of Paris, June 6th–August 25th, 1944* (New York, 1982).

Knox, MacGregor. *Hitler's Italian Allies: Royal Armed Forces, Fascist Regime, and the War of 1940–1943* (New York, 2000).

Large, David Clay. *Berlin* (New York, 2000).

Leighton, Richard M. "OVERLORD Revisited: An Interpretation of American Strategy in the European War, 1942–1944," *American Historical Review* 68, no. 4 (1963): 919–37 (also available online at JSTOR; requires paid subscription).

Lewis, Adrian. *Omaha Beach: A Flawed Victory* (Chapel Hill, NC, 2001).

May, Ernest R. *Strange Victory: Hitler's Conquest of France* (New York, 2000).

Müller, Rolf-Dieter, and Gerd R. Ueberschär, *Hitler's War in the East, 1941–1945: A Critical Assessment* (New York, 2001).

Neillands, Robin. *The Bomber War: The Allied Air Offensive against Nazi Germany* (Woodstock, NY, 2001).

Overy, Richard. *The Battle of Britain: The Myth and the Reality* (New York, 2001).

Parker, Danny. *Hitler's Ardennes Offensive: The German View of the Battle of the Bulge* (Mechanicsburg, PA, 1997).

Powers, Stephen T. "The Battle of Normandy: The Lingering Controversy," *Journal of Military History* 56, no. 3 (1992): 455–71 (also available online at JSTOR; requires paid subscription).

Rolf, David. *The Bloody Road to Tunis: Destruction of the Axis Forces in North Africa, November 1942–May 1943* (London, 2001).

Tout, Ken. *The Bloody Battle for Tilly: Normandy 1944* (New York, 2000).

Vaccaro, Tony. *Entering Germany: 1944–1949* (New York, 2001).

World War II: The War in Europe (DVD from the History Channel, 2000).

Young, Desmond. *Rommel: The Desert Fox* (New York, 1986).

CHAPTER 4

PACIFIC THEATER OF OPERATIONS

The war in the Pacific covered one-third of the globe. In the end the fact that the American economy was ten times bigger than Japan's—and grew during the war—meant that only one power could overcome the logistical challenge. Militarily the war saw a sudden Japanese blitzkrieg in the first ninety days that was phenomenally successful. At Pearl Harbor, Isoruko Yamamoto won the greatest and most one-sided naval victory since his great hero, Admiral Heihachiro Togo, sank the Russian fleet in 1905—or, indeed, since Horatio Nelson sank the French at Trafalgar in 1805. Both the Japanese and American navies were firm believers in Admiral Alfred Thayer Mahan's doctrine of sea power. They both believed that the nation that knocked out the opponent's naval power in a decisive fleet battle would win the war. Yamamoto's highly innovative use of naval aviation at Pearl Harbor had indeed destroyed the American battleship fleet, but both sides suddenly realized that naval aviation would fight the decisive battle, not the old battle wagons. America's small carrier fleet had not been damaged; FDR rushed ahead with the construction of a vast fleet of aircraft carriers, which the Japanese could never dream of matching.

Meanwhile, Japanese air power sank the British fleet and allowed land forces to seize Singapore, the major remaining Allied stronghold west of San Francisco. The Japanese also destroyed MacArthur's air force and invaded and captured the Philippines as well as Guam, numerous islands, and Hong Kong. The Dutch and Australian forces were likewise demolished, as Japanese fleets steamed toward India and Australia. The

Zero fighter plane—light, versatile, and very long range—proved remarkably successful. The Americans captured a crashed model in Alaska and reverse engineered it to discover its flaws. The Zero gained its long range by lack of armor, so Grumman Aviation built 11,000 Hellcats to defeat the Zero—the Hellcat had shorter range but was faster, climbed well, was armored, and carried six machine guns to riddle any Zero in its sights (see http://www.cris.com/~Twist/airwar/f6f/f6f-3.shtml). The Japanese failed to significantly improve the Zero or any of their weapons systems, nor did they borrow German technology. Meanwhile, the Americans made dramatic advances in aircraft design, anti-aircraft systems (especially proximity fuzes and radar), and, of course, the atomic bomb.

The Allies quickly recovered and stopped Japanese advances at the Battle of Coral Sea in May 1942—the first great naval battle fought entirely by aircraft. The Japanese were by now badly overextended. They had the fighting power to win battles but not the logistical support for their forward bases, which were spread over millions of square miles. Yamamoto unwisely decided to seize the central island of Midway. Now that the war was so fluid, he had to rely primarily on radio communications. The American "MAGIC" cryptography program decrypted enough of the radio messages so Allied forces knew Midway was the target, and Admiral Ernest King (the Chief of Naval Operations) gambled everything by concentrating all his forces in defense of Midway in June 1942. The Japanese admirals were confused regarding their mission and divided their forces, and this time they were caught by surprise. Japan lost four irreplaceable carriers; just six months after Pearl Harbor, the Japanese were on the defensive and would never recover. Japan did not pull back into a defensible perimeter, allowing King to launch his submarines against the Japanese logistics and eventually sink most of its tankers and many of its supply ships and troop transports. At Guadalcanal the overextended Japanese were slowly pushed back as the Americans gained overall strength and concentrated their forces at a critical point. Japan had plenty of submarines, but it remained locked into a Mahanian theory that only a decisive fleet battle matters. Therefore, it did not attack American logistics but saved its submarines for a fleet battle that never came.

Admiral Chester Nimitz in the central Pacific and General MacArthur in the southwest Pacific now began a series of moves to forward island bases, bypassing major Japanese strongholds. The strategy was to seize selected small Japanese bases by an overwhelming attack with heavy navy bombardment, close air support of ground troops, and marine or army landings over the beaches. Some of the battles were very bloody, but the Americans won every one. The critical battle came at Saipan in June 1944. Japan sent its fleet to protect the vital islands but mishandled its command system and was massacred at the Battle of Philippines Sea. The Americans now built huge airfields for their new secret weapon, the very long-range B-29, which could dump huge bomb loads on Japanese cities and fly so high that Japanese defenses were ineffective. Fifty major industrial centers were targeted, and Japan was forced to evacuate nonessential civilians. Combined with submarine attacks on oil supplies, the air raids ruined Japanese industrial capability. By spring 1945, they were able to produce only Kamikaze airplanes and enough fuel for one-way trips.

The worst American strategic mistake was the belief that China's one-half billion people could neutralize Japan if only they were well armed and commanded. Therefore, the United States poured billions of dollars into China to support a hopeless regime that never contributed to the war effort. Through the entire war, the Japanese maintained firm control of the Chinese theater.

After the loss of Saipan, Emperor Hirohito demanded more and more sacrifices from the Japanese people. Fearful that defeat would endanger his position as emperor, he pushed his people to the very limit. The Allies decided to invade Japan in the fall of 1945, but first they needed closer bases. Iwo Jima was captured after an incredibly bloody battle in February 1945 and Okinawa after an even worse battle that spring. The Japanese had finally learned how to fight the Americans—rather than trying to win, they caused as many casualties as possible. Indeed, the Americans were terrified of the suicidal banzai attacks on land and the Kamikaze suicide planes from the sky. No one knew how many tens of thousands of Americans would die in the invasion—nor how many million Japanese would be killed. At the critical moment Secretary of War Stimson came forward with an alternate plan to end the war by shocking the Japanese high command. The first atomic blast at Hiroshima baffled the Japanese high command, until they decided that atomic energy was so expensive that the Americans could only have one bomb. The second bomb on Nagasaki crushed Japan's last hope.

Hoping that Soviet intervention would succeed where the Chinese had failed, Roosevelt begged Stalin to intervene in Japan and in the process weakened his bargaining power regarding postwar Europe. Stalin did intervene on schedule, a few days after Hiroshima. The battle-hardened Red Army pushed back the weakened Japanese forces in Manchuria and seized Korea, setting the stage for the Cold War in Asia and the Korean War. With the collapse of its armies in Manchuria, Tokyo's cause was now hopeless, and the emperor decided the only way to save himself was to surrender. MacArthur accepted the surrender of Japan aboard the USS *Missouri* in Tokyo Bay on September 2, 1945. As proconsul in Japan, he decided that the emperor needed to remain in power in order to insure the full cooperation of the Japanese people. Therefore, MacArthur made certain that Hirohito's top advisors were executed, but the emperor himself stayed on the throne (he died in 1989 after a 62-year reign).

The Chinese, British, and Australian forces also fought against Japan. On China see http://www.army.mil/cmh-pg/books/wwii/11-9/CBI.htm. The British war was fought mostly in Burma, and information can be found at http://www.burmastar.org.uk/links.htm. Most Australian units fought under MacArthur (see http://www.awm.gov.au/atwar/ww2.htm and http://home.st.net.au/~dunn/).

WEB SITE REVIEWS

G E N E R A L

The Center for Military History WWII Online Bookshelves
http://www.army.mil/cmh-pg/collections/USAWW2/USAWW2.htm

For the full review of this site, see p. 8, and for a review of the material pertaining to the European/Atlantic/Mediterranean theater of operations, see p. 41.

Eleven of the U.S. Army's Green Books are devoted to the war in the Pacific. At the time of this review only two have been posted online, but *Guadalcanal: The First Offensive* and *Okinawa: The Last Battle* are both must visits. The volume on Guadalcanal includes numerous maps as well as such interesting features as a Japanese analysis of American combat methods. The volume on Okinawa runs more than five hundred pages and contains an even broader collection of maps and illustrations.

Twenty of the World War II Commemorative Brochures focus on campaigns in the Asian-Pacific theater, and the full texts can be found at http://www.army.mil/cmh-pg/collections/WW2-Broch.htm. In addition to the two Green Books and twenty commemorative brochures, the site includes ten additional publications that pertain to the Pacific theater. The complete list and full text of these publications can be found at http://www.army.mil/cmh-pg/online/Bookshelves/WW2-List.htm.

CONTENT   ★ ★ ★ ★
AESTHETICS   ★ ★ ★
NAVIGATION   ★ ★ ★ ★

Hyperwar: A Hypertext History of the Second World War
http://www.ibiblio.org/hyperwar

Webmaster Patrick Clancy envisions Hyperwar as "primarily [a] military history of the Second World War, completely cross-referenced via hypertext links and enhanced, where appropriate, by various multi-media computer technologies." As Clancy himself acknowledges, Hyperwar remains very much a project in development. He has only begun to scratch the surface of what he hopes to build, but, nevertheless, he has created a site of interest to serious students of World War II.

Hyperwar is divided into four main sections. The first, entitled Political Papers, Policy Statements, Treaties, includes important primary materials from Neville Chamberlain's 1938 "Peace in Our Time" speech to Japanese surrender documents. Military/Service Histories draws material from official army, navy, air force, and marine corps accounts of the war. Although most of this information is available elsewhere, Hyperwar offers the advantage of pulling it together onto one site. Separate sections entitled Pacific and European Theater of Operations include after action reports and accounts of the war's most important battles.

Unfortunately, many of the indexed documents are not yet available online. Hyperwar is a one-man labor of love and, therefore, necessarily slow in its development. Although the detail of each index hints at what Clancy eventually hopes to build, researchers are likely to become frustrated when they discover the discrepancy between what is listed and what is actually available. To date, Clancy has focused most of his attention on the Pacific theater of operations. Consequently, the most valuable information pertains to operations at Wake Island, Midway, and Guadalcanal. He intends to turn his attention in the second phase of Hyperwar's development to the China-India-Burma theater, and in phase three, he will add to the already available material on the European theater of operations.

CONTENT ★ ★ ★ ★
AESTHETICS ★ ★ ★
NAVIGATION ★ ★ ★

World War II in the Pacific

http://historyplace.com/unitedstates/pacificwar/index.html

One of many World War II pages hosted by The History Place, World War II in the Pacific is a superb collection of fifty photographs, all of which come from the files of the National Archives. Although many of these images appear on multiple web sites, researchers will appreciate a chance to find such quality images, all from the war in the Pacific, assembled on one site. A thumbnail sketch and brief textual description of each image allows visitors to scroll quickly through the index; a full-size version of the photograph can be viewed by clicking on the smaller image.

Many of the images depict fierce battle scenes on Okinawa, Iwo Jima, the Solomon Islands, and other islands (including the famous image of marines raising the flag over Iwo Jima). Visitors will see Allied POWs with their hands bound behind their backs during the infamous Bataan Death March in April 1942. Other pictures depict the American surrender at Corregidor the following month and American POWs celebrating July 4, 1942, despite the threat of death from their captors.

The site includes a number of images from the decks of American ships as planes take off from aircraft carriers and gunners shoot at kamikazes. One image captures a Japanese plane being shot down, while another records the mayhem on the deck of the USS *Bunker Hill* after it was struck by two kamikazes within thirty seconds, resulting in more than 600 casualties.

Additional photographs of note document two soldiers taking a cigarette break in their foxhole on Peleliu, a surgeon plying his trade in an underground bunker on one of the Solomon Islands, and Colonel Paul Tibbetts, pilot of the Enola Gay, waving as he prepares to take off from Tinian Island to deliver the first atomic bomb.

CONTENT   ★ ★ ★ ★
AESTHETICS   ★ ★ ★ ★ ★
NAVIGATION   ★ ★ ★ ★

PEARL HARBOR

Pearl Harbor Photo Archive
http://www.ibiblio.org/memory

Hosted by ibiblio.org, the "public's visual archive" and home to both Hyperwar (see p. 58) and World War II Resources (see p. 10), Pearl Harbor Photo Archive contains 150 photographs, posters, and cartoons from the National Archives and Records Administration. Researchers will find an extensive collection of photographs taken during and soon after the surprise attack. The archive includes an eerie photograph taken from the air by a Japanese pilot; numerous images of American warships exploding, burning, and sinking; and shots of the salvage operations that began in the immediate aftermath of the attack.

The images in the archive, however, are not limited to the attack on December 7, 1941. In fact, one of the strengths of this collection is the inclusion of numerous posters and cartoons produced later in the war, which urge Americans to "Remember Pearl Harbor" and "Avenge Pearl Harbor" by purchasing war bonds, joining the Coast Guard, and lending general support to the war effort. In addition, visitors to the archive will find photographs of such luminaries as Franklin and Eleanor Roosevelt and Douglas MacArthur on visits to Pearl Harbor.

The 150 images are organized into groups of twenty-five. Unfortunately, no index is available for the site at this time; consequently, researchers must scroll through the entire collection to see what is available. Each thumbnail image is accompanied by a title, date, and National Archives control number. Clicking on the thumbnail produces a larger image of the photograph or poster.

Anyone interested in visual imagery related to Pearl Harbor will consider Pearl Harbor Photo Archive a must visit.

CONTENT   ★ ★ ★
AESTHETICS   ★ ★ ★
NAVIGATION   ★ ★

WWII Resources: The Pearl Harbor Attack Hearings
http://www.ibiblio.org/pha

For a full review of this site, see p. 10.

For a full review of this site, see p. 10.

WWII Resources: The Pearl Harbor Attack Hearings includes extensive material pertaining to the Japanese attack on Pearl Harbor. In particular, researchers will want to consult 5,000 pages of documents and testimony from the official Pearl Harbor Attack Hearings. The product of nine separate investigations that culminated in a congressional inquiry at the war's end, the final report ran to more than 25,000 pages, all of which webmaster Larry Jewell will ultimately post on WWII Resources. Visitors can read all eight of the investigations that preceded the joint congressional hearings and inundate themselves with details of the conditions at Hawaii, Allied prewar planning, Japanese planning and policy, and, of course, details of the actual attack.

The Pearl Harbor Attack Hearings can be reached directly via http://www. ibiblio.org/pha/pha/index.html. Navigation between the various hearings is straightforward, although accessing the Pearl Harbor Attack Hearings directly will prevent visitors from linking to the main index of WWII Resources, which includes other material of significance, such as general orders and directives, a map of Pearl Harbor on the morning of December 7, 1941, and documents pertaining to the American entrance into the war. Consequently, researchers interested in the full range of offerings are better off connecting to http://www. ibiblio.org/pha and scrolling down to the Pearl Harbor Attack Hearings.

CONTENT   ★ ★ ★ ★ ★
AESTHETICS   ★ ★ ★
NAVIGATION   ★ ★ ★ ★

THE U.S. AND JAPANESE NAVIES

D. L. James' Naval, Maritime, and Aviation Pages
http://www.odyssey.dircon.co.uk/nm.htm

David James has actually created four separate web sites of interest to researchers of the war in the Pacific, all of which can be accessed through the above address.

Individual pages on Guadalcanal, the Battle of the Philippines Sea, the Battle of Leyte Gulf, and aircraft of the Pacific war each merit a visit. The information on James's sites comes from scholarly sources, particularly Samuel Eliot Morison's *History of United States Naval Operations in World War Two*, a multivolume work that Morison produced at the behest of the navy and that has effectively served as the navy's official history of the war. Given that neither the Naval Historical Center nor its trade publisher has yet to make Morison's massive history available online, researchers ought to take note of James's contribution.

Although providing but a brief summary in comparison to Morison's complete work, James's sites offer a much needed official narrative of key naval battles that researchers will find especially useful as a companion to the numerous first-person accounts that dominate the web. While the diaries and memoirs of sailors and soldiers put a human face on the war, they often lack the context and perspective more readily available in official accounts.

James's narratives of Guadalcanal and the Battle of Leyte Gulf are more complete than his account of the Battle of the Philippine Sea. Not only does he provide a thorough history of the Guadalcanal campaign from the initial Allied attack in August 1942 to the Japanese evacuation in February 1943 (most of the fighting had actually ended in December), but he also places Guadalcanal within the context of earlier Pacific engagements. In particular, he devotes significant attention to the June 1942 Battle of Midway, where American naval forces sank four of six Japanese aircraft carriers and thus scored their first significant victory in the Pacific. Similarly, James explains Leyte Gulf in detail and discusses separately each of the four engagements that took place between October 23 and 26, 1944, as Allied forces reconquered the Philippines two and one-half years after the fall of the Bataan Peninsula in April 1942. Although not as thorough, his page on the Battle of the Philippine Sea, fought on June 19–20, 1944, is important and worth a visit. Finally, researchers will appreciate James's attention to the aircraft used by both Allied and Japanese forces in the Pacific.

CONTENT   ★ ★ ★ ★
AESTHETICS   ★ ★ ★
NAVIGATION   ★ ★ ★ ★

Imperial Japanese Navy Page
http://www.combinedfleet.com

Created and managed by a naval enthusiast, the Imperial Japanese Navy Page provides comprehensive data on the ships, guns, and aircraft of the Japanese navy. Although the site does not contain primary documents relating to naval strategy, it will appeal to researchers interested in the physical dimensions and capabilities of the Japanese navy.

An attractive index directs visitors to sections entitled Images, Data, and Special Features. Although most of the images are scanned from models rather than photographs, the collection is extensive and includes aircraft carriers, battleships, heavy cruisers, light cruisers, destroyers, and submarines. Data contains separate pages on naval guns, radar, and torpedoes, a short description of the importance of each piece of equipment to overall Japanese strategy, and a comprehensive chart of the specifications of each type of gun, radar, or torpedo in the Japanese arsenal. Data also includes brief biographies of critical Japanese naval officers with links to the major battles and campaigns in which they participated.

The Special Features section contains a Guns n' Armor Page; an analysis of naval aviation; separate operational histories of Japanese aircraft carriers, destroyers, and battleships; and an extensive collection of maps. A section entitled The Pacific War in Maps contains images of the thirty-five most important battles and campaigns in the Pacific theater, including Pearl Harbor, Midway, Guadalcanal, and Leyte Gulf. The maps are accompanied by short descriptions of each battle, along with a count of the number of vessels involved on both sides and the number of losses sustained in each engagement.

CONTENT ★ ★ ★
AESTHETICS ★ ★ ★ ★
NAVIGATION ★ ★ ★ ★

The Merchant Marine in World War II
http://usmm.org/index.html#anchor252856

For a full review of this site, see p. 42.

The official web site of the U.S. Merchant Marine includes extensive information on the war in the Pacific. As this site details, merchant mariners played roles just as critical in the Pacific as they did in the Atlantic. Merchant mariners figured prominently in the invasions of Okinawa and Mindaro, in the Battle of Leyte Gulf, and in the planned invasion of the Japanese mainland. The merchant mariners, in fact, suffered more casualties in the invasion of Mindaro than all other American service branches combined.

Just like their brethren in the navy, merchant mariners combated the ever-present threat posed by Japanese kamikaze pilots and submarines. The officers and crew of the SS *Richard Hovey*, for example, were torpedoed by a Japanese submarine in the Arabian Sea in March 1944. As they abandoned ship and loaded onto lifeboats, they faced machine-gun fire from the Japanese submarine as a Japanese sailor filmed the entire episode. Satisfied with the capture of the captain and three others (all four were eventually repatriated), the Japanese left the men of the *Richard Hovey* to their own devices. After seventeen days at sea, the men were rescued, sixty-three of the seventy-one having survived the attack and subsequent ordeal.

CONTENT   ★ ★ ★ ★
AESTHETICS   ★ ★ ★
NAVIGATION   ★ ★ ★ ★

Navy Historical Center: World War II
http://www.history.navy.mil/wars/index.html#anchor12058

Navy Historical Center: World War Two contains a wealth of information likely to interest students of the Pacific theater of operations. The site does not, however, include the navy's official history of World War II, *History of Naval Operations in World War II*, by Samuel Eliot Morison, which is not available on the web. Consequently, visitors should not expect the thousands of pages of official reports that define the online offerings of The Center for Military History: WWII Online Bookshelves.

Despite the shortage of official documentation, the Navy Historical Center's web page is certainly worth a visit. Ever wonder what happens when a submariner needs an appendectomy and there is no doctor on board? Find out here; the site includes an oral history with a pharmacist's mate who performed just such a surgery. Other fascinating oral histories, including several with women, provide an intimate look at all the major naval battles in the Pacific, as well as the invasion of Normandy and the naval war in the Atlantic. Most of this site, however, is devoted to the war in the Pacific. Entries on engagements such as Pearl Harbor and Midway contain action reports, survivor reports, photographs, and naval medical activities. Visitors will find information on the effect of typhoons on naval operations as well as a sketch on the five Sullivan brothers, who were all killed in November 1942 when their ship, the USS *Juneau*, went down.

A separate index of photographs from the Pacific can be accessed via http://www.history.navy.mil/branches/org11-2.htm. Select Events and WWII in the Pacific for an array of photographs from Pearl Harbor, the Coral Sea, Midway, Guadalcanal, and the Japanese surrender.

CONTENT   ★ ★ ★ ★
AESTHETICS   ★ ★ ★
NAVIGATION   ★ ★ ★ ★

The Pacific War: The United States Navy
http://www.microworks.net/pacific

An excellent overview of the war in the Pacific, Tim Lanzendorfer's web site is divided into twelve sections: Road to War, Bases, Ships of the Fleet, Armaments, Naval Aviation, Equipments, Biographies, Intelligence, Battles, Pictorial History, Statistics, and Personal History. Although The Pacific War: The United States Navy as a whole contains relatively few primary materials, students of the Pacific theater nonetheless will find it informative, thorough, and well worth a visit.

Complete with the text of critical treaties and documents, Road to War is a welcome diplomatic history of American-Japanese relations from 1853 to 1941. Lanzendorfer reminds visitors that American-Japanese tensions in the Pacific began in the nineteenth century, not the 1920s or 1930s. The Battles section will prove useful to any visitor looking to keep straight the numerous engagements that constituted the four-year war in the Pacific. Separate chapters on more well-known battles such as Guadalcanal, Midway, and Leyte Gulf appear alongside information on lesser-known engagements. The chapter entitled Armaments is especially thorough.

As is the case with most web sites, The Pacific War remains a work in progress. For instance, although close to 100 naval commanders are listed in Biographies, links to actual content appear in only fifteen cases. Nonetheless, the biographies are useful and will become even more so as additional content is added.

CONTENT	★ ★ ★ ★	
AESTHETICS	★ ★ ★ ★	
NAVIGATION	★ ★ ★ ★	

THE ATOMIC BOMB

Atomic Bomb: Decision
http://www.dannen.com/decision

A relatively small but terrific collection of primary documents, Atomic Bomb: Decision details internal White House, War Department, and Manhattan Project deliberations with an emphasis on the objections of leading scientists and government officials who came to oppose the bomb's use. Drawn primarily from the National Archives, the site's twenty documents include the minutes of a "target committee" meeting held in Robert Oppenheimer's office in May 1945, memorandum relating to the bomb's testing on July 16, 1945, and accounts of the test from a number of witnesses, including Enrico Fermi.

One of the most valuable features of Atomic Bomb: Decision is the inclusion of extensive documentation addressing the increased apprehension of Manhattan Project insiders. In June, scientists at the University of Chicago issued the Franck Report, in which they urged that the bomb only be exploded "before the eyes of representatives of all United Nations, on the desert or a barren island." Soon after, Undersecretary of the Navy Ralph Bard condemned any unannounced use of the bomb as contrary to "the position of the United States as a great humanitarian nation." Perhaps most famously, Leo Szilard, one of those who signed the Franck Report, circulated a draft petition asking fellow scientists to join him in urging the president to disavow the bomb's use. Ultimately, nearly seventy scientists at the Chicago Metallurgical Laboratory signed his petition, while scientists at other Manhattan Project facilities adopted similar resolutions.

President Harry Truman, of course, ultimately decided to test and drop the atomic bomb. Atomic Bomb: Decision includes the accounts of seven eyewitnesses who heard Truman inform Stalin of the bomb's existence. In addition, visitors can both read and hear Truman's address to the nation after the first bomb was dropped on Hiroshima. Finally, the site contains the text of an interview with Leo Szilard in 1960 as well as a link to a companion site devoted entirely to Szilard's life. The Szilard site and Atomic Bomb: Decision are maintained by Gene Dannen, a scholar who has spent the past twenty years working on a book about Szilard's role in the birth of the nuclear age.

CONTENT   ★ ★ ★
AESTHETICS   ★ ★ ★
NAVIGATION   ★ ★ ★ ★

The Decision to Drop the Atomic Bomb
http://www.trumanlibrary.org/whistlestop/study_collections/bomb/large/bomb.htm

Designed as a teaching tool for advanced high school students as part of Project Whistlestop (see Chapter 2), The Decision to Drop The Atomic Bomb provides teachers and students with hundreds of pages of primary materials relating to the decision to drop atomic bombs over Hiroshima and Nagasaki. Presented in their original form, the documents include minutes from internal White House meetings, commission reports, letters to and from various military officials with regard to testing and targeting, official press releases, presidential diary entries, and more. In addition to a trove of primary resources with tremendous educational value, this well-organized, user-friendly site offers teaching units, lesson plans, and classroom activities.

The documents are organized into nearly a dozen folders, each of which contains an index with a brief description of the contents of the folder and a link to each item. Truman and the Bomb: A Documentary History is a 21-chapter analysis of the documents by Truman scholar Robert Ferrell. The Groves Report discusses targeting decisions made in the spring and summer of 1945. Materials in the Interim Committee folder pertain to the deliberations of a group put together by Secretary of War Henry Stimson, while Testing the Bomb includes original drawings made by a witness to the successful test of the bomb over the New Mexico desert in July 1945. Strategic Bombing includes the full text of a 51-page report of the United States Strategic Bombing Survey.

In Truman Diary Entries, students and teachers can read President Truman's thoughts in July 1945 as he debated when to inform Stalin about the bomb. Official Releases includes various White House and War Department press releases issued on August 6, 1945. One of the most fascinating sources in the collection is an exchange between Senator Richard Russell and Truman, which can be found in Opinions and Responses. On August 7, 1945, the day after the first bomb was dropped, Russell telegrammed Truman and urged him not to show restraint or issue any more warnings, but to force Japan to come "groveling" and accept unconditional surrender. Truman responded, "I know that Japan is a terribly cruel and uncivilized nation in warfare but I can't bring myself to believe that, because they are beasts, we should ourselves act in the same manner." Furthermore, added Truman, "I certainly regret the necessity of wiping out whole populations because of the 'pigheadedness' of the leaders of a nation and, for your information, I am not going to do it unless it is absolutely necessary." Truman concluded that he wanted only to save American lives.

CONTENT   ★ ★ ★ ★
AESTHETICS   ★ ★ ★ ★
NAVIGATION   ★ ★ ★ ★

SUGGESTED READINGS

Aldrich, Richard J. *Intelligence and the War against Japan* (New York, 2000).

Alexander, Joseph H. *Edson's Raiders: The 1st Marine Battalion in World War II* (Annapolis, MD, 2000).

Allen, Louis. *Burma: The Longest War, 1941–1945* (London, 2000).

Alperovitz, Gar. *The Decision to Use the Atomic Bomb and the Architecture of an American Myth* (New York, 1995).

Appleman, Roy E., et al. *Okinawa: The Last Battle* (Washington, DC, 1949).

Bergerud, Eric M. *Touched with Fire: The Land War in the South Pacific* (New York, 1997).

——. *Fire in the Sky: The Air War in the South Pacific* (Boulder, CO, 2001).

Berry, Henry. *This Is No Drill! Living Memories of the Attack on Pearl Harbor* (New York, 2001).

Blair, Clay, Jr. *Silent Victory: The U.S. Submarine War against Japan* (Annapolis, MD, 2001).

Bradley, James, with Ron Powers. *Flags of Our Fathers* (New York, 2000).

Center for Military History, *American Military History* (http://www.army.mil/cmh-pg/books/AMH/amh-toc.htm).

Clausen, Henry, and Bruce Lee. *Pearl Harbor: Final Judgment* (Cambridge, MA, 2001).

Costello, John. *The Pacific War, 1941–1945* (New York, 1981).

Craven, Wesley Frank, and J. L. Cate. *The Army Air Forces in World War II,* 7 vols. (Chicago, 1948–1958).

Cutler, Thomas J. *The Battle of Leyte Gulf* (New York, 1994).

Daws, Gavan. *Prisoners of the Japanese: POWs of World War II* (New York, 1992).

Dower, John W. *War without Mercy: Race and Power in the Pacific War* (New York, 1986).

Flanagan, General E. M., Jr. *Corregidor: The Rock Force Assault, 1945* (Novato, CA, 1988).

Frank, Richard B. *Guadalcanal* (New York, 1990).

———. *Downfall: The End of the Imperial Japanese Empire* (New York, 2001).

Hersey, John. *Hiroshima,* 2d ed. (New York, 1985).

Iriye, Akira. *The Origins of the Second World War in Asia and the Pacific* (White Plains, NY, 1989).

Ishida, Jintaro. *The Remains at War: Apology and Forgiveness* (Manila, 2001).

Josephy, Alvin M., Jr. *The Long and the Short and the Tall: Marines in Combat on Guam and Iwo Jima* (Springfield, NJ, 2000).

Kessler, Lynn S., and Edmond B. Bart. *Never in Doubt: Remembering Iwo Jima* (Annapolis, MD, 1999).

Lee, Loyd E., ed. *World War II in Asia and the Pacific and the War's Aftermath, with General Themes* (Westport, CT, 1997).

Lord, Walter. *Day of Infamy* (New York, 2001).

Miller, Thomas G., Jr. *The Cactus Air Force* (New York, 1981).

Morison, Samuel Eliot. *The Two-Ocean War: A Short History of the United States Navy in the Second World War* (Boston, 1989).

Prange, Gordon W. *At Dawn We Slept: The Untold Story of Pearl Harbor* (New York, 1982).

———. *The Verdict of History: Pearl Harbor* (New York, 1991).

Rhodes, Richard. *The Making of the Atomic Bomb* (New York, 1995).

Sides, Hampton. *Ghost Soldiers: The Forgotten Epic Story of World War II's Most Dramatic Rescue Mission* (New York, 2001).

Smith, George W. *Carlson's Raid: The Daring Marine Assault on Makin* (Novato, CA, 2001).

Spector, Ronald H. *Eagle against the Sun: The American War with Japan* (New York, 1985).

——. *At War, At Sea: Sailors and Naval Combat in the Twentieth Century* (New York, 2001).

Toland, John. *Infamy: Pearl Harbor and Its Aftermath* (New York, 1982).

Tsouras, Peter G., ed. *Rising Sun Victorious: The Alternate History of How the Japanese Won the Pacific War* (London, 2001).

Wels, Susan. *Pearl Harbor: America's Darkest Day* (San Diego, CA, 2001).

World War II: War in the Pacific (DVD from the History Channel, 2000).

Wright, Derrick. *The Battle for Iwo Jima* (New York, 1999).

CHAPTER 5

THE
SOLDIERS'
STORIES

The web sites reviewed in this chapter depict—sometimes in poignant detail—the life of the common American soldier in World War II. His feelings and opinions, fears and hopes hit us square in the face as we read the memoirs, diaries, and caches of letters reproduced on these sites. The open nature of the web enables the "publication" of these valuable resources, which most likely would never have been published in traditional formats.

Our vision of the common soldier probably has been shaped over the years more by movies than anything else. The 1940s was the golden age of motion pictures. It was a great art form for actors, authors, and directors, and millions of people walked to nearby theaters every week for the cheap and convenient entertainment. The newsreels provided vivid coverage of the previous week's events around the world (rather like the evening news programs on television today). The cartoons might have featured Bugs Bunny or Donald Duck in combat against the "Japs." Feature films, however, had the greatest impact on the audience. Shot in black and white, they portrayed a recent event that had been well publicized in the newspapers and magazines. The plots had been approved by a government censor at the Office of War Information, and usually the military cooperated and participated in some way. *Casablanca* (1942) was the first great film of the war, as Rick (Humphrey Bogart) exemplified the ambiguity of American neutrality before Pearl Harbor.

Movie depictions of hand-to-hand fighting began with *Bataan* (1943) starring Robert Taylor, Desi Arnez, Thomas Mitchell, and Lloyd Nolan, setting the standard early for future combat films. Bataan was the peninsula in the Philippines where American and Filipino infantrymen held off the Japanese invasion in late 1941 and early 1942 and ultimately were forced to surrender. The scenes of hand-to-hand jungle combat were excruciatingly realistic for the 1940s and for decades to come would shape common ideas of what combat was like. Today, we live in an era of special effects, and *Bataan* would be rejected by audiences for its poor production values (it was filmed on a Hollywood lot).

As was typical of wartime films, the Japanese in *Bataan* are depicted as faceless, cruel, subhuman monsters especially adapted to jungle warfare. "Those no tail baboons," says Taylor, "they're skillful. They can live and fight for a month on what wouldn't last you guys two days." They possess overwhelming firepower—sophisticated hardware used with barbaric cruelty. (MacArthur thought the Japanese outnumbered him 2 to 1; actually, he had more men.) In *Bataan,* the only way to defeat the Axis is by teamwork. The typical unit is depicted as a dozen or so representatives of all facets of American life. The melting pot in *Bataan* features one Pole, one Irishman, one Jew, one Black, two Filipinos, and six generic Yankees. The Yankees range from an elite West Pointer to an innocent farm boy, a gangster, and a pacifist. The West Pointer is killed right away, thus allowing the natural leadership to emerge in democratic fashion. *Bataan,* like all combat movies, dwells on rituals of the home front (Christmas dinner) and the battlefield (cleaning the rifle). Individual heroism is applauded, but it does not win the war. Teamwork, in conjunction with ultimately irresistible American industrial prowess, brings victory. Viewers loved *Bataan* and perhaps bought some war bonds in the lobby after the show.

Once the war was over it was no longer necessary to stimulate home front audiences to patriotism. Most subsequent war movies are full of action, but the biggest hit of 1946 and winner of seven Academy Awards, *The Best Years of Our Lives,* focused on the returning veterans and their adjustments to a society that had changed radically since they were drafted (see http://www.filmsite.org/besty.html).

Some later movies probed the subtle psychological tensions that World War II soldiers experienced. A favorite theme was the contradiction between a chain of command that must be obeyed and democratic, egalitarian values. *Mr. Roberts* (1955) starred Henry Fonda as the eager warrior trapped on a navy supply ship commanded by an obsessive bureaucrat, played by James Cagney (see the comments at http://www.kollman-saucier.com/oped2.shtml). *Twelve O'Clock High* (1950) starred Gregory Peck as an air force general who teaches his men that effective action requires rigid obedience to the rules (see the guide to the film at http://www. teachwithmovies.org/guides/twelve-oclock-high.html). Humphrey Bogart's stunning depiction of Captain Queeg in *The Caine Mutiny* (1954) suggests that rigidity led to insanity (see http://www.homevideos.com/revclas/9b.htm).

British and Americans dominate the war movie genre, but one German film is worthy of special attention. Wolfgang Petersen's sympathetic *Das Boot* (1981; see http://movie-reviews.colossus.net/movies/d/das_boot.html) portrays a U-boat attacking and being attacked as the crew tries to survive day by day, hour by hour, in the claustrophobic confines of their small, vulnerable boat. Were they heroes or victims of war? The film leaves the question open.

The antiwar mood of the 1960s led to a new kind of war film; outsiders revolting against the system were portrayed as heroes, and the U.S. Army as an organization either was ignored or became the villain. *The Dirty Dozen* (1967) was one of many films showing the heroic achievements of a group of outcasts and misfits who destroy the scientifically "perfect" German war machine.

A new dimension of realism appeared with *Saving Private Ryan,* directed by Stephen Spielberg in 1999. The opening scenes offer unforgettably graphic depictions of the horrors of war and what the common soldier was asked to endure (see http://www.rzm.com/pvt.ryan/). Historian Stephen Ambrose discusses the realism in this film at http://private-ryan.eb.com/page1.html.

Of course, movies are problematic in that they do not show life as it really happens; in many ways they reveal more about the audiences that laugh, cry, boo, and cheer with the film. A good introduction to the life of the GI is Lee Kennett's *G.I.: The American Soldier in World War II* (1987). For specific information on rations visit http://www.qmfound.com/food_wwII.htm, and for clothing http://www.qmfound.com/army_clothing_history.htm#WorldWarII. Note that the one detail Hollywood almost always gets right is clothing. See http://www.rtbb.com/~korteng/SmallArms/m1rifle.html for material on the GI's primary weapon, the Garand M1.

Real history of the soldiers comes from other sources, such as letters sent home and oral histories. The military systematically censored letters, in part to eliminate information that might be useful to the enemy, and in part to monitor exactly what the men were thinking. Censorship seemed at first a natural job for the WAC, but too many women were stunned and nauseated by the contents of the mail and had to be replaced by men. Local historical societies actively collect files of letters, and we can expect them to start showing up on the web. Several web sites reviewed in this chapter offer powerful oral histories from people who lived through the 1940s.

The opportunity to create your own oral history should not be passed up. People who remember the 1940s are growing older; most of them are happy to talk about their experiences with a tape recorder or videotape recorder on. (Some combat soldiers, however, are still tight lipped about the horrors they experienced.) The war was a huge cooperative enterprise, and everyone played a role. Those who lived through the 1940s have vivid memories of the little episodes and telling incidents that combined make the story of the war years come alive. For those creating an oral history, ask if the interviewee has photographs, scrap books, or old letters or can put you in touch with a friend who can talk in more detail about the war. For some excellent basic tips on how to conduct your own oral history interview, visit http://bancroft.berkeley.edu/ROHO/rohotips.html or http://www.ancestry.com/library/view/columns/tips/66.asp.

WEB SITE REVIEWS

GENERAL ORAL HISTORY

The Drop Zone Virtual Museum

http://www.thedropzone.org

"Once you got into conflict you start to understand death and the smell of death." So begins Jack Williamson, a staff sergeant with the 101st Airborne's 327th Glider Infantry Regiment, as he relates his experience at the Battle of the Bulge to Drop Zone's creator and webmaster, Patrick O'Donnell. A business consultant and self-described "volunteer historian," O'Donnell and his corps of volunteers have built an impressive site devoted to chronicling the exploits of American Rangers and other airborne troops. O'Donnell has conducted more than 500 interviews, although only a fraction appear online at any one time. His subjects saw action in both Europe and the Pacific, while others such as the all-black 555th Parachute Infantry Battalion, the "Triple Nickels," remained stateside throughout the war, fighting forest fires in the Pacific Northwest. One particularly unique feature of Drop Zone is the inclusion of a handful of oral histories from Axis troops who fought American airborne units.

The best accounts, such as Jack Williamson's, are riveting and provide deep insights into the fears, thoughts, and grim reality of young men in battle. Furthermore, O'Donnell has made every effort to ensure the accuracy of the information posted on his site, employing an array of primary and secondary sources to confirm details of the stories told by his subjects. While most of the interviews are quite informative, others are less useful, particularly those that provide but a brief account of a specific incident. In addition, visitors to Drop Zone will find that these interviews focus almost exclusively on actual combat experience.

For the most part, the site is easy to navigate, although the photographs are clunky and the "time portal" confusing. In addition, the home page is dominated by a distracting advertisement for O'Donnell's recently published book, which is based on his interviews. Despite these limitations, Drop Zone remains an impressive and valuable web site.

CONTENT   ★ ★ ★ ★ ★
AESTHETICS   ★ ★ ★ ★
NAVIGATION   ★ ★ ★

The Rutgers Oral History Archives of World War II
http://fas-history.rutgers.edu/oralhistory/orlhom.htm

Established by the History Department at Rutgers University in 1994, this project has succeeded in its mission to increase understanding of World War II from the perspective of average service men and women: the junior officers, sailors, soldiers, airmen, nurses, defense industry workers, and even those who entertained the troops. In many respects, the launching of the Rutgers project anticipated the surge in popularity in the late-1990s of books, videos, and films that chronicled the memories and experiences of the generation that came of age during the Great Depression and faced down the Axis powers. To date, the project has limited its 218 interviews (new interviews are added regularly) to men who attended Rutgers College and women who attended the New Jersey College for Women. Some subjects graduated just before the war and entered the armed services as junior officers, while others first went to war as enlisted personnel and were able to attend college later only because of the GI Bill, a vivid reminder that World War II transformed American society in multiple ways.

The interviews are superb, by far the best available on the web, and contain a wealth of information that places the war within its broader historical context. Each interview begins with detailed information on the childhood and family background of the participant, including a discussion of what it was like to grow up during the Great Depression. Some provide a fascinating glimpse of campus life in the 1930s. The interviews then turn to the war itself, and researchers find themselves sharing the harrowing combat experiences, as well as the lighter moments, of men and women who served in Europe, the Pacific, China, Burma, India, and on the home front. The interviewers should be commended for allowing the participants to tell their stories without interruption. After reading several of these oral histories, one is left with an understanding of the simple but powerful truth of one soldier's remark that: "A lot of lucky things happen. That's how you get through a war."

In addition to the interviews, the site contains an easily navigable chart that lists the branch of service and theater of operation for each individual. A separate chart provides links to some of the infantry units and air groups in which the interviewees served. The site also contains useful links to other World War II and oral history sites. The handful of photographs and other images, however, do not live up to the quality of the interviews themselves.

For a review of material on this site pertaining to the home front, see p. 98, and for women and African Americans in World War II, see p. 114.

CONTENT   ★ ★ ★ ★ ★
AESTHETICS   ★ ★ ★ ★
NAVIGATION   ★ ★ ★ ★

Tankbooks.com
http://www.tankbooks.com

Tankbooks.com is the creation of Aaron Elson, who committed himself to collecting the stories of World War II veterans after attending a reunion of the 712th Tank Battalion, his father's unit. Billed as the "first oral history web site," Tankbooks.com is certainly one of the best. Elson has posted more than fifty in-depth interviews and 125 related stories. Although veterans of the 712th Tank Battalion appear more often than those who served in other units, Elson has extended his research to include tailgunners, paratroopers, pilots, infantrymen, and prisoners of war who participated in the most intense battles in both Europe and the Pacific. In addition, Elson has included interviews with several women who discuss their experiences as single mothers on the home front.

Readily accessible and of interest to a general audience, the site includes a useful index with a brief description of each subject. Unlike many of the firsthand accounts found on the web, each of the oral histories on Tankbooks.com is extensive and includes details of the subject's life before and after the war. Without a doubt, however, the emphasis lies on combat experiences, crash landings, forced marches endured by POWs, and other harsh realities of war.

Elson has published four books based on his interviews, and web viewers can read excerpts from them. In addition, Tankbooks.com contains a number of useful links to other World War II sites.

CONTENT	★ ★ ★
AESTHETICS	★ ★ ★
NAVIGATION	★ ★ ★ ★

EUROPEAN/ATLANTIC/MEDITERRANEAN THEATER

"Dad" Rarey's Sketchbook Journals
http://www.rareybird.com

In early 1942, George Rarey was drafted into the army air forces and eventually assigned to the 379th Fighter Squadron. A cartoonist and commercial artist prior to his induction, Rarey catalogued his war experience in a series of sketchbooks, producing hundreds of drawings between 1942 and his death in the skies over France just weeks after D-Day. Known as "Dad" to the rest of the squadron because, at twenty-five, he was older than most of them, Rarey also painted nose art on the planes of many of his squadron mates.

This site, run by Rarey's son, who was but a few months old when Rarey was shot down, contains many of Rarey's sketches accompanied by excerpts of letters from Rarey to his wife, her memoirs, and the recollections of members of the 379th Fighter Squadron. Visitors can follow Rarey's journey from his induction, when he drew "a quick and telling cartoon of a bewildered disheveled little civilian saying adieu to the world as he had known and loved," to flight school, to the trip across the Atlantic, and into combat. While in England training for the impending invasion of France, Rarey learned of his son's birth, an occasion that prompted him to write, "This happiness is nigh unbearable . . . what a ridiculous and worthless thing a war is in the light of such a wonderful event."

On June 21, 1944, Rarey wrote to his wife:

> Every night I crawl into my little sack and light up the last cigarette of the day and there in the dark with the wind whippin' around the tent flaps I think of you—of your hair and eyes and pretty face—of your lovely young body—of your warmth and sweetness. It isn't in the spirit of frustration but of fulfillment. I've known these things and knowing them and having them once, I have them forever. That wonderful look in your eyes when we'd meet after being apart for a few hours—or a few weeks—always the same—full of love. Ah, Betty Lou, you're the perfect girl for me—I love ya, Mama!

A sketch that accompanied the letter proved to be Rarey's last. He died several days later.

In addition to Rarey's sketchbooks, the site includes images of the nose art and numerous portraits that Rarey drew of other pilots. A brief but telling excerpt from his wife's memoir tells of their days together in New York City just prior to his induction.

CONTENT   ★ ★ ★ ★
AESTHETICS   ★ ★ ★ ★
NAVIGATION   ★ ★ ★ ★

Dad's War: Finding and Telling Your Father's WWII Story
http://members.aol.com/dadswar/index.htm

One of the most unique sites on the web, Dad's War documents the efforts of one man to discover his own father's experience in World War II. More important, however, Dad's War offers concrete advice and proposes a specific course of action for those interested in their own dad's war.

In the early 1990s, Wesley Johnston set out to discover the wartime history of his father, Walter, who served in an antitank platoon of Company B of the 38th Armored Infantry Battalion of the 7th Armored Division. Walter saw action at St. Viths, Belgium, in the Battle of the Bulge, and in Germany during the European war's final days. In response to his findings, Johnston created several web pages, the most notable of which focuses on the Battle of the Bulge (one page includes an interesting map with the location of all American units involved in the battle), while another page serves as the unofficial page of the 7th Armored Division. Although poor health has slowed his efforts in recent months, Johnston continues to add links and update the sites.

What is most clear from Dad's War is that Johnston has spent considerable time finding his way through the maze of government records that, taken together, shed light on the story of each individual soldier. Johnston offers a list of first steps for those interested in finding and telling the story of their own dad's war, but he reserves his most detailed instructions and advice for those willing to purchase his workbook. Although not a useful site for serious researchers of World War II battles, campaigns, or leaders, Dad's War is an obvious starting point for those who, like Wesley Johnston, want to learn more about their father's war experience.

CONTENT   ★ ★ ★
AESTHETICS   ★ ★ ★
NAVIGATION   ★ ★ ★

Diaries and Photos of Two German Soldiers
http://www.geipelnet.com

The diaries and photos of German soldiers Karl and Otto are part of a family web site that includes photographs of vacations and other family events. Visitors may find it frustrating not to learn more about Karl and Otto's connection to the hosts of the site; webmaster Barry Geipel explains only that they were uncles but offers no information, for instance, that explains when family members moved to the United States. No last name is provided for either Karl or Otto. Nonetheless, the site provides an interesting juxtaposition with the wartime experiences of American soldiers, which predominate on the web.

Otto served on the Russian front with a battalion of tank hunters from June 1941 through the end of the war. Karl, by contrast, served in the Luftwaffe. Of the two, Otto's album is by far the more interesting. His diary entries and photos begin on June 21, 1941, the launch of Operation Barbarossa, the German invasion of the Soviet Union. By the end of the war, Otto was no longer the smiling youth of four years earlier. The webmaster concedes that, by contrast, Karl's album is rather dull. Stationed in Alsace-Lorraine with an anti-aircraft artillery unit, his war experience appears sedate when compared to Otto's.

While Otto's diary and photos in particular will draw the attention of those interested in understanding the war through the experiences of the men who fought the battles, the navigation of this site is difficult. Viewers can only scroll through Otto's album one day at a time, moving forwards or backwards. Unfortunately, there is no index or calendar that allows one to skip around or even return to the home page. Furthermore, interested viewers will have to log onto the family web site, scroll down to Family History, and then link to the war albums page—there is no direct link to Otto and Karl's diaries and photos.

CONTENT   ★ ★ ★
AESTHETICS   ★ ★ ★
NAVIGATION   ★ ★ ★

Memoir of Sgt. William Heller
http://www.warfoto.com

A war photographer with the 3rd Infantry Division, William Heller captured the war through pictures rather than words. This site, run by his son, contains over 200 photographs that chronicle the 3rd Division's march from Casablanca in North Africa to Hitler's Eagle Nest in Berchtesgaden. Along the way, the 3rd Division took part in the invasions of Sicily, Italy, and Southern France before marching across Germany. Heller took most of the photographs on this site, while other photographers assigned to the 3rd Division contributed the rest.

The photos document nearly every aspect of army life: combat, including amphibious landings and maneuvers in the Italian Alps; the United Service Organizations (USO) appearances of such stars as Bob Hope, Jack Benny, and Marlene Dietrich; daily experiences of GIs, including their attendance at prayer services; and generals reviewing the troops and plotting strategy. The most graphic images include the dead on the battlefields and medics treating wounded soldiers. No pictures, however, capture the horror of World War II as clearly as Heller's shots of dead children in Dachau. Other memorable photographs include a picture of the French Resistance shaving the head of a woman who fraternized with German soldiers and a group of war correspondents holding up Hermann Göring's pajamas after the capture of Hitler's guest house.

A logically organized table of contents allows for straightforward navigation. Although the photographs themselves are exceptional in their quality, the site's design is rather busy and somewhat distracting. Taken as a whole, however, the pictures available on Memoir of Sgt. William Heller provide a riveting look at the war.

CONTENT   ★ ★ ★ ★
AESTHETICS   ★ ★ ★
NAVIGATION   ★ ★ ★ ★

Mud and Guts
http://mariposa.yosemite.net/mudnguts/index.htm

Devoted to the World War II recollections of Arthur J. Clayton, a private from Missouri who saw action with the 409th Regiment of the 103d Division from late 1944 through the end of the war, Mud and Guts combines recollections with intensely moving letters written from the front. Clayton himself acknowledges that his stories may differ from others, because, in his words, "in combat each day is a nightmare and no two people see the same things in the same light and many times no one actually does know what happened nor how." Nevertheless, Clayton's account is especially valuable and is a must visit for those interested in the war as experienced by the soldiers. No doubt aware that time would erode his ability to remember events, Clayton recorded his recollections in the immediate aftermath of the war.

Along with his own memories, Mud and Guts includes a number of clippings from Clayton's hometown newspaper. An editor of the Brunswick, Missouri, paper before joining the army, Clayton wrote a number of extended letters expressly intended for publication. One might, therefore, treat Clayton's observations as combining the experiences of Private Ryan and Ernie Pyle. When creating the website in the 1990s, Clayton added a few editorial comments and recollections from platoon mates to supplement his original letters and immediate postwar memories. These more recent additions appear in italics throughout the text, a welcome device that enables the viewer to keep the various sources straight.

Clayton's keen eye and eloquent prose, no doubt forged by his journalistic training, provide an account of the war that far surpasses what is available on most web sites. From basic training in California, to combat in Belgium and Germany, to the liberation of Dachau, Clayton offers deeply personal insight into the nature of combat. His account of the liberation of Dachau is simply horrifying. His letter from a hospital bed in France, where he recovered from wounds before returning to the front, speaks for itself of the meaning of friendship forged in the worst of circumstances:

> Many nights in foxholes we have slept peacefully, trusting our life to the alertness of another then trading posts and doing the same for him. There have been times when we shared small bits of crackers or a square of chocolate when no other food was to be found, the last swallow of water in a canteen, slept "spoon fashion" on the cold ground for mutual warmth. We've raced across open fields to take a town, running with pounding hearts and legs of lead while enemy machine guns seemed to blaze in our very faces. It's experiences like those that cement friendships that can never be broken. Yet now, back in a hospital, I'll probably never see those boys

again while over here. I may go back to my old outfit, probably not, but even so, many of those I left will be gone.

CONTENT   ★ ★ ★ ★
AESTHETICS   ★ ★ ★ ★
NAVIGATION   ★ ★ ★ ★

Private Art

http://www.private-art.com

Arthur Pranger, a native of Covington, Kentucky, served in the 86th Mortar Battalion and saw action in France, Belgium, and Germany from June 1944 until the end of the war in Europe. Run by Pranger's wife, Rose, this site contains hundreds of letters that Art wrote or received from the time he began training in Texas in 1943 until he returned home. His correspondents include his mother and father, brother and sister, and family friends, such as a British couple he stayed with while in England.

Numerous sites contain recollections of combat experience, but Private Art's letters are valuable because they reveal a different side of the war. From the beginning, Art, who continued to sign his letters Pfc. (private first class) even after being promoted, wrote to his family in understated terms clearly intended to put them at ease. Despite his mother's obvious and understandable anxiety about his arrival in France three weeks after D-Day, Art wrote: "I'm now in France. I'm in the fighting now but don't worry, I'm alright so far and it's not too bad. I sure was sorry to leave England though." That December, mired in the Ardennes Forest in the midst of the Battle of the Bulge, Art told his family to have a good Christmas and not to worry: "Nothing is much different up here excepting that the Germans are getting a little rough."

Another outstanding strength of this site is the inclusion of letters written to Private Art from anxious family and friends on the home front. More often than not, the experiences of those on the battlefield and those on the home front are represented as separate entities, but the exchange of letters presented here sheds light on the interconnection that existed throughout World War II. A monthly calendar serves as a user-friendly index and ensures easy navigation. Attractive graphics enhance what is already a site worth exploring.

For a review of the material on this site relating to the home front, see p. 104.

CONTENT   ★ ★ ★ ★
AESTHETICS   ★ ★ ★ ★
NAVIGATION   ★ ★ ★ ★

A World War II Experience: The Story of Colonel William M. Slayden II at the Battle of the Bulge
http://www.grunts.net/wars/20thcentury/wwii/slayden/slayden.html

On December 15, 1944, staff officer William Slayden was stationed along the Allied front in Belgium and training a recently arrived division with no combat experience. Unbeknownst to Slayden and the Allies, the Germans secretly moved 200,000 troops, 500 tanks, and 1,900 guns into position that night. Attacking along a 60-mile front before dawn on December 16, the Germans launched the Ardennes Offensive, or the Battle of the Bulge. Caught by surprise, outnumbered 3 to 1, and unable to take advantage of superior air power because of poor weather, the Allies spent a desperate week on the defensive. Just before Christmas the weather cleared, reinforcements arrived, and the Allies stemmed the German attack, finally securing their lines three weeks later.

Drawing upon original diary entries and recollections, William Slayden provides a riveting account of his experience in every stage of the Battle of the Bulge. He maintains a calm and measured tone and relates the utter confusion that suffused the Allies in the initial days of the battle as German troops—dressed in American uniforms and speaking English—infiltrated American lines and changed road signs. As Allied fortunes changed after the first week, Slayden reminds readers of the cost of war: "The death and destruction are horrible. The dead are frozen in horrible positions, the towns and villages are utterly destroyed, and dead animals are lying around everywhere. Once our tanks break through the opposition nothing seems to stop them. They run over anything in the way, even the enemy dead where they have fallen."

Slayden's memoir, which includes a few photographs but no maps or other related material, makes for a wonderful companion piece to the more comprehensive Battle of the Bulge site run by CRIBA (see Chapter 3). Slayden's experience provides convincing support for Winston Churchill's declaration in the British House of Commons that the Battle of the Bulge "is undoubtedly the greatest American battle of the war and will, I believe, be regarded as an ever-famous American victory."

CONTENT   ★ ★ ★ ★
AESTHETICS   ★ ★ ★
NAVIGATION   ★ ★ ★

PACIFIC THEATER

Frankel-y Speaking About World War II in the South Pacific
http://www.frankel-y.com

In his introduction to this impressive memoir, Stanley Frankel notes with obvious irony that "like most American men in my generation I was not brought up to be a soldier. My first twenty-three years ill-prepared me to be plunked down as a World War II infantryman." Furthermore, Frankel had led demonstrations against participation in the war in Europe while a student at Northwestern University. Nonetheless, after being drafted into the army in January 1941, Frankel spent the duration of the war "in the dank jungles of the Solomon Islands, in the lethal streets and buildings of Manila and on the frightening, winding mountain roads leading up to Baguio in the Philippines." By war's end, the one-time antiwar protester had become an officer in the United States Army and had led troops in some of the worst engagements in the Pacific.

Frankel neglects to mention in his introduction that he was not just an anti-war protester at Northwestern; he was, according to *Time* magazine, the student leader of the national peace movement. Nor does Frankel hint that after his service in World War II he had a career as a writer and journalist, including stints as a speechwriter for both Adlai Stevenson and Hubert Humphrey. Given his career as a writer, it is not surprising that Frankel eventually wrote a memoir of his years in the army, the complete text of which is reproduced on this web site.

Although Frankel shies away from blandishing his later accomplishments, his penchant for writing shines throughout his memoir. In fact, while many memoirs suffer from the passage of time and the fogginess of memory, Frankel's recollections benefit from the prolific correspondence that he produced during the war. Throughout his three and one-half years in the South Pacific, Frankel sent material to a New York literary agent, most of it written in the immediate aftermath of combat operations. Some of this correspondence was published, although army censors consequently took a closer look at everything Frankel wrote. Just as critical as a source for this memoir, Frankel wrote nearly every day to his future wife. At the end of the war, she presented him with 1,232 letters that he had written. The bulk of the material in the twenty chapters that constitute this memoir, therefore, comes directly from wartime observations.

Frankel emphasizes that he was both a participant and observer in the South Pacific. As an officer he not only led men into battle but also had to inform families of the deaths of their sons. Throughout his memoir, Frankel approaches each of these tasks with a deep desire to hold on to his humanity. He recognizes that

unspeakable acts are committed in war and yet never ceases to struggle internally with the same impulses that led him to oppose the war in Europe while a
college student. Some of Frankel's most reflective thoughts appear in the final
chapter, in which he attempts to come to terms with the war and his participation in it. Ultimately, Frankel recognizes World War II as a "good war" that had
to be won by whatever means. He makes an interesting distinction between
Japanese forces, who fought to win the war, and the Germans, whose devotion
to the Final Solution had nothing to do with winning the war and, in fact, diverted men and equipment away from the war effort. Consequently, Frankel cannot bring himself to forgive the Germans. Despite his recognition of World War
II as necessary, Frankel remained a pacifist at heart. He was so opposed to the
Vietnam War that he led a group called Businessmen for Peace in Vietnam, a
position that resulted in his inclusion on Richard Nixon's enemies list.

CONTENT   ★ ★ ★ ★
AESTHETICS   ★ ★ ★
NAVIGATION   ★ ★ ★ ★

A Marine Diary: My Experiences on Guadalcanal
http://www.gnt.net/~jrube/intro.html

As a result of its intensity and duration, no battle in the Pacific has produced more
firsthand online accounts than Guadalcanal. James R. "Rube" Garrett, who
served in the Solomon Islands with the First Marine Division throughout the
duration of the campaign, from August until December 1942, has created one
of the very best sites on Guadalcanal. Fortunately for students of the American experience in the South Pacific, Garrett kept a diary that he has posted
online. Garrett sets the tone for what readers should expect when he explains
that "some pages of my diary were blank because we were just too busy shooting or being shot at. We were scared a lot of the time. The weeks and months
of anxiety and tension . . . long days of tedious work, night watches at the edge
of the jungle suddenly punctuated by sheer terror."

Garrett's diary and extensive photographs from Guadalcanal form the heart of this
web site. Entries discuss the horrific as well as the mundane. In addition, Garrett
and his son have supplemented the diary entries with excerpts from conversations
recorded after the war, as well as historical footnotes from scholarly works and official marine accounts of the campaign. The Garretts have thoughtfully and faithfully identified this additional information through the use of italics and quotation
marks. The net result is a more valuable account of Guadalcanal that in no way
compromises, but rather enhances, the integrity of the diary entries.

Well indexed and easily navigable, the site also includes a number of interesting
photographs of the ships and planes that engaged the Japanese offshore while the

marines were hunkered down on land. Graphic images of combat and its after-math, including pictures of dead Japanese soldiers, are also posted on A Marine Diary. One particular photograph serves as a less graphic, but nonetheless vivid, reminder of the costs of war. Taken in September 1940 during boot camp at Quantico, Virginia, Garrett and his platoon mates posed for a formal portrait. A note under the photograph indicates that less than one-half of the men returned.

CONTENT ★ ★ ★
AESTHETICS ★ ★ ★ ★
NAVIGATION ★ ★ ★ ★

To Hell and Back: A Guadalcanal Journal

http://users.erols.com/jd55/guadalcanal.html

As a 21-year-old serving in the First Marine Division, Pfc. James A. Donohue kept a diary of his harrowing experience at Guadalcanal. Not until his death more than one-half century later did his family learn of its existence. The opening page of To Hell and Back presents excerpts from Donohue's journal along with useful commentary from his daughter. The rest of the site consists of the journal itself, presented in its entirety and without interruption.

From August 7, when American forces captured the island, until early December, Donohue and his mates remained at the front line, fighting Japanese forces on the beaches, in the jungle, and in the hills. From the first entry, one gets a palpable sense of the awful conditions they endured. "The second day was murder," Donohue writes. The following days offered little respite. Nearly every day, Japanese troops attacked from land, air, and sea, prompting Donohue to remark, "bombs, bombs, one goes nuts." Forced at times to lie in a foxhole for thirteen or fourteen hours at a time, the marines endured unrelenting pressure. Donohue's descriptions are so vivid that visitors will feel the gratitude he expressed to the navy in late November for intercepting a Japanese convoy bound for Guadalcanal with 30,000 additional troops.

When not writing about the struggle to stay alive, Donohue fills his journal with tales of mosquitoes, flying ants, fleas, dysentery, and hunger. He also describes the savage cruelty of Japanese troops and the effect it had on American soldiers. The very real possibility of death pervaded every movement; the less likely possibility of getting home by Christmas offered the barest, but essential, sliver of hope. Unfortunately, most of Donohue's entries are not dated, leaving the reader confused at times about the actual chronology. Nevertheless, To Hell and Back is a must read.

CONTENT ★ ★ ★ ★
AESTHETICS ★ ★ ★
NAVIGATION ★ ★ ★

Twelve Hundred Days
http://home.attbi.com/~rgrokett/POW/index.htm

A native of Kansas, Russell Grokett Sr. spent 1,200 days as a Japanese POW after his capture on the Bataan Peninsula in April 1942. A chilling account, Twelve Hundred Days chronicles Grokett's capture, the notorious Bataan Death March, a sea voyage from the Philippines to Formosa to the Korean Peninsula, and his eventual imprisonment at a Japanese labor camp in Mukden, Manchuria.

The first page of the 21-page diary begins with an entry from day 285 of captivity, presumably sometime in January 1943 and several months after Grokett's arrival at Mukden: "Bad day. Diesinger died." Grokett explains that his best friend's corpse and those of other prisoners remained stacked in piles in anticipation of the spring thaw. "When is this ever going to end?" he wonders. But 900 more days of captivity awaited Grokett, who adds that "Mukden was built on the presumption that Japan not only would win the war but would keep many prisoners at work for years to come. When we arrived at Hoten compound, the Japs told us that if we obeyed orders for the next 10 or 20 years to come, our relatives would be permitted to visit us!"

While the conditions in Manchuria were brutal—cold, hunger, and insufficient clothing afflicted the men all winter—Grokett's description of the Bataan Death March is simply horrifying. As their Japanese captors organized the march, American and Filipino prisoners, along with Filipino civilians, withered in the heat and were not fed for twenty-four hours or more. Those too weak to stand were bayoneted. Once the march began, Japanese captors amused themselves by pushing prisoners over the cliffs. According to Grokett's account: "Their screams ended only when they hit jagged rocks below. The Filipinos fared even worse. Young girls were pulled out of ranks and raped repeatedly. Anyone who resisted was shot. Frightened mothers would rub human dung on their daughters' faces to make them unattractive to the guards." Guards ordered their captives to quicken their pace; those unable to keep up were killed. Prisoners who tried to come to the aid of their weaker comrades were shot.

Grokett's account is a must read for anyone interested in the experience of American POWs in the Pacific. Researchers, however, may find the organization and uncertainty over the narrative voice somewhat frustrating. Grokett died in 1982; although the web site is primarily the work of his grandson, the home page makes it clear that Twelve Hundred Days is Grockett's own account, presumably dictated before his death. Portions of the diary appear in italics, and these are clearly Grokett's own words. Most of the text is not italicized, however, and while the majority of the diary appears to be in Grokett's voice, he is referred to in the third person often enough to raise doubts. Furthermore, for no obvious reason, the creators of the site eschewed a strict chronological approach. The site opens with day 285 of captivity; day 1, the capture at Bataan, appears on page 7. Last, the internal navigation is somewhat clumsy. Researchers can move forward and backward and always have the option of returning to the home page, but it is not possible to jump to a noncontiguous page.

CONTENT   ★ ★ ★ ★
AESTHETICS   ★ ★ ★ ★
NAVIGATION   ★ ★ ★

When Victory Is Ours: Letters Home From the South Pacific, 1943–1945
http://www.topshot.com/dh/Victory.html

While serving as commander of a small transport vessel in the South Pacific, Morris D. Coppersmith penned numerous letters to his parents. Moving, insightful, prophetic, and wide ranging, Coppersmith's letters constitute one of the most remarkable collections of wartime correspondence available on the web. Although presented in abridged form (the original collection runs to some 85,000 words), the thirty letters that make up When Victory Is Ours should not be missed.

The primary responsibility of Coppersmith and his crew aboard LCI 432 was to ferry as many as two hundred troops at a time into position for onshore assaults. Consequently, during the first year of his correspondence, Coppersmith did not directly experience combat, a fact that disappointed his brother and sister who hoped for accounts of the "real" war. Free from the immediate concern with survival that preoccupied frontline troops, Coppersmith's detachment provided him a unique perspective on the war. From the outset, Coppersmith recognized that he and his men had no cause for complaint when compared to the wretched combat conditions faced by those they transported. In particular, Coppersmith writes in moving terms of raggedy Australian troops, four-fifths of whom he estimated would not have met the lowest American standards for combat readiness. His admiration for these men, some of whom were sixty years old and veterans of World War I, is clearly genuine.

In May 1944, Coppersmith and his crew finally participated directly in a combat assault. Other such engagements soon followed. Visitors will appreciate the difficulty with which Coppersmith carried out orders to effectively unload troops to their certain death. While moored in the Leyte Gulf next to the USS *Achilles*, Coppersmith and his crew watched as a Japanese suicide bomber crashed into the ship. Coppersmith also describes his visit to the recently overrun Palawan prison camp and the absolute horror of discovering that Japanese guards had burned their prisoners alive. When Coppersmith arrived, charred bones and hanging flesh remained visible.

Despite such compelling testimony, Coppersmith's most remarkable insights are not combat related. In one letter that alone would merit this site's review, Coppersmith rages against the forces of anti-Semitism that he knows will lead to the questioning of his and other Jews' patriotism. For this reason, he asks his parents to recognize the importance of his younger brother's military service and to hold back their tears as another son goes off to war. Furthermore, while deeply moved by the efforts of Australian troops, he expresses dismay that Australia as a nation refused to allow black or Jewish immigrants to participate in the war despite a need for more troops. Finally, in the one letter written after the war, Coppersmith explains that a single African American served among his crew of twenty-one members. Due to the tight quarters, the entire enlisted crew slept in one compartment, a situation that did not please the four white southerners on board. According to Coppersmith, it was fortunate that "Willie knew his place," a clear reminder of the extent to which prejudice and custom defined race relations, even in the South Pacific.

In one of his final letters, Coppersmith looked forward with great prescience to what American troops would face when they returned home. "The serviceman will present many interesting problems," he wrote.

> Politicians, corporations, chambers of commerce, loud speakers and countless others wax eloquently with promises of what a utopia is open for the men upon their return. It will take no little time to make these men realize that the world does not owe them a living simply because of their participation. Even the loans they will make must be repaid. A completed college education takes effort and sacrifice in the way of study and deprivation of an otherwise possible married normal family life. So, too, there is no guarantee of future success, even after graduation, unless they be adequately and properly constituted. Bonuses are soon spent and are paid but once. Jobs may be promised and guaranteed upon their return, but they are available only where there is a continued demand for labor, and it is up to the man to hold and retain the job he returns to.

CONTENT　　★　★　★　★　★
AESTHETICS　★　★　★
NAVIGATION　★　★　★

A World War II Diary in the Pacific
http://www.sinclair.edu/sec/his103/103d01.htm

Jack "Weary" McKnight served aboard the USS *Essex* from April 1943 to December 1945. The first aircraft carrier of its class and thus critical to Allied efforts in the Pacific, the *Essex* and its crew took part in numerous engagements, including in the Mariannas and at Eniwetok, Guam, Palau, and, perhaps most importantly, Leyte Gulf and Okinawa. Throughout his time on board, McKnight kept a diary, which his son has transcribed and posted online. Although McKnight's diary reads like a log—factual notations on maneuvers, number of enemy planes shot down, etc.—and contains little in the way of personal reflections or feelings, it nonetheless provides fascinating insight into the constant activity of an aircraft carrier and its crew.

One of McKnight's earliest entries reads "destination unknown," a vivid reminder of the uncertainty that faced sailors in the Pacific. What follows is a rapid series of engagements and movements that never seems to slow except during brief periods of leave. McKnight's diary is well indexed by month and therefore easily navigable from one month to the next and back. A series of footnotes, presumably added by McKnight's son, provides useful information and links to relevant sites. For instance, when McKnight mentions another ship in a convoy—and such references appear frequently—a link is provided to a brief history of that vessel. Similar links are provided for major engagements. In addition, A World War II Diary in the Pacific includes a number of photographs that enhance the very events McKnight describes as well as other interesting graphics, such as a menu from Thanksgiving dinner.

The single most fascinating aspect of this site centers on the events of November 25, 1944. While cruising 100 miles east of Luzon, a Japanese kamikaze struck the flight deck of the *Essex*, killing fifteen and wounding forty-five of its crew. Numerous photographs of the attack are available, including one of the attack plane just before it struck and one that shows a gaping hole in the flight deck. Most spectacularly, film footage of the attack, shot by seamen on a neighboring ship, is available and well worth the time needed for downloading.

CONTENT   ★ ★ ★ ★
AESTHETICS   ★ ★ ★ ★
NAVIGATION   ★ ★ ★ ★ ★

SUGGESTED READINGS

Ambrose, Stephen. *Citizen Soldiers: The U.S. Army from the Normandy Beaches to the Bulge to the Surrender of Germany, June 7, 1944 to May 7, 1945* (New York, 1998).

———. *Band of Brothers: E Company, 506th Regiment, 101st Airborne from Normandy to Hitler's Eagle Nest* (New York, 2001).

———. *Wild Blue: The Men and Boys Who Flew the B-24s over Germany, 1944–45* (New York, 2002).

Bartov, Omer. *Hitler's Army: Soldiers, Nazis and War in the Third Reich* (New York, 1992).

Blunt, Roscoe E., Jr. *Foot Soldier: A Combat Infantryman's War in Europe* (New York, 2000).

Boyington, Gregory. *Baa Baa Black Sheep* (Blue Ridge, PA, 1990).

Brokaw, Tom. *The Greatest Generation* (New York, 1998).

Carroll, Andrew, ed. *War Letters: Extraordinary Correspondence from American Wars* (New York, 2001).

Crosby, Harry H. *A Wing and a Prayer: The "Bloody 100th" Bomb Group of the U.S. Eighth Air Force in Action over Europe in World War II* (New York, 1993).

Daddis, Gregory A. *Fighting in the Great Crusade: An 8th Infantry Artillery Officer in World War II* (Baton Rouge, LA, 2002).

Dower, John W. *War without Mercy: Race and Power in the Pacific War* (New York, 1987).

Drez, Ronald J. *Voices of D-Day: The Story of the Allied Invasion Told by Those Who Were There* (Baton Rouge, LA, 1994).

Ellis, John. *On the Front Lines: The Experience of War through the Eyes of Allied Soldiers in World War II* (New York, 1991).

Greene, Bob. *Duty: A Father, His Son, and the Man Who Won the War* (Madison, WI, 2001).

Hynes, Samuel Lynn. *The Soldiers' Tale: Bearing Witness to Modern War* (New York, 1998).

Jackson, Carlton. *Allied Secret: The Sinking of HMT* Rohna (Norman, OK, 2002).

Johnson, J. E. *Wing Leader: Top-Scoring Allied Fighter Pilot of World War Two* (Toronto, 2000).

Johnson, Robert S. *Thunderbolt! An Extraordinary Story of a World War II Ace* (New York, 1997).

Kennett, Lee. *G. I.: The American Soldier in World War II* (New York, 1987).

Leckie, Robert. *Helmet for My Pillow: The Best Selling Account of Marine Combat in the Pacific* (New York, 2001).

Lee, Loyd E. "Personal Narratives of Sailors, Soldiers and Civilians," in *World War II in Europe, Africa, and the Americas, with General Sources* (Westport, CT, 1997).

Linderman, Gerald F. *The World within War: America's Combat Experience in World War II* (New York, 1997).

Luza, Radomir. *The Hitler Kiss: A Memoir of the Czech Resistance* (Baton Rouge, LA, 2002).

MacDonald, Charles B. *Company Commander* (Washington, DC, 1947).

MacKenzie, S. P. "Prisoners of War and Civilian Internees." In *World War II in Asia and the Pacific and the War's Aftermath, with General Themes,* edited by Loyd E. Lee (Westport, CT, 1997).

Manchester, William. *Goodbye Darkness: A Memoir of the Pacific War* (Boston, 1979).

Mauldin, Bill. *Up Front* (New York, 1968).

Morgan, Col. Robert, with Ron Powers. *The Man Who Flew the Memphis Belle: Memoir of a WWII Bomber Pilot* (New York, 2001).

Mullener, Elizabeth. *War Stories: Remembering World War II* (Baton Rouge, LA, 2002).

Pyle, Ernie. *Ernie Pyle's War: America's Eyewitness to World War II* (Lawrence, KS, 1998).

Richard, Oscar G., III. *Kriegie: An American POW in Germany* (Baton Rouge, LA, 2000).

Sledge, Eugene B. *With the Old Breed: At Peleliu and Okinawa* (New York, 1990).

Springer, Joseph A. *The Black Devil Brigade: The True Story of the First Special Service Force* (Pacifica, CA, 2001).

Wilson, George. *If You Survive* (New York, 1997).

Zumbro, Derek S. *In Deadly Combat: A German Soldier's Memoir of the Eastern Front* (Lawrence, KS, 2000).

CHAPTER 6

THE HOME FRONT

More important in determining victory than all the battles was the war for industrial production. The United States, Great Britain, and the Soviet Union won the war because they crushed Germany and Japan under an avalanche of warplanes, ships, artillery, and tanks. Furthermore, the Americans and British bombed the Axis industrial structure into oblivion, as recounted in graphic detail in the United States Strategic Bombing Surveys, compiled in 1946. Copies of the original *Summary Reports* that detail the tremendous damage done to the industrial and transportation infrastructures are available online at http://www.anesi.com/ussbs02.htm and http://www.anesi.com/ussbs01.htm. For the most part the study of the Allies' industrial production is a prosaic recital of statistical accomplishments, but for a lively example of wartime production see the British site at http://www.iwm.org.uk/online/sinews/intro.htm. Oil was the most important munition of the war. Two-thirds of all supplies shipped abroad consisted of oil. The United Stated pumped nearly two-thirds of the world's oil supply from its rich Texas and California fields—and it was cheap at only $1.15 a barrel (the dollar in the early 1940s was worth about 10 present-day dollars). Shipping the oil was problematic because of the German submarines off the U.S. coast. The nation's tanker capacity by war's end reached 11.4 millions tons (compared to 2.5 million tons in 1941). Civilian demand for gasoline was cut 28 percent by rationing, and increased production (up 29 percent from 1941 to 1945) fueled the war effort. In 1942, Japan cut off 90 percent of its rubber supplies to the United States. Despite early confusion, by late 1943 a highly successful synthetic rubber industry met the nation's increased war demands. For an account of the vital importance of petroleum during the war, see http://www.qmfound.com/fuels_wwII.htm.

In five years the United States produced $181 billion worth of munitions, of which aircraft comprised 24 percent; ships, 22 percent; food, clothing, and medicine, 20 percent; tanks and trucks, 12 percent; ammunition, 10 percent; guns and fire control equipment, 6 percent; and radio and radar, 6 percent. Employment in the munitions industry as a whole peaked at 8.8 million in late 1944; 29 percent of the workers were women, and 8 percent were African American. The world gasped in 1940 when Roosevelt promised to build 50,000 airplanes. In the end, 300,000 were built, at a cost of $45 billion. The air force took 185,000; the navy, 60,000; Britain, Canada, Australia, and New Zealand, 33,000; the Soviet Union, 18,000; and China, 4,000. Measured by weight, the production totaled 2.9 billion pounds, of which 61 percent was bombers and 22 percent fighters. For the models produced see http://www.wpafb.af.mil/museum/air_power/ap.htm.

The rifles, cannons, shells, and ammunition for the forces were made primarily in government arsenals. The arsenals were set up in small towns known to have a surplus of labor, and they employed 486,000 workers in 1943, contrasted to 22,000 in 1940. Shipyards launched 88,000 landing craft, 215 submarines, 147 aircraft carriers, and 952 other warships, aggregating 14 million tons. Ships traditionally had been hand crafted by skilled workers, with riveting used to hold the steel plates together. Blueprints were standardized for wartime production, and simplified construction techniques were developed. Welding replaced riveting, thereby allowing the shipyards to employ unskilled labor with a few weeks of training. The assembly line process was a triumph, producing 5,200 merchant ships totaling 39 million gross tons.

All major countries developed high-powered propaganda machines to stress to their populations the importance of production in winning the war. Hundreds of American posters supporting wartime production can be found online, as well as a few from other countries. Recently, high-quality paper reproductions of these posters have come on the market; they can be found on ebay.com by searching under "war poster," "world war poster," or "war bonds." Like television commercials today, the posters were ubiquitous during the war. Shopkeepers put them in their windows; they were in schools, factories, post offices, and train stations. Smaller versions were in buses. The posters had to be succinct, clear, and accessible to the average person (who had not graduated from high school). People hurrying by could grasp their message with a quick glance. Most of the posters were produced and distributed by federal government agencies, but some were designed and sold to factories by private sign companies. They often urged more labor-management cooperation. All posters reflected the "official" line on a topic. Information was a weapon; indeed, movies and radio broadcasts were also coordinated or censored by the federal government. The result was that antiwar posters or any sort of alternative message was not allowed and was not seen. On censorship see http://xroads.virginia.edu/~CLASS/am485_98/lane/media/censor.htm.

The posters probably did not change anyone's mind; instead, they reinforced the official position, giving it added legitimacy. In America the patriotism level was quite high; defeatism was rampant in many other countries, however, and their governments tried to control it through propaganda. One serious problem was that of rumors. Many of the posters available on the web contain dire warnings against spies—they seem to be listening everywhere and will immediately report every bit of gossip to lurking submarines, who will strike hard using that information ("Loose Lips Might Sink Ships"). In reality, the government did not fear spies at all, but the warnings were used in an effort to stop defeatism and negative rumors. The great majority of all wartime rumors were negative, derogatory, or defeatist—like stories of hospital ships secretly returning filled with quadriplegics. The best way to stop this defeatism was to keep everyone quiet and hope that people would only repeat what they learned from public sources, which was always upbeat and optimistic. Discussions with those who lived through the war, however, often reveal people who to this day obey the posters and refuse to talk about their "secret" activities during the war.

On a more positive note, the posters celebrated industrial production. Factory workers were proud—the posters correctly emphasized that they were as vital to the war effort as the front line soldiers. Of course, guilt themes were omnipresent—do not slack off or a soldier will die because of your failure. Many workers were unfamiliar with factory life and had to be warned to avoid accidents. A special category of posters focused on encouraging women to join the paid labor force (see Chapter 7 for a discussion of women's roles in the war). Farm production should not be overlooked; far more Americans lived on farms in the '40s than today, and their contribution was vital too.

It is surprising to discover that there were few posters encouraging men to sign up for the draft. That was because the draft was very well organized and met with little resistance. There were posters, however, encouraging men to sign up for glamorous—but high risk—elite roles such as flier.

Many posters emphasized teamwork and national unity as hallmarks of patriotism. Many stressed the international character of the war and tried to neutralize persistent rumors to the effect that the Americans were pulling British chestnuts out of the fire, or that Uncle Joe Stalin was really a nasty Communist. The government responded to these rumors with posters showing the horribleness of the Nazis and Japanese. Interestingly, very few wartime posters mentioned the Holocaust—that horrible event did not reach public consciousness in a major way until the 1960s.

The politics of the home front saw "Dr. Win the War" replace "Dr. New Deal," as President Roosevelt himself said. There are rich resources available for the New

Deal era, and some valuable materials for the war years as well, in the major New Deal site at http://newdeal.feri.org/. Those interested in this era will also find valuable material on the NEWDEAL email list, whose archives can be browsed at http://listserv.uic.edu/archives/newdeal.html. Subscription is free and can be done by email; subscribers receive daily reports and can ask scholars and specialists questions. The site is especially strong on biographies and reviews of recent scholarly books.

Cartoons provide a wonderful insight into how people thought during the war. Unlike government-approved posters, the editorial cartoonists in American newspapers had freedom of speech and were often quite critical of the failures of the government and industry. Labor unions that went on strike during the war were favorite targets of editorial wrath. Among the greatest cartoonists of the 1940s were Herblock, Vaughan Shoemaker, Ding Darling, and Jim Berryman in America and David Low in Britain. Niskayuna High School in upstate New York has been scanning editorial cartoons from newspapers all over the country housed at the Roosevelt Presidential Library and has created a wonderful online resource at http://www.nisk.k12.ny.us/fdr/FDRcartoons.html. Doubtless the most horrible miscarriage of justice on the home front was the relocation of the Japanese away from the West Coast. For a history of the decision to relocate Japanese Americans, see http://www.army.mil/CMH-PG/BOOKS/70-7_05.htm. Several sites reviewed in this chapter also deal with this topic.

Scholarly and popular interest in the home front experience during World War II has been increasing in recent years. The outstanding web sites reviewed in this chapter offer rich resources for those who want to know more than just the "guns and trumpets" history of the war.

 EB SITE REVIEWS

GENERAL

American Memory from the Library of Congress
http://rs6.loc.gov/ammem/amhome.html

American Memory, the Library of Congress's digital archive, includes more than 7 million items from more than 100 separate collections. Among the vast holdings are several collections and hundreds of items of deep relevance to researchers, educators, and students interested in the American home front during World War II.

"America from the Great Depression to World War II: Photographs from the FSA-OWI, 1935–1945" (http://memory.loc.gov/ammem/fsowhome.html) is perhaps the single most important collection of American documentary photography ever assembled. In the mid- to late 1930s, the Farm Security Administration (FSA) hired the nation's most accomplished documentary photographers—including Dorothea Lange, Margaret Bourke-White, and Walker Evans, among others—to record the experience of Americans as they struggled to cope with the Great Depression. With the onset of war, the corps of photographers shifted their attention to home front mobilization, producing thousands of images for the Office of War Information (OWI). All told, the FSA-OWI collection contains more than 160,000 black and white and 1,600 colored photographs.

The immense size of the collection is both its greatest strength and weakness. The corps of photographers captured every conceivable aspect of World War II mobilization. Images abound of aircraft assembly lines and female war workers. And although the collection is searchable by subject, creator, and geographic location, "World War II" does not appear in the subject index. Consequently, certain researchers, depending on what they hope to find, face a daunting task as they sift through the photographs. The much smaller collection of colored photographs provides the same search options, but it does include "World War II, 1939–1945" in the subject index, making it more manageable for researches of the war.

"By the People, for the People: Posters from the WPA, 1936–1943" (http://memory.loc.gov/ammem/wpaposters/wpahome.html) contains more than 900 of the original 2,000 posters, lithographs, and woodcuts produced at the behest of the New Deal's Works Progress Administration (WPA). Hired to publicize a variety of New Deal–era health, cultural, and educational programs, the artists, like the photographers, turned their attention to the war effort in the early 1940s. The collection's subject index includes war blackouts, war bonds and funds, war posters, and war work. Researchers may also search the collection by keyword or creator.

In addition to these resources, American Memory includes literally hundreds of items from assorted collections that pertain to the American experience in World War II. The biggest challenge is to find these items. From the American Memory home page (http://rs6.loc.gov/ammem/amhome.html), visitors should choose "Collection Finder" and then "Time 1930–1949." A search engine allows one to search all of the library's online collections. A search for "World War II," for instance, produces 215 items, while a search for "World War" produces the maximum 500 hits. A thorough examination of the American Memory collections requires substantial time, but the offerings are well worth it.

CONTENT   ★ ★ ★ ★
AESTHETICS   ★ ★ ★
NAVIGATION   ★ ★ ★

The Rutgers Oral History Archives of World War II
http://fas-history.rutgers.edu/oralhistory/orlhom.htm

For a full review of this site, see p. 75, and for a review of material pertaining to women and African Americans, see p. 114.

Although the 218 interviews in this superb archive focus on the experiences of men and women who went overseas during World War II, researchers interested in the American home front should not overlook this site, as many of the interviews provide fascinating accounts of the wartime contributions of men and women who never left the United States. In fact, an easy-to-navigate chart that lists the branch of service and theater of operation for each individual indicates those who remained on the home front (look for "HF"). Visitors to The Rutgers Oral History Archives of World War II will find interviews with women who worked as nurses and with the USO and men who made maps, trained pilots, guarded German POWs in the United States, and joined the army but never made it overseas. Interviewees discuss rationing, blackouts, and air raids. Furthermore, many of the interviews provide an in-depth look at the American home front in the immediate postwar period.

CONTENT   ★ ★ ★ ★
AESTHETICS   ★ ★ ★
NAVIGATION   ★ ★ ★

U.S. Army Signal Corps Photograph Collection
http://eagle.vsla.edu/signal.corps

More than 1.5 million men and women departing for and returning from service in World War II passed through the Hampton Roads Port of Embarkation in Newport News, Virginia. Photographers with the U.S. Army's Signal Corps dutifully recorded the movements of these legions; more than 3,500 of their images are now housed in the Library of Virginia's U.S. Army Signal Corps Photograph Collection (SCC). This massive photographic archive, available online in its entirety, details "the preparation and loading of war materials, the activities of the U.S. Quartermaster Corps, U.S. military personnel arriving and departing through the ports of Hampton Roads, civilian employees, Red Cross workers, wounded personnel, entertainers, animals, and German and Italian prisoners of war."

The SCC is so extensive that first-time visitors may feel overwhelmed. The site has an excellent search engine designed for a variety of types of searches, but it lacks an index with predetermined categories that would facilitate navigation. Consequently, researchers without a clear sense of what or who they are looking for may find it difficult to navigate the site. Nevertheless, once embarking upon a search, the engine will produce a number of hits, each of which provides a thumbnail sketch of the relevant images and brief descriptions. Clicking on the number of each hit will produce a full description of all known information, and larger images can be accessed by clicking on the thumbnails. The Signal Corps photographers faithfully recorded the names of their subjects; consequently, individuals in most images are identified by name, and their names are cross-listed with the search engine. For example, visitors can search for Red Skelton and will be led to two images of Private First Class Richard "Red" Skelton. On the other hand, a visitor would have to know to search for Skelton; otherwise, one would have no way of finding his picture but for sheer chance.

The Library of Virginia's SCC is one of the most extensive collections of World War II photographs available on the web. The variety and richness of images make this site a must visit.

For a review of material on this site relating to women and African Americans, see *p. 115.*

CONTENT   ★ ★ ★ ★ ★
AESTHETICS   ★ ★ ★ ★
NAVIGATION   ★ ★ ★ ★

World War II: The Home Front
http://library.thinkquest.org/15511/index.htm

One of more than four thousand entries on ThinkQuest, "an online community where young people learn, teach, mentor, discover, research and grow," World War II: The Home Front is an interactive site created by students for students. Valuable not only in what it teaches about the American home front, the site also provides a rich example of the web-based learning possibilities for students of all ages.

The brainchild of high school students in Galesburg, Illinois, and Amherst, New York, World War II: The Home Front allows visitors to enmesh themselves in the lives of five fictional American families during the 1943–44 school year; this year was chosen because the war effort was at full force but its outcome not yet certain. The creators are the first to acknowledge that their site provides little insight into the causes of the war; instead, it focuses on "day-to-day life and period culture."

The heart of this site is found in a section entitled Simulation. Students and other visitors are introduced to five families from around the country of different ethnic, economic, and political backgrounds (curiously and noticeably, none of the families are African American). Participants in the simulation then embark on a series of exercises, such as journal writing, in which they draw upon various resources to respond to a series of situational questions. Participants are also asked to make posters and buttons and devise radio announcements that address important social and political issues.

A brief but useful timeline, organized by year, discusses the major events of the war and provides useful background information for the simulation. The WWII Encyclopedia, located in a section entitled Resources, contains short but thorough entries on significant persons and events. The Museum section further enhances the simulation with artifacts, posters, and graphics that provide insight into the popular culture of the World War II home front. Communications, entertainment, civil defense, victory gardens, fashion, and even children's toys are all represented in the Museum.

CONTENT   ★ ★ ★ ★
AESTHETICS   ★ ★ ★ ★
NAVIGATION   ★ ★ ★ ★

INTERNMENT ON THE HOME FRONT— JAPANESE AMERICANS AND POWS

Confinement and Ethnicity: An Overview of World War II Japanese-American Relocation Sites
http://www.cr.nps.gov/history/books/gnrlpub.htm

Produced by the National Park Service, this online book provides a terrific history of the forced relocation and confinement of 120,000 Japanese Americans during World War II. Three introductory essays, including one written by Eleanor Roosevelt in 1943, trace the 1942 exodus of Japanese Americans from their homes in the western United States, to the seventeen temporary "assembly centers," to the ten "relocation" camps that became home for some American citizens for as long as three years. The introduction includes a useful map that shows the areas of the United States affected by relocation as well as the locations of the camps and assembly centers. Each essay reminds the reader of the devastating effect relocation had on the lives of those who were displaced.

One of the strengths of Confinement and Ethnicity is that it has separate, and extensive, chapters on each of the ten relocation camps: Gila River, Granada, Heart Mountain, Jerome, Manzanar, Minidoka, Poston, Rohwer, Topaz, and Tule

Lake. Researchers interested in a specific camp, or in the camps as a whole, will find detailed information on nearly every aspect of camp life, from organization, to work, to recreation. Each chapter contains photos and detailed maps.

Additional chapters cover other locations where Japanese Americans were forcibly housed during World War II—assembly centers, isolation centers, Department of Justice and U.S. Army camps, and even prisons. Appendix C contains a series of Corps of Engineer drawings of buildings at the various camps and centers.

A user-friendly sidebar serves as a table of contents/index and allows visitors to navigate smoothly from one chapter to the next. Unlike the case with many online books, researchers will not get stuck in the middle of a chapter because navigation only allows one to move forward or backward one page at a time. Instead, visitors to Confinement and Ethnicity always have the option to escape to the home page or to any of the other chapters. The site has its own URL (http://www.cr.nps.gov/history/online_books/anthropology74/), but, for whatever reason, visitors must first link to the National Park Service's list of general publications at http://www.cr.nps.gov/history/books/gnrlpub.htm and then connect to Confinement and Ethnicity.

CONTENT   ★ ★ ★
AESTHETICS ★ ★ ★
NAVIGATION ★ ★ ★ ★

Evacuation and Internment of San Francisco Japanese
http://www.sfmuseum.org/war/evactxt.html

Throughout March and April 1942, the *San Francisco News* covered the heightened harassment and eventual forced removal of the city's Japanese American population. Designed and run by the Museum of the City of San Francisco, this site contains more than seventy original news reports that portray a city gripped by the most potent and destructive combination of war hysteria and fear. Led by Lieutenant General John DeWitt, the commander of the San Francisco Presidio, business and political leaders worked together to ensure the destruction of the city's Japanese community.

In addition to the news reports, the site includes a remarkable array of primary documents certain to interest researchers, educators, and students. Visitors to Evacuation and Internment of San Francisco Japanese might consider beginning with the Chronology of 1942 San Francisco War Events. Not only does the timeline provide useful political context for the news reports, but it has links to key documents, such as Roosevelt's Executive Order No. 9066 and General DeWitt's subsequent instructions to all persons of Japanese descent to voluntarily relocate.

Other primary documents include DeWitt's "Final Report on the Evacuation of the Japanese" and the War Relocation Authority's (WRA) "Relocation of Japanese Americans." Dorothea Lange's photographs of the evacuation are both riveting and haunting, as are images from the Manzanar camp, to which many San Francisco Japanese were sent. A May 21, 1942, headline from the *San Francisco Chronicle* summed up the effectiveness of the campaign: "S.F. Clear of All But 6 Sick Japanese."

The Museum of the City of San Francisco has, in effect, created a community study of Japanese American removal and relocation. Most web pages devoted to Japanese American relocation focus on the camps themselves, but this site provides a vivid reminder of what was lost, destroyed, and left behind. User-friendly and easy to navigate, it is a must visit.

In addition to Evacuation and Internment of San Francisco Japanese, researchers will want to peruse a related exhibit: The Home Front—San Francisco during World War II. Accessible at http://www.sfmuseum.org/hist1/index0.2.html#war, The Home Front exhibit includes an extensive chronology, newspaper articles, instructions for civil defense and air raid warnings, and opinion pieces on various aspects of the domestic war effort. Like the exhibit on Japanese-American evacuation and internment, the museum's home front resources provide an excellent look at one community's experience during the war.

CONTENT   ★ ★ ★ ★
AESTHETICS   ★ ★ ★ ★
NAVIGATION   ★ ★ ★ ★

Kriegsgefangen: The German Prisoners of World War II
http://www.kriegsgefangen.de

Few Americans think of the continental United States as home to German and Axis POWs. Of the 3,800,000 Germans prisoners in American custody, however, more than 360,000 were interned at camps in the United States. The first of these prisoners were members of the German Africa Corps, who were captured in Tunisia in 1943; the rest were captured on the western front after the Allied invasion of June 1944.

Part of a larger web site ("kriegsgefangen" is German for prisoner of war) devoted to recording the experience of German POWs in countries throughout the world, this site does not contain extensive material on German POWs in the United States. In addition, errors in the translation from German to English may frustrate some visitors. Nonetheless, this site offers information not available elsewhere on the web and suggests a need to expand our conception of the home front.

Visitors to the home page of Kriegsgefangen: The German Prisoners of World War II should click on the American flag (after choosing English as the language with which to view the site) to reach the section devoted to German prisoners in the United States. The organization of what follows is somewhat confusing, but two of the four possible links will prove useful: Prisoners in the USA and Multimedia. Prisoners in the USA provides a brief history and notes that the overwhelming majority of POW camps in the United States were in the South. Consequently, it is unfortunate that all of the information here pertains to Camp Farragut in Idaho.

In addition to the brief history provided by the webmaster, the site offers a series of articles from *Die Lupe*, the newspaper of Camp Farragut. Among the articles are the reflections of a German prisoner who spent ten months at Farragut, as well as Christmas wishes exchanged between the prisoners and the camp commandant. As the prisoners prepared to leave the camp at the war's end, they expressed a desire to overcome "the ruins of our fatherland and the illness of our nation," while the camp commander expressed hope that time in the camp had provided "a little view of democratic life, a new courage to face the problems of tomorrow, a memory of a peaceful Christmas where you had freedom of speech, religion, want, and fear."

Numerous photographs enhance the musings from *Die Lupe*, while the Multimedia section includes three short films: one on camp life in general; one showing efforts to teach English to German prisoners; and one entitled "Controlling German Prisoners of War." Finally, on the home page, the Content link accesses some additional sketches from another POW camp in the United States.

CONTENT ★ ★ ★
AESTHETICS ★ ★ ★
NAVIGATION ★ ★ ★

War Relocation Authority Photographs of Japanese-American Evacuation and Resettlement, 1942–1945
http://www.oac.cdlib.org/dynaweb/ead/calher/jvac

Between 1942 and 1945, WRA staff photographers recorded more than 7000 images of all aspects and phases of Japanese American internment. Pictures depict Japanese American merchants closing their shops in advance of their evacuation; mounds of baggage in city centers awaiting transport to resettlement centers; and, of course, evacuees themselves boarding buses headed for assembly centers and camps. Photographers also recorded Japanese Americans at the seventeen assembly centers to which they were sent before being transported to the ten relocation camps. The bulk of the photographs in the collection, not surprisingly, portray life inside the camps. A final batch of images documents the resettlement of Japanese Americans after the camps' closings.

Downloading the site's large files requires patience, but navigation is otherwise quite easy. The collection is exceedingly well organized into eighteen series. Each of the ten relocation camps has its own series, while the others depict pre-evacuation activities, assembly centers, relocation, and resettlement. Each series, in turn, is divided into numerous groups. The images in each group are identified by caption, name of the photographer, date taken, and WRA identification number. Clicking a small icon next to the caption produces the actual image.

The WRA photographs are simply staggering in their number and scope. Researchers and educators interested in visual representations of Japanese American internment will make this site their first, and perhaps last, stop on the web.

CONTENT   ★ ★ ★ ★ ★
AESTHETICS   ★ ★ ★ ★
NAVIGATION   ★ ★ ★ ★

LETTERS FROM THE HOME FRONT

Private Art

http://www.private-art.com

For a full review of this site, see p. 81.

For a full review of this site, see p. 81.

Private Art contains the correspondence of Arthur Pranger and his family during his service in Europe from June 1944 until the end of the war. As the letters reveal, family and friends on the home front worried a great deal about their loved ones in the war, but they simultaneously made every effort to go about their lives. Art's father wrote to his son about funerals, vacations, and house chores, signing one letter "good luck." His mother passed on news about the rise of the river and fears of an impending flood and happily reported that the nephew of a family friend had been discovered alive in the Philippines after three years as a POW. Art's brother wrote about the results of his Latin test.

CONTENT   ★ ★ ★ ★
AESTHETICS   ★ ★ ★ ★
NAVIGATION   ★ ★ ★ ★

PUBLICATIONS AND POSTERS

Dr. Seuss Went to War: A Catalog of Political Cartoons by Dr. Seuss
http://orpheus.ucsd.edu/speccoll/dspolitic

Theodore Geisel, better known as Dr. Seuss, earned fame and fortune as an author and illustrator of children's books. Few fans think of Dr. Seuss as a political cartoonist, but from 1941 to 1943, he was the chief editorial cartoonist for *PM*, a New York newspaper. During his tenure, Geisel produced 400 cartoons, all of which are now housed in the special collections library at the University of California at San Diego. Most of the cartoons in the collection are relevant to World War II.

Visitors to Dr. Seuss Went to War will instantly recognize Dr. Seuss's distinctive style. All of the characters in these drawings, including Roosevelt, Hitler, Stalin, and the ever-present animals, look like they would feel right at home in Dr. Seuss's more famous children's books. The site is well organized and allows visitors to search the cartoons by date or subject. The date index is subdivided by year, month, and day. The subject index is organized into four subgroups: People, Countries/Regions, War/Domestic Issues, and Battles and Battlefields. Visitors will find sketches of many important World War II political and military leaders, including more than 100 of Hitler. No major aspect of the war escaped Dr. Seuss's attention. From the isolationist American First Committee, led by Charles Lindbergh, to the attack on Pearl Harbor, to war industries and racism, Dr. Seuss covered it all. The only unfortunate aspect of this collection is that Dr. Seuss did not remain at *PM* through the end of the war. One can only imagine what he might have drawn during the final two and one-half years of the war.

CONTENT   ★ ★ ★ ★
AESTHETICS   ★ ★ ★ ★
NAVIGATION   ★ ★ ★

Government Publications From World War II
http://www2.smu.edu/cul/ww2/title.htm

Hosted by Southern Methodist University's Digital Library, Government Publications From World War II contains the full text of more than forty government publications, almost all of which pertain to civilian life on the home front. The reports are organized alphabetically rather than by subject; consequently, visitors must scroll through the single index until finding an appropriate title. Furthermore, many of the documents must be read or downloaded as Adobe PDF files and thus can take time.

A significant number of the publications reflect not only the extent to which women transformed the work place during World War II but also the lingering uncertainty and assumptions about the ability of women to do the work effectively. Titles include "Boarding Homes for Women War Workers," "Choosing Woman for Industry Jobs," "Night Work for Women and Shift Rotation in War Plants," "Safety Caps for Women Machine Operators," "Safety Shoes for Women Workers," and "Women's Effective War Work Requires Time for Meals and Rest."

Other reports emphasize the necessity of a vigilant homeland defense. "Defend American Freedom," "The Defense Program: A Handbook for Speakers," and "The Home Front in National Defense" are all included in full. Planners in the Agriculture Department concentrated on maximizing the food supply. In addition to offering tips to farmers in "Produce More Meat, Milk and Leather with No More Feed," the department created a "Victory Garden Insect Guide."

The ability of children and soldiers to negotiate the transition from wartime to peacetime concerned policymakers. In response, the Children's Bureau of the Commission on Children in Wartime published "Goals for Children and Youth: In the Transition from War to Peace," while the War Department provided "Additional Information for Soldiers Going Back to Civilian Life: A Supplement Explaining Provisions of the 'GI Bill of Rights.'"

CONTENT   ★ ★ ★ ★
AESTHETICS   ★ ★ ★
NAVIGATION   ★ ★ ★

Powers of Persuasion: Poster Art From World War II
http://www.archives.gov/digital_classroom/lessons/powers_of_persuasion/powers_of_persuasion.html

Part of a larger exhibit displayed at the National Archives in the mid-1990s, Powers of Persuasion contains thirty-three posters and one sound file that represent what the site's curators refer to as a "constant battle for the hearts and minds of the American citizenry." Throughout the duration of the war, propaganda and persuasion "became a wartime industry, almost as important as the manufacturing of bullets and planes." The posters in this collection are divided into two groups: one set of posters aims to instill pride and patriotism, while the other presents a shocking, harsh view of war, in particular the consequences of an Axis victory. These latter images, according to the exhibit, "appeal to darker impulses, fostering feelings of suspicion, fear, and even hate."

Among the posters that instill pride, patriotism, and general confidence in the American war effort, researchers will find appeals to strong men to "man the guns" and to patriotic women to "get a war job." In an attempt to minimize the effect of pervasive and overt discrimination at home, images of black and white war workers, along with a personal message from heavyweight champion Joe Louis, attempt to convey the importance of racial solidarity. Appeals to conserve gas include the admonition that "when you ride alone, you ride with Hitler." In addition, Norman Rockwell's famous Four Freedoms prints are included along with an excerpt from Roosevelt's speech on the same subject.

A second set of images attempts to instill fear in an American public physically removed from the war itself. Claiming that "our homes are in danger now," threatening and brutal caricatures of Hitler and a Japanese leader loom over the United States. Menacing talons imprinted with a swastika and rising sun reach for a blond American mother and her baby. Warning Americans to be alert to domestic spies while tapping into assumptions about the propensity of women to gossip, one image depicts a typical American woman on a wanted poster; her crime: "Murder: Her Careless Talk Costs Lives."

CONTENT   ★ ★ ★ ★
AESTHETICS   ★ ★ ★ ★
NAVIGATION   ★ ★ ★ ★

Produce for Victory: Posters on the American Home Front, 1941–1945
http://www.americanhistory.si.edu/victory

Organized by the Smithsonian Institution's National Museum of American History, this online companion to an exhibition of the same name includes more than forty posters issued by federal agencies, businesses, and private organizations. Intended to mobilize those on the home front to recognize war aims as their "personal mission," the posters urged workers and families to do their part to boost production in the factories and at home. The collection is organized into six groups: Every Citizen a Soldier; The Poster's Place in War Time; Retooling for Victory: The Factory Front; Efficient Workers; War Aims through Art: The U.S. Office of War Information; and Fighting for an Ideal America. Each section includes a brief but helpful introduction that considers the most prominent themes and uses of imagery. The title, original dimensions, and name of the artist or sponsoring agency accompany a thumbnail sketch of each image, which, when clicked, provides a larger version of the poster.

Major corporations such as General Motors (GM) and Oldsmobile produced posters urging their employees to work harder and more efficiently. One GM poster proclaimed "It's a Two Fisted Fight" against an image of two hands holding a rifle and a wrench. Set against a silhouette of a hand with a crochet needle, an artist hired by the WPA urged Americans to "Remember Pearl Harbor:

Purl Harder." Another government-sponsored artist urged Americans to "Grow It Yourself: Plan a Farm Garden Now."

Idealized images of the American family pervaded World War II poster art. A series of "This Is America ... Keep It Free" posters proclaimed the virtue of small-town, wholesome individuals and their families. The Kroger Grocery Company produced a poster of children wearing gas masks with the prayer "Dear God, Keep Them Safe" above the children. An artist hired by Oldsmobile painted an image of a mother reading to her children with the intonation "Don't Let Anything Happen to Them ... Keep Firing."

CONTENT   ★ ★ ★ ★
AESTHETICS   ★ ★ ★ ★
NAVIGATION   ★ ★ ★ ★

World War II Poster Collection
http://www.library.nwu.edu/govpub/collections/wwii-posters

The Northwestern University library has gathered together a superb collection of more than 325 posters issued by various federal agencies from 1941 through 1945. From the home page, visitors can search the site by date, title, topic, or keyword, which will generate thumbnail pictures of the relevant posters with the titles, dates, and agencies that created them. Visitors can then choose to display a more complete record as well as a larger JPEG file for the poster itself. Northwestern University does not sell reproductions of these posters, but the National Archives and Records Administration does.

Despite the various options, searching World War II Poster Collection can appear daunting simply because of the size of the archive. Visitors not looking for a particular image should begin with a search by topic. The designers have sensibly organized the collection into the following categories: War Bonds, Don't Talk, Victory Gardens/Save the Forest, Canning/Rationing, Defense Work, Conserve Materials for War Effort, Home Efforts, Stay Healthy, Civil Defense, and Office of Price Administration.

The posters provide a terrific look at the various components of home front mobilization, from conservation and rationing, to civil defense, to warnings against gossip for fear the enemy may be lurking nearby. The art itself is worth a visit; the posters as a whole are an invaluable resource for understanding the concerns of a society at war.

CONTENT   ★ ★ ★ ★ ★
AESTHETICS   ★ ★ ★ ★
NAVIGATION   ★ ★ ★ ★

SUGGESTED READINGS

Adams, Michael C. C. *The Best War Ever: America and World War II* (Baltimore, MD, 1994).

Azema, Jean-Pierre, et al. *Collaboration and Resistance: Images of Life in Vichy France 1940–1944* (New York, 2000).

Bailey, Beth, and David Farber. *First Strange Place: The Alchemy of Race and Sex in World War II Hawaii* (Baltimore, MD, 1994).

Berube, Allan. *Coming Out Under Fire: The History of Gay Men and Women in World War II* (New York, 1990).

Blum, John Morton. *V Was for Victory: Politics and American Culture during World War II* (New York, 1976).

Bukey, Evan Burr. *Hitler's Austria: Popular Sentiment in the Nazi Era, 1938–1945* (Chapel Hill, NC, 2000).

Capeci, Dominic, Jr. *The Harlem Riot of 1943* (Philadelphia, PA, 1977).

Clive, Alan. *State of War: Michigan in World War II* (Ann Arbor, MI, 1979).

Costello, John. *Virtue Under Fire: How World War II Changed Our Social and Sexual Attitudes* (New York, 1987).

Daniels, Roger. *Prisoners without Trial: Japanese Americans in World War II* (New York, 1993).

Editors of Time-Life Books. *Decade of Triumph: The 40s* (Alexandria, VA, 1999).

Ehrenberg, Lewis A., and Susan E. Hirsch, eds. *The War in American Culture: Society and Consciousness during World War II* (Chicago, 1996).

Gellately, Robert. *Backing Hitler: Consent and Coercion in Nazi Germany* (New York, 2001).

Goodman, Jack, ed. *While You Were Gone: A Report on Wartime Life in the United States* (New York, 1946).

Hoffman, Daniel. *Zone of the Interior: A Memoir, 1942–1947* (Baton Rouge, LA, 2000).

Hoopes, Roy, ed. *Americans Remember the Home Front: An Oral Narrative of the World War II Years in America* (New York, 2002).

Irons, Peter. *Justice at War: The Story of the Japanese American Internment Cases* (New York, 1983).

Jeffries, John W. *Wartime America: The World War II Home Front* (Chicago, 1996).

Kennedy, David M. *Freedom from Fear: The American People in Depression and War, 1929–1945* (New York, 1999).

Koppes, Clayton R., and Gregory D. Black. *Hollywood Goes to War: How Politics, Profits, and Propaganda Shaped World War II Movies* (New York, 1987).

Kryder, Daniel. *Divided Arsenal: Race and the American State during World War II* (New York, 2000).

Laurie, Clayton D. *The Propaganda Warriors: America's Crusade against Nazi Germany* (Lawrence, KS, 1996).

Leonard, Hal. *I'll Be Seeing You: 50 Songs of World War II* (Milwaukee, WI, 1995).

Lichtenstein, Nelson. *Labor's War at Home: The CIO in World War II* (New York, 1987).

Mazon, Mauricio. *The Zoot-Suit Riots: The Psychology of Symbolic Annihilation* (Austin, TX, 1984).

Millar, James R., and Susan J. Linz. "The Cost of World War II to the Soviet People: A Research Note," *Journal of Economic History* 38, no. 4 (1978): 959–62 (also available online at JSTOR; requires paid subscription).

Minear, Richard H. *Dr. Seuss Goes to War: The World War II Editorial Cartoons of Theodor Seuss Geisel* (New York, 2001).

Muir, Malcolm, ed. *Human Tradition in the World War II Era* (Wilmington, DE, 1999).

O'Brien, Kenneth Paul, and Lynn Hudson Parsons, eds. *The Home-Front War: World War II and American Society* (Westport, CT, 1995).

O'Neill, William L. *A Democracy at War: America's Fight at Home and Abroad in World War II* (New York, 1993).

Polenberg, Richard. *War and Society: The United States, 1941–1945* (Philadelphia, 1972).

Roeder, George H., Jr. *The Censored War: American Visual Experience during World War Two* (New Haven, CT, 1993).

Robinson, Greg. *By Order of the President: FDR and the Internment of Japanese Americans* (Cambridge, MA, 2001).

Rubenstein, Harry R., and William L. Bird. *Design for Victory: World War II Posters on the American Home Front* (New York, 1998).

Shirer, William L. *"This Is Berlin": Radio Broadcasts, 1938–1940* (New York, 1999).

Shulman, Holly Cowan. *The Voice of America: Propaganda and Democracy, 1941–1945* (Madison, WI, 1991).

Starr, Kevin. *Embattled Dreams: California in War and Peace, 1940–1950* (New York, 2002).

Steele, Richard W. *Free Speech in the Good War* (New York, 1999).

Tateishi, John, ed. *And Justice for All: An Oral History of the Japanese-American Detention Camps* (Seattle, WA, 1999).

Terkel, Studs. *"The Good War": An Oral History of World War II* (New York, 1984).

Tuttle, William. *Daddy's Gone to War: The Second World War in the Lives of America's Children* (New York, 1993).

Waters, Mary. *Illinois,* 2 vols. (Springfield, IL, 1951).

Winkler, Allan. *The Politics of Propaganda: The Office of War Information, 1942–1945* (New Haven, CT, 1978).

——. *Home Front U.S.A.: America during World War II,* 2d ed. (Wheeling, IL, 2000).

Wynn, Neil A. *The Afro-American and the Second World War* (New York, 1993).

CHAPTER 7

NEW OPPORTUNITIES

WOMEN AND AFRICAN AMERICANS IN WORLD WAR II

The war years brought a remarkable increase in the roles women were encouraged to play in American society. In the depression years, the feeling was strong—among both men and women—that employment opportunities were strictly limited. Therefore, if a husband and wife were both employed, they would be taking a job desperately needed by some unemployed breadwinner. Unemployment vanished by 1943, and with 12 million men taken into the services, there was a desperate shortage of workers. Married women were encouraged to work; high wages pulled many students out of high schools and colleges. The great majority of jobs were gender-typed as appropriate for men or for women but seldom for both. Most of the new women employees went into the female job sector. Enticing women to take munitions jobs was problematic, so these positions were re-engineered so that unskilled women could learn them quickly. Thus, airplane construction was redesigned to emphasize riveting, which could be quickly taught. Munitions jobs paid very well—double the usual rates—and war plants made available new services, such as child care and transportation. The government also launched a major propaganda campaign to persuade women to take these jobs. The Redstone Arsenal in Alabama was run directly by the army, but most war plants were operated by private companies. The defense plants were located in larger cities, especially on the West Coast. Therefore, millions of families were uprooted in the search for high-paying, patriotic jobs.

There was money aplenty in the defense plants, but housing was scarce; many people lived with another family or in trailers. Teenagers (the very word was new) had less supervision, more opportunity for employment, and the role model of older brothers in the service. They were creating a new youth culture that nervous commentators feared would result in a wave of juvenile delinquency, and when teenagers married soldiers, the commentators worried that divorce rates would skyrocket. It was a sober age, however; juvenile delinquency was not a major problem, and the divorce rate rose only slightly. What most women seemed to want was a return to normalcy—to companionate marriages, with the men at home and preferably a new home in the suburbs, which people hoped would be built as soon as the war ended.

The most successful propaganda appeal was probably the idea that this terrible war would end faster, and the menfolk would come home sooner, if women donned overalls. This theme appealed also to the pacifistic sentiments that were stronger among women. (To appeal to men, the posters stressed vengeance—"Kill the bastards!")

Most adult women remained at home as housewives, and many posters were directed to them. It was essential that they support the total war America had entered by complying with the rationing and price controls and willingly sending their men off to war. The nation allocated about 40 percent of its total economic output to the war effort, so shortages of numerous products were frequent. Little or no new housing, cars, or appliances were available. Rationing was imposed on shoes, meat, sugar, coffee, gasoline, and many other consumer products. For example, to buy a pair of new shoes the shopper had to have three things: cash for the purchase price (which was held down by government price controls), ration coupons (which were distributed equally to men, women, and children through schools), and the shoe store had to have them in stock. If any one element was lacking, there was no sale. Europe also had rationing, but in many European countries, large "black markets" emerged where one could buy scarce items illegally (at a much higher price, with no ration coupons). There was very little black market activity in the United States, however; consumers supported the war effort. Often that meant "Use It Up, Wear It Out, Make It Do Or Do Without!"

A total war meant the military had to make effective use of womanpower. Copying the British example, the services set up auxiliary units: the Women's Army Corps (WAC), the Navy's Women Accepted for Volunteer Emergency Services (WAVES), the Women's Air Force (WAF), the Coast Guard SPARs (SPARs is from the Coast Guard motto, "Semper Paratus," which means "Always Ready"), and the women marines. The Army Nurse Corps and Navy Nurse Corps greatly expanded to be ready to handle the hundreds of thousands of feared casualties in an invasion of Japan that never happened. In all, some 300,000 women served. None were in combat, and most had traditional female jobs such as nurse, nurse's aid, secretary, or telephone operator. The Women Airforce Service Pilots (WASP) were a group of civilian women who flew airplanes—not in combat, but from factories to the coast for transfer overseas.

At war's end the munitions factories closed, and the workers had to find new jobs. Some of the women stayed in the paid labor force, but most became housewives again. Historians agree that gender roles were not drastically altered by the war. While some women expressed disappointment that they had to give up their jobs, postwar surveys consistently showed that the women who had exhausted themselves by playing multiple roles as workers, housewives, and mothers in difficult circumstances seemed eager to shed the worker role and let their husbands be breadwinners again.

Segregation of blacks and whites continued through the war years with few exceptions. (Segregation would not change until the civil rights laws of the 1960s.) Therefore, separate posters were designed for the African American community. They featured race heroes such as Dorie Miller (a navy messman who grabbed a machine gun to shoot at Japanese planes at Pearl Harbor) and heavyweight boxing champion Joe Louis. See the American Memory materials at the Library of Congress at http://memory.loc.gov/ammem/aaohtml/exhibit/aopart8.html#08a for more information.

The leaders of the African American community promoted a "double V" agenda—victory abroad over Germany and Japan, and victory at home over racial discrimination. Demanding not so much integration as equal opportunity to obtain defense jobs, they threatened a "March on Washington" in 1941. They never actually marched, but President Roosevelt responded to the threat with Executive Order 8802, which stated that there should be "no discrimination in the employment of workers in defense industries or Government because of race, creed, color, or national origin." Roosevelt also established a Committee on Fair Employment Practices to discuss discrimination complaints; it had no enforcement powers, however, and was disbanded after the war. Meanwhile, millions of African Americans left the very low-paying farm jobs in the cotton South and headed toward industrial cities. The migration was permanent—it was good riddance to the rural Jim Crow (segregated) South. The economic status of blacks improved sharply, as millions moved from unemployment in the city or underemployment in the cotton South to manual labor jobs vacated by whites. By 1944, 10.1 percent of male and 9.1 percent of female employees were African American, and their wages had increased to 46 percent of the rate for white men and 42 percent for women. Except for government-run munitions plants, blacks were the last hired and the first fired. Segregation still was ironclad in the South and prevailed in practice in the North. Rioting in Detroit in 1943 (see http://detnews.com/history/riot/riot.htm) killed thirty-four as the acute housing shortage pitted newly arrived black families against newly arrived Appalachian whites. Observers were convinced that far more interracial bloodletting was inevitable, but apart from a few limited incidents in Mobile, Alabama, and Beaumont, Texas, there was no major violence.

According to national policy, blacks were drafted in proportion to their percentage of the total American population (about 10 percent). Most were assigned to noncombat duties, but the air force set up an elite flying unit based in Tuskegee, Alabama (see http://www.coax.net/people/lwf/ta_his1.htm and http://members.aol.com/hqtai/tai/tai.html). The merchant marine was not officially part of the military, but blacks found many opportunities there (see http://www.usmm.org/african-americans.html).

The navy—more hidebound by traditions than other branches of the military—was probably the most reluctant to use blacks in anything but menial roles. The question of desegregating the services came up late in the war when Eisenhower was running short of combat soldiers in France and asked for volunteers, who served in partially integrated units.

At war's end, there were 695,000 black men enlisted in the army and air force, with 7,800 black officers; 165,000 were enlisted in the navy, and sixty were marines. President Truman opened up equal opportunities in 1948 and finally, after the Korean War, the separate black and white units were integrated. An excellent resource for studying integration is the highly detailed reference book written by black scholar Ulysses Lee as part of the official army history (see http://www.army.mil/cmh-pg/books/wwii/11-4/).

 EB SITE REVIEWS

GENERAL

The Rutgers Oral History Archives of World War II
http://fas-history.rutgers.edu/oralhistory/orlhom.htm

For a full review of this site, see p. 75, and for a review of material pertaining to the home front, see p. 98.

Among the over 200 interviews posted on this site, established by the History Department at Rutgers University, visitors will find more than twenty interviews with women who contributed to the war effort in a variety of capacities. Interviewees served as nurses, bandage wrappers for Johnson & Johnson, and store clerks. One woman worked as a film librarian for the Office of War Information, while another served with the USO. The interviews include discussions of air raids, rationing, and blackouts, as well as marriages that took place as their husbands headed off to war. Some of these marriages survived the war; others did not. Each of the interviewees attended the New Jersey College for Women (now part of Rutgers University) either before or after the war. In addition to the interviews, the site contains a user-friendly chart that lists the branch of service and theater of operation for each individual, including a designation for home front (HF).

CONTENT   ★ ★ ★ ★ ★
AESTHETICS   ★ ★ ★ ★
NAVIGATION   ★ ★ ★ ★

U.S. Army Signal Corps Photograph Collection
http://eagle.vsla.edu/signal.corps

For a full review of this site, see p. 98.

More than 1.5 million men and women departing for and returning from service in World War II passed through the Hampton Roads Port of Embarkation in Newport News, Virginia. Photographers with the U.S. Army's Signal Corps faithfully documented their every move and, in the process, created an invaluable archive of images.

Many of the images in this collection depict women filling a variety of jobs at Hampton Roads—female administrators, clerks, mechanics, nurses, photographers, and USO performers are represented. The collection also contains photos of members of the WAC, female officers and enlisted personnel, French women volunteers, and Chinese Army medical officers. African American officers, enlisted men, nurses, and chaplains are also portrayed.

CONTENT   ★ ★ ★ ★ ★
AESTHETICS   ★ ★ ★ ★
NAVIGATION   ★ ★ ★ ★

AFRICAN AMERICANS

African Americans and the U.S. Navy—World War II
http://www.history.navy.mil/photos/prs-tpic/af-amer/afa-wwii.htm

Part of the Online Library of Selected Images of the U.S. Navy Historical Center (see Chapter 4), this site contains several dozen photographs, but no significant text. The navy remained the most thoroughly segregated branch of the military through World War II, and the photographs depict the narrow range of jobs available for blacks. Consequently, many of the images depict black mess stewards such as Cook Third Class Doris "Dorie" Miller, who won the Navy Cross for his heroism during the attack on Pearl Harbor.

The images in the two parts of World War II Service at Pacific Bases depict black construction battalions, logistics support companies, and supply depot personnel on Guam, Okinawa, and other islands. A series of photos show black enlisted men in training at various stateside facilities. So restrictive was the navy that the one image of blacks firing weapons in World War II Shipboard Service actually depicts mess attendants at play while the USS *Copahee* sailed from California to the southwest Pacific. A click of the thumbnail sketch produces a larger image that clearly shows the men horsing around.

Visitors to African Americans and the U.S. Navy—World War II should not expect a wealth of information, but they will find important images of African Americans serving in the U.S. Navy. Links from the site will take visitors to the Navy Historical Center's home page.

CONTENT   ★ ★ ★
AESTHETICS   ★ ★ ★
NAVIGATION   ★ ★ ★

African Americans in World War II
http://www.historyplace.com

Maintained by The History Place, African Americans in World War II is a small but important collection of thirty-three photographs. Unlike most of the World War II images of African Americans in the Navy Historical Center's collection, which depict blacks as mess stewards and manual laborers, the photographs posted to this web site emphasize the combat contributions of African Americans in Europe and the Pacific.

By selecting African Americans in WWII on the home page, visitors will find neatly arranged images of infantrymen firing at nests of German machine guns in Italy, a tank crew awaiting orders in Germany, a squadron preparing for the day's mission from its base in Italy, troops guarding a German prisoner, marines preparing to face the Japanese in the Pacific, and a marine patrol cautiously making its way through the jungle on a Japanese-held island. Additional photos highlight the contributions of African American women, who served in the military as nurses and also as welders, machine operators, and mechanics at defense factories on the home front.

CONTENT   ★ ★ ★
AESTHETICS   ★ ★ ★ ★
NAVIGATION   ★ ★ ★ ★

Integration of the Armed Forces
http://www.redstone.army.mil/history/integrate/welcome.html

Although the integration of the armed forces did not occur until after World War II, this site, which is maintained by the Redstone Arsenal, will interest students of the war. From the home page, link first to History of Black Military Service and then to From WWI through WWII. Researchers will find a detailed, three-part chronology of the period; portions of Part 1 and all of Parts 2 and 3 are devoted to World War II. Part 3 includes a useful bibliography. Although the site does not contain primary documents, the chronology contains a wealth of useful information regarding every aspect of black service in the military, from recruitment, to D-Day, to service at sea, to the end of the war. The chronology is accompanied by thumbnail sketches of numerous photographs and recruiting posters. Among those depicted are General Benjamin Davis, the Tuskegee Airmen, Private Joe Louis, and Army Lieutenant John Roosevelt "Jackie" Robinson, one of the few black officers in the 761st "Black Panther" Tank Battalion. Researchers should be aware that most of the internal links, which feature additional information on key individuals, do not work.

The most fascinating aspect of Integration of the Armed Forces is the Multimedia section. Visitors can watch *The Negro Soldier*, a 1944 U.S. Army training film produced by director Frank Capra that was the first training film to depict African American servicemen in a favorable light. On the other hand, visitors can also review *The Navy Steward*, a much less flattering portrayal of African Americans produced by the U.S. Navy. Finally, researchers can watch *African Americans in World War II: A Legacy of Patriotism and Valor*, produced more recently by the Department of Defense.

Integration of the Armed Forces also includes a section entitled Integration Chronology. Condensed from the work of Morris MacGregor, researchers will get a great deal more out of a visit to the original, unedited version, available online at Integration of the Armed Forces, 1940–1965 (see below).

CONTENT   ★ ★ ★
AESTHETICS   ★ ★ ★
NAVIGATION   ★ ★ ★ ★

Integration of the Armed Forces, 1940–1965
http://www.army.mil/cmh-pg/books/integration/IAF-fm.htm

Part of the U.S. Army's CMH's Defense Studies Series, Integration of the Armed Forces, 1940–1965 replicates the text and tables, but not the illustrations, of Morris MacGregor's book of the same name. A leading scholar in the field,

MacGregor's previous works include the 13-volume *Blacks in the United States Armed Forces: Basic Documents*, which he co-edited with Bernard C. Nalty. Running at well over 600 pages, *Integration of the Armed Forces, 1940–1965*, is as detailed an account of the subject as researchers are likely to find, at least on the web.

In his forward, MacGregor refers to the book as "an administrative history" that examines the "fall of the legal, administrative, and social barriers to the black American's full participation in the military service of his country." As MacGregor points out, his book is not "a study of racial attitudes," black or white; his research did not include the autobiographical accounts or oral histories necessary for such a study.

Although concerned primarily with the postwar integration of the American military, three chapters will prove especially useful to researchers interested in the participation of blacks in World War II and official military policy toward their participation. "World War II: The Army," "World War II: The Navy," and "World War II: The Marines and the Coast Guard" provide researchers with ample material on the decision of top brass to affirm segregation as official military policy, but MacGregor also pays attention to early stirrings of reform. The online version of *Integration of the Armed Forces, 1940–1965*, comes complete with citations.

CONTENT   ★ ★ ★ ★
AESTHETICS   ★ ★ ★
NAVIGATION   ★ ★ ★ ★

Lest We Forget: African Americans in World War II
http://www.coax.net/people/lwf/ww2.htm

In Lest We Forget, webmaster Bennie McRae has compiled an extensive online resource for the history and culture of "African Americans, other ethnic, non-ethnic groups and individuals." Lest We Forget includes a section devoted to the African American experience in World War II. Visitors who want to peruse McRae's entire collection may prefer to reach the World War II material via the home page (http://www.coax.net/people/lwf/default.htm) and then scroll down to Military-Veterans: World War II. Alternatively, visitors may skip the home page and proceed directly to the World War II material via the URL listed above.

Lest We Forget offers a comprehensive collection of articles, documents, and general information on the African American experience in World War II. McRae has neatly organized the site into sections entitled Home Front, European Theater, and Pacific Theater, with additional pages devoted to special reports and requests and a list of links to relevant publications from the CMH. Most of the information on the site is copyrighted by Lest We Forget, although significant portions are available via links to other sites; unfortunately, a number of these external links are broken.

Among other material, the Home Front includes biographies of black military leaders as well as features on the National Airmen's Association of America, a precursor to the Tuskegee Airmen, and the Men of Montford Point, the first black marines. The European Theater and Pacific Theater include extensive lists of black units that served in the respective theaters and more detailed studies of the activities of units that particularly distinguished themselves.

Visitors to Lest We Forget should not expect to find significant primary documents. There do not appear to be any oral histories or photographs, except those accessible via links to other sites. Nevertheless, Lest We Forget provides a good starting point for researchers intent on getting a sense of the breadth of African American contributions to World War II.

CONTENT ★ ★ ★ ★
AESTHETICS ★ ★ ★
NAVIGATION ★ ★ ★ ★

WOMEN AT HOME, AT WORK, AND AT WAR

WASP on the Web
http://www.wasp-wwii.org/wasp/home.htm

During World War II, nearly 2000 women contributed to the war effort as Women Airforce Service Pilots (WASP). The first women in American history trained to fly military aircraft, the WASP were assigned to bases throughout the United States, where they performed a variety of tasks. The online component of Baylor University's Wings Across America project, WASP on the Web is devoted to preserving the history of these women.

Eventually, the site will include interview transcripts with dozens of former WASP. To date, directors of the Wings Across America project have finished more than seventy such interviews, but none of them are available online. In the meantime, WASP on the Web contains a variety of primary source material. The home page is cluttered, but researchers will want to take a look at three sections in particular: Gallery, Resources, and Records.

The Gallery includes songs sung by the WASP; an extensive scrapbook of training photos, cartoons, and posters; and audio and video clips of interviews and speeches by and about the WASP. Barry Goldwater and Janet Reno are among those who have sung the praises of the group. In addition, the audio clips allow visitors to hear the sounds of the various planes flown by the WASP. The Resources section contains a glossary of World War II terms, a timeline of events significant in WASP history, a comprehensive roster of WASP by training classes, and reprints of the *Fifinella Gazette*, a newspaper published by WASP trainees and later renamed *The Avenger*. In Records, one will find official statements and summaries of WASP activities, training requirements, a cost/benefit analysis of flight training, a comparison of officers' pay, official checklists carried by all WASP, and instructions for night flying.

CONTENT   ★ ★ ★ ★
AESTHETICS   ★ ★ ★
NAVIGATION   ★ ★ ★

What Did You Do In The War, Grandma?

http://www.stg.brown.edu/projects/WWII_Women/tocCS.html

Aside from being one of the best-named web sites, What Did You Do In The War, Grandma? is among the top online collections of oral histories specifically devoted to the experience of women during World War II. Initiated as a class project at South Kingstown (Rhode Island) High School, this site will prove valuable to researchers interested in the life of women in Rhode Island before, during, and after World War II. Just as important, What Did You Do In The War, Grandma? ought to inspire teachers to recognize the value of such projects in the education of their own students. As conveyed in an introductory essay by Linda Wood, the school librarian and codirector of the project, the students who conducted these interviews learned more about their subjects, and themselves, than they had imagined possible.

The twenty-six women whose interviews are presented experienced World War II in a variety of ways. One played professional baseball, another was a journalist, while a third had to raise six children alone. "Nearly all of those interviewed in this project shared in the patriotism of the war," writes University of Rhode Island professor Sharon Strom in an eloquent essay that accompanies the interviews. "But the devastation in Europe, the unleashing of atomic weapons on Japan, the deaths of loved ones, and the emotional difficulties many men faced in coming home, made women question war as a means of solving international problems. Although many knew the war had opened new opportunities to them and their loved ones, it also brought abiding sorrow and a sense that the world had entered a new phase of its history."

The home page contains user-friendly links to each of the twenty-six interviews that form the heart of this online archive. Also via the home page, visitors can access several introductory essays, a timeline, and a glossary of frequently used terms. Significant events, people, and terms that appear in the text of the interviews are linked directly to the glossary and timeline.

CONTENT   ★ ★ ★ ★ ★
AESTHETICS ★ ★ ★ ★
NAVIGATION ★ ★ ★ ★

Women at War: Redstone's WWII Female "Production Soldiers"
http://www.redstone.army.mil/history/women/welcome.html

In 1941 the United States Army broke ground on a new ordnance facility in Huntsville, Alabama. By the height of the war, several thousand women, mostly white but some black, were employed at the facility known as the Redstone Arsenal. Women at War tells the story of Redstone's establishment, hiring policies, labor practices, and general operations, all with an emphasis on the multiple ways in which the lives of women in Huntsville were transformed as they moved out of the fields and into the factory.

Unlike most sites reviewed in this book, Women at War is not a collection of primary sources. The story of the Redstone Arsenal, however, is told via a scholarly paper based on primary research and presented to the Conference of Army Historians in 1992. The full text of the paper is posted here—although curiously enough the footnotes have been omitted. The paper, in effect, serves as a community study, a thorough look at one particular munitions plant and the women whose labor was indispensable to its operation. The site includes a short film based on the paper.

At the end of the paper, visitors can link to a collection of more than 125 photographs taken at Redstone during World War II. Many of the photographs in the Redstone WWII Photo Archive depict women, including numerous images of women working at different points on the assembly line. Unfortunately, there is no index to the photo archive, and most of the photographs lack captions. Consequently, visitors must scroll through the images one by one. The Redstone WWII Photo Archive and the essay on Redstone's female production aoldiers are part of a larger site devoted to the history of Redstone Arsenal (http://www.redstone.army.mil/history/welcome.html). Researchers interested in women and World War II will find it easier to access the World War II photos via the link from Woman at War than through the site's home page.

CONTENT   ★ ★ ★
AESTHETICS ★ ★ ★
NAVIGATION ★ ★ ★

Women in the United States Army: The Army Nurse Corps
http://www.army.mil/cmh-pg/books/wwii/72-14/72-14.htm

and Women's Army Corps
http://www.army.mil/cmh-pg/brochures/wac/wac.htm

More than 59,000 women served in the U.S. Army's Nurse Corps during World War II. According to this publication of the U.S. Army's Center for Military History (CMH) "nurses served under fire in field hospitals and evacuation hospitals, on hospital trains and hospital ships, and as flight nurses on medical transport planes." The nurse corps served in every theater of operations— Europe, the Mediterranean, North Africa, and the Pacific—and on occasion were taken prisoner. Without a doubt, the abilities of these nurses and their courage in working so close to the front lines kept postinjury mortality rates among American forces to a minimum.

By contrast, more than 150,000 women served in the Women's Army Corps (WAC) during World War II. Originally created by Congress in the wake of Pearl Harbor as the Women's Army Auxiliary Corps (WAAC), the corps was not considered part of the regular army, a significant organizational distinction that denied personnel compensation in the event of injury and protection in the event of capture by the enemy. In July 1943, as the army's manpower needs grew in anticipation of the invasion of Europe, Congress converted the WAAC into the WAC and provided full benefits and protection for all members. Throughout the war, members of the WAC filled critical jobs and served with distinction as communication specialists, radio operators, switchboard operators, clerks, typists, drivers, cryptographers, and interpreters.

Part of the CMH's commemoration of the fiftieth anniversary of World War II, these publications serve as a vivid reminder that the contributions of women to the war effort were not limited to the home front. While neither site contains primary source material beyond a handful of photographs, they nonetheless provide the most thorough online history of women in the United States Army during World War II. Furthermore, both web pages have a list of suggested readings, including first-person accounts from former nurses and WAC members.

CONTENT   ★ ★ ★
AESTHETICS   ★ ★ ★
NAVIGATION   ★ ★ ★ ★

Women in the U.S. Navy
http://www.history.navy.mil/faqs/faq48-1.htm

Although not an extensive collection and not focused entirely on World War II, this Naval Historical Center page contains valuable information pertaining to the service of women in World War II. An extensive bibliography of works relating to women in the navy during World War II is provided, along with a list of relevant archival records. Unfortunately, few documents pertaining to the service of women in World War II are available online at this time.

Despite the paucity of documents, researchers will be particularly interested in the four oral histories, all of U.S. Navy nurses, that are available on this site. Ruth Ericson was stationed at Pearl Harbor during the Japanese attack. Ann Bernatitus served in the Philippines, including Bataan, was evacuated from Corregidor, and later served aboard a ship off Okinawa during that campaign. Dorothy Danner spent more than three years as a POW in the Philippines. Finally, Helen Pavlovsky and Sara Marcum worked at a base hospital during the Normandy invasion.

In addition to the oral histories, Women in the U.S. Navy contains a collection of close to fifty naval recruiting posters from World War II. Most of the posters were aimed at recruiting women to join WAVES—Women Accepted for Voluntary Emergency Services. Similar to the WAC, WAVES filled a number of essential positions and served as radio operators, clerks, stenographers, air traffic controllers, machinists, and pharmacists. As several of the posters point out, each WAVE performed a job that allowed one more sailor to man the guns.

Photographs of WAVES, including their training, meals and quarters, recreation, shipboard orientation, transportation, and various occupations, are presented. Brief textual introductions accompany the images. Given the significant role that WAVES played in World War II, it is unfortunate and surprising that the Naval Historical Center has not yet added oral histories of these women to the valuable accounts of the nurses noted above.

CONTENT   ★ ★ ★ ★
AESTHETICS   ★ ★ ★
NAVIGATION   ★ ★ ★

Women in World War II From the National Archives
http://www.nara.gov/nara/searchnail.html

This online collection from the massive holdings of the National Archives consists of 150 photographs, posters, and textual documents. Taken together, this material provides a rich record of the experience of American women in World War II.

Unfortunately, the site does not have its own URL and therefore cannot be bookmarked. Researchers first must go to the above address, click on "NAIL Digital Copies Search," and then enter keywords "women" and "world war ii." Be sure that both "media" and "NARA units" are set to "all media" and "all units" respectively. A successful search should produce 150 hits. Although it is possible to refine a search, researchers will discover that there is no index and thus no alternative to scrolling through the results of a search. This process, however, is made considerably less cumbersome by choosing "display all hits," which allows access to twenty-five search results at a time, each of which includes a thumbnail sketch, title, and control number as well as easy links to a full description and larger image.

Despite such navigational difficulties, researchers will quickly appreciate the value of this site. Numerous photographs show women at work in the defense plants, manning the rivet guns and welding torches, building assault boats, and forging weapons casings. White and black women appear side by side, as do women and men. The collection includes photographs of nurses bandaging injured troops, members of the WAC enjoying a little rest and relaxation in North Africa, and nurses with the army air forces undergoing training exercises.

A number of posters issued by federal agencies to engender support for the war effort are also available. Trumpeting the contributions of women of all ages as nurses, industrial workers, and mothers, these posters encouraged women to join the military, get a defense job, and "harvest war crops." An entire series of posters entitled "Women's Place in War," issued by the WAC, shows women performing a variety of tasks, from repairing radios, to observing the weather, to drafting maps.

In addition, a handful of textual documents serve as a reminder that the experience of women in World War II was not always positive. A series of documents details complaints filed by black women against Pratt and Whitney Aircraft for job discrimination. An all-too-familiar experience for African American women and men, the company's personnel office repeatedly told black women that there were no positions available in their training schools but that jobs were available in the cafeteria.

CONTENT   ★ ★ ★ ★
AESTHETICS   ★ ★ ★ ★
NAVIGATION   ★ ★ ★

SUGGESTED READINGS

Anderson, Karen. *Wartime Women: Sex Roles, Family Relations, and the Status of Women during World War II* (Westport, CT, 1981).

Astor, Gerald. *The Right to Fight: A History of African Americans in the Military* (Cambridge, MA, 2001).

Buchanan, Albert Russell. *Black Americans in World War II* (Santa Barbara, CA, 1977).

Campbell, D'Ann. *Women at War with America: Private Lives in a Patriotic Era* (Cambridge, MA, 1984).

Capeci, Dominic, Jr. *The Harlem Riot of 1943* (Philadelphia, PA, 1977).

Dalfiume, Richard M. "The 'Forgotten Years' of the Negro Revolution," *Journal of American History* 55, no. 1 (1968): 90–106 (also available online at JSTOR; requires paid subscription).

——. *Desegregation of the U.S. Armed Forces* (Columbia, MO, 1969).

Fessler, Diane Burke. *No Time for Fear: Voices of American Military Nurses in World War II* (Lansing, MI, 1996).

Flynn, George Q. "Selective Service and American Blacks During World War II," *Journal of Negro History* 69, no. 1 (1984): 14–25 (also available online at JSTOR; requires paid subscription).

Gluck, Sherna B. *Rosie the Riveter Revisited: Women, the War, and Social Change.* (Farmington Hills, MI, 1987).

Godson, Susan H. *Serving Proudly: A History of Women in the U.S. Navy* (Annapolis, MD, 2002).

Green, Ann Bosanko. *One Woman's War: Letters Home from the Women's Army Corps, 1944–1946* (St. Paul, MN, 1989).

Hartmann, Susan. *The Home Front and Beyond: American Women in the 1940s* (Boston, 1982).

Havens, Thomas R. H. "Women and War in Japan, 1937–45," *American Historical Review* 80, no. 4 (1975): 913–34 (also available online at JSTOR; requires paid subscription).

Honey, Maureen. *Creating Rosie the Riveter: Class, Gender, and Propaganda during World War II* (Amherst, MA, 1984).

Honey, Maureen, ed. *Bitter Fruit: African American Women in World War II* (Columbia, MO, 1999).

Lee, Ulysses. *The Employment of Negro Troops* (Washington, DC, 1966).

Litoff, Judy Barrett, and David C. Smith. *American Women in a World at War: Contemporary Accounts from World War II* (Wilmington, DE, 1997).

——. *We're in This War, Too* (New York, 1994).

MacGregor, Morris J., Jr. *Integration of the Armed Forces, 1940–1965* (Washington, DC, 1981).

MacGregor, Morris J., and Bernard C. Nalty, eds. *Blacks in the U.S. Armed Forces: Basic Documents* (Wilmington, DE, 1976).

———. *Blacks in the Military: Essential Documents* (Wilmington, DE, 1981).

McGuire, Phillip, ed. *Taps for a Jim Crow Army: Letters from Black Soldiers in World War II* (Lexington, KY, 1993).

Meyer, Leisa D. *Creating G.I. Jane: Sexuality and Power in the Women's Army Corps during World War II* (New York, 1996).

Milkman, Ruth. *Gender at Work: The Dynamics of Job Segregation by Sex during World War II* (Champaign, IL, 1987).

Miller, Grace Porter. *Call of Duty: A Montana Girl in World War II* (Baton Rouge, LA, 1999).

Monahan, Evelyn M., and Rosemary Neidel-Greenlee. *All This Hell: U.S. Nurses Imprisoned by the Japanese* (Lexington, KY, 2000).

Morden, Bettie J. *The Women's Army Corps, 1945–1978* (Washington, DC, 1990).

Myrdal, Gunnar. *An American Dilemma: The Negro Problem and American Democracy* (New York, 1944).

Nalty, Bernard C. *Strength for the Fight: A History of Black Americans in the Military* (New York, 1989).

Rupp, Leila J. *Mobilizing Women for War* (Princeton, NJ, 1978).

Sarnecky, Mary T. *A History of the U.S. Army Nurse Corps* (Philadelphia, PA, 1999).

Sigmund, Anna Maria. *Women of the Third Reich* (Richmond Hill, ON, 2000).

Treadwell, Mattie. *Women's Army Corps* (Washington, DC, 1954).

White, Walter. *A Rising Wind* (Garden City, NY, 1945).

Wynn, Neil A. *The Afro-American and the Second World War* (New York, 1993).

CHAPTER 8

THE HOLOCAUST AND WAR CRIMES

The Nazis violently hated all Jews and everything they stood for. They worked relentlessly toward the goal of removing all possible Jewish influences. Starting in the 1920s (when they were a small party) with a violently anti-Semitic rhetoric that blamed Jews for all the problems of Germany and the modern world, the Nazis defined Jews as a permanent "race" that would never change and could never be improved. The Nazis also strongly disliked Christianity as being too Jewish, and their goal was to return to a pre-Christian, all-Aryan (imaginary) world. The second stage of Nazi policy concerning Jews, lasting from 1933 to 1938, when Hitler was dictator in peacetime Germany, involved the removal of Jews from all public offices. The Nazis encouraged the Jews to immigrate and half of the Jewish population in Germany did so (including Albert Einstein and the teenaged Henry Kissinger). The Nazis opened Dachau and other concentration camps to punish thousands of their political enemies—including many Jews. About 1,000 Jews were murdered in concentration camps inside Germany before 1939; these were distinct from the killing camps that were opened in 1942 in Poland. Stage three, from 1938 to 1941, involved increasingly severe and humiliating restrictions for Jews. Kristallnacht in November 1938 was a systematic violent attack on all synagogues. World public opinion grew hostile to the Nazis, who responded by supporting pro-Nazi, anti-Semitic political movements in France and other countries, including the German-American Bund. After invading Poland in 1939, the Nazis forced 2 million Jews into a few ghettoes with below-starvation food allotments.

The fourth stage of Nazi aggression began when the Germans invaded Russia in June 1941. Special field units called Einsatzgruppen were developed. Seven of these units rounded up and shot Polish Catholic priests, intellectuals, and political leaders. Another five units (with 3,000 men) followed the Red Army and executed Communist commissars and partisans and about 600,000 Russian Jews. The Wannsee Conference in January 1942 began stage five of Nazi power; it was then that top Nazis decided on a "Final Solution"—to round up and secretly execute all the Jews of Europe. Killing centers were opened in Poland, and thousands of trainloads of Jews were transported there and gassed immediately upon arrival. Over 3 million Jews (and many gypsies and members of other hated groups) were murdered, mostly in 1942–43.

The sixth and final stage of Nazi policy came when the Soviet armies overran the Polish concentration camps in 1944–45 and liberated the survivors. In all, 6 million Jews were murdered; most of the 300,000 survivors emigrated to the United States or Israel.

Analytically, the people involved in the Holocaust can be divided into the following groups.

Victims. Millions were victimized by the Nazi regime during the Holocaust. The Jews were always its principal target; however, the Nazis also systematically hunted down and murdered the Roma people (gypsies). They also targeted special enemies, including Communist activists, Jehovah's Witnesses, homosexuals, and people with disabilities. The last group was the target of euthanasia programs carried out in German hospitals from 1939 to 1941. These programs were stopped when German Christian leaders mobilized public opinion against them.

Perpetrators. Under the guidance of an all-powerful führer (Hitler), the Nazis believed fervently in force, violence, and terror as their best weapons. The most fanatical Nazis joined the SS, which carried out most of the executions. The Final Solution was directed by Heinrich Himmler, commander of the SS and minister of the interior. He was captured in 1945 and committed suicide before his war crimes trial began. His top aide was Reinhard Heydrich, head of the Gestapo and, after 1939, of all the secret police agencies grouped into the Reich Security Main Office (RSHA); he was assassinated by Czech commandos with British help in 1942. Adolph Eichmann was the senior SS bureaucrat in charge of deportation and transportation. However, regular German army police units also systematically killed large numbers of civilians and POWs on the eastern front. After the war, West Germany recognized its guilt and made large financial payments to Israel, but communist East Germany refused to do the same.

Bystanders. In recent years much controversy has arisen over when Roosevelt learned what about the Nazis activities, and what he did or did not do about them.

Switzerland was neutral and accepted some refugees, but it also made large profits by trading and banking with Germany; in the 1990s, the Swiss were forced to make reparation payments.

Collaborators. In rounding up Jews the Nazis sometimes had the enthusiastic cooperation of pro-Nazi governments (as in France and Slovakia). A few countries, including Italy and Hungary, tried to stall the Nazis, but the Germans took power directly and seized the Jews. Only Bulgaria and Denmark succeeded to a large extent in protecting their Jews.

Resisters. Resistance took many forms, from individual acts to hundreds of examples of organized, armed resistance. The most famous episode was the month-long uprising of the 60,000 remaining Jews in the Warsaw Ghetto in April 1943. At the Sobibor death camp, an uprising in October 1943 allowed 600 prisoners to escape.

Rescuers. Rescuers hid potential victims as best they could; the story of Anne Frank is the most famous. The Danish people managed to ferry their entire Jewish population to neutral Sweden in one night under the noses of the Nazis. The pope helped protect some Italian Jews; it is still being debated whether or not he could have done much more. The most famous rescuer is Oskar Schindler; *Schindler's List* tells the true story of how he saved 1,100 Jews from the Nazis by setting up factories that produced defective munitions. For further information, see http://www.teachwithmovies.org/guides/schindlers-list.html.

Liberators. The Allies liberated the concentration camps in 1945, but the question remains whether they could have bombed the camps or otherwise stopped the Final Solution. The main war criminals were tried at the International War Crimes Tribunals at Nuremberg in 1945–1947 and at smaller trials throughout Europe. The Holocaust was mentioned at the trials, but the major allegation against defendants was the systematic planning of an unjust war. The Far East War Crimes Trials were held from 1946 to 1948 and resulted in the conviction of twenty-five Japanese generals and high officials accused of crimes against peace. Over 2000 local and regional trials convicted 4000 Japanese officers of mistreating prisoners and civilians.

Survivors. The survivors of the Final Solution were very quiet about their experiences until about 1961, when Adolph Eichmann was captured in South America by Israel, tried in Jerusalem, and executed. Since then the Holocaust has become recognized as the most horrible episode of the twentieth century and it has been analyzed in numerous books, courses, museums, and movies. The most important museums are the Holocaust Museum in Washington and the Museum of Tolerance in Los Angeles, each of which have excellent websites (see reviews below).

WEB SITE REVIEWS

THE HOLOCAUST

The Holocaust from the Jewish Virtual Library

http://www.us-israel.org/jsource/index.html

Part of a comprehensive site devoted to all periods in Jewish history, The Holocaust from the Jewish Virtual Library provides excellent information on the Holocaust. From the library's main page, The Holocaust section leads to an alphabetized list of topics. Visitors would be wise to begin with History of the Holocaust, which provides a thorough and useful overview of key persons and events. Internal links to other pages allow visitors to explore various people and topics in greater depth. Some entries, such as the one for the Gestapo, are limited to brief encyclopedic descriptions. Other subjects, however, are explored in depth through the use of primary and secondary source material. A list of sources accompanies all material on the site.

The information on the Final Solution, for example, is particularly rich. Researchers will find the Wannsee Protocol along with proclamations and orders from Adolf Hitler, Heinrich Himmler, and Hermann Göring. An SS statistical report on the evacuation of Jews is chilling precisely because of the assumed ordinariness of the language. Separate pages on the gas chambers and concentration camps provide a look at the various aspects of the Nazi's machinery of extermination.

Extermination was by no means limited to the gas chambers. Material on the Einsatzgruppen, a special "mobile killing unit" within the SS charged with liquidating the Third Reich's political enemies, traces the systematic killing of Jews, communists, and Roma throughout Poland and the Ukraine. Separate pages contain operations reports; a secret Nazi document on the use of special "gas vans," which served as mobile gas chambers; and information on the efforts of the Einsatzgruppen to hide the bodies of their victims.

The Jewish Virtual Library includes an important section concerning Holocaust deniers. Drawn primarily from the Nizkor Project (see below), the material includes Answers to the 66 Questions of Holocaust Deniers, Holocaust Denial on Campus, Holocaust Denial in the Syrian Media, and the Soap Allegations.

CONTENT	★ ★ ★ ★	
AESTHETICS	★ ★ ★ ★	
NAVIGATION	★ ★ ★ ★	

Mauthausen Memorial

http://www.mauthausen-memorial.gv.at/engl/index.html

Constructed in 1938 in northeastern Austria just after the Anschluss, the Mauthausen concentration camp housed 200,000 Jews, gypsies, homosexuals, political opponents of the Third Reich, and common criminals; approximately half of them were murdered by the Nazis or died of other causes. Although not as large as other concentration camps, Mauthausen earned a tough reputation as the only camp classified as Stage 3—reserved "for accused felons, incorrigibles and at the same time hardened criminals and asocial individuals, in other words, hardly educable detainees." Maintained by the Austrian Ministry of the Interior, Mauthausen Memorial is a must visit for those who want to understand the inner workings of a concentration camp and the horrors faced by camp inmates on a daily basis.

Visitors should not be worried when the home page appears in German; the entire site is available in English as well. The most effective means of navigating the site, although relatively easy, is not immediately obvious. Visitors should select the English version of the home page, choose The Mauthausen Concentration Camp 1938–1945, scroll down to the bottom of the first page that appears, and select List of all Pages. An accessible, logically organized table of contents appears. The first few listings provide an informative overview of Mauthausen's history, including its construction by the first group of detainees. The rest of the site is organized into sections that focus on the architecture and layout of the camp; daily life; the camp population; the SS; forced labor; disease, violence, and death; statistical data; and excerpts from oral histories.

The Compound Mauthausen includes maps and photographs that detail the layout of the main camp and the astonishing number of satellite camps that supported it. A key to the main camp allows researchers to select different buildings—the prisoners' brothel, the kitchen, the women's barracks, and the gas chamber among them—and link to a textual description of each. Life in the Camp includes separate pages on the prisoners' arrival; the barracks; nutrition; everyday life; women, children, and adolescents; and attempts to escape. Camp Population details the categories and nationalities of the 200,000 prisoners, as well as efforts at self-government.

A section entitled The SS includes information on Mauthausen commanders, including a chilling description of the camp doctors and the medical experiments they performed. Fifteen oral histories are available in Excerpts from Reports by Former Prisoners. Drawn from the official Mauthausen Concentration Camp Memorial Archive, these firsthand accounts provide intensely moving, and often horrific, details about the inhumane treatment endured by prisoners on a daily basis; whippings, murders, shaving of heads, and forced prostitution are all discussed.

Internal links appear throughout the site and allow researchers to move easily from one page to another. In addition, high-quality photographs supplement most of the textual descriptions.

CONTENT   ★ ★ ★ ★
AESTHETICS   ★ ★ ★
NAVIGATION   ★ ★ ★

Museum of Tolerance Online
http://www.wiesenthal.com/mot/index.cfm

Housed at Los Angeles's Simon Wiesenthal Center, the Museum of Tolerance has created an online archive extraordinary in its scope, yet at times difficult to navigate on account of inconsistent organization. Designed to serve as a learning tool for students and teachers as well as an online archive for researchers, the site is organized into several main sections, each of which is easily accessible via the home page.

Billed as a "comprehensive resource on the Holocaust and World War II," the Multimedia Learning Center should garner the most attention from students. Thousands of text files and tens of thousands of photographs are organized into units entitled The Jews, The Nazis, World War II, Antisemitism and the Final Solution, Resistance and Rescue, The World Response, Righteous Among the Nations, and After the War. Each unit, in turn, is subdivided into chapters—People, Places, Organizations, and Topics—which contain dozens of individual pages with encyclopedic descriptions, links to other topics and some combination of maps, photographs, and primary documents.

While the amount of available information is impressive, the organization of it into prefabricated units without the inclusion of a comprehensive index of sources limits overall access to the site's resources. For example, the Multimedia Learning Center contains no separate, comprehensive index of the primary documents, maps, and photographs that are attached to the various pages. Consequently, visitors are left with no choice but to work their way through the individual pages and look for a particular image or document. Fortunately, an index to the collection's tens of thousands of photographs, which alone make the Museum of Tolerance Online a must visit, is available at http://history1900s.about. com/library/holocaust/aa122299a.htm?iam+ask&terms=german+tokyo+rose. Organized alphabetically by subject, the index provided by About.com links directly to the Museum of Tolerance's online photographic archive. It remains unclear why access to the photographs in the same sensible manner is not possible directly from the Museum of Tolerance's home page.

Teachers and educators also will want to peruse Teacher's Resources, where they will find a glossary of terms, places, and personalities related to the Holocaust; a timeline of significant events; answers to the most frequently asked questions; and lists of relevant articles and books. Scholars and researchers will find more than 13,000 documents in Special Collections. Drawn from the collections of the Institute of Documentation in Israel, the materials in Special Collections are organized into ten groups and indexed by subject; under each subject heading is the number of documents in the set and the language in which they appear (German, English, or Hebrew). Researchers should be aware that while a significant number of the documents are in English, the majority are not. At this point, the site's organizational difficulties emerge again. For instance, Collection 1 includes an entry called Long Dark Nazi-Years with 388 documents in English. But once researchers click on Long Dark Nazi-Years, they will find a series of numbers, 1 through 388, with no indication whatsoever of the content of the individual files. The only option is to wade through the entire series. One can only hope that the Museum of Tolerance will find the time and resources to adequately index this remarkable collection.

CONTENT ★ ★ ★ ★ ★
AESTHETICS ★ ★ ★ ★
NAVIGATION ★ ★ ★

The Nizkor Project
http://www.nizkor.org

Affiliated with the League for Human Rights of B'nai Brith, Canada, the Nizkor Project is dedicated to combating Holocaust deniers who, in the words of historian Deborah Lipstadt, "count on the fact that the vast majority of readers will not have access to the documentation or make the effort to determine how they have falsified or misconstrued information." In response, the creators of this site have made such documentation available. From the home page or the site map, researchers can access a trove of book excerpts, essays, photographs, drawings, and primary documents, all of which challenge the distortions and lies endemic to Holocaust denial.

The Nizkor Project is organized into six sections. Holocaust Research Guides provides extensive documentation on the gas chambers and ovens of Auschwitz-Birkenau, as well as evidence of the medical experiments performed there. The Leuchter Report, a well-known denier tract, is refuted point by point. A section on camps includes separate entries for Buchenwald, Mauthausen, Nordhausen, Dachau, Bergen-Belsen, and Auschwitz-Birkenau. Visitors will want to pay particular attention to U.S. Army photographs of Auschwitz, an army film of the liberation of Mauthausen, and a collection of haunting drawings by a female prisoner at Auschwitz that were used as evidence in Adolf Eichmann's trial.

People: From A to Z contains short biographies of key German officials and more substantial material relating to Adolf Hitler and Adolf Eichmann. Researchers will find primary documents that describe Hitler's preparation for war against Poland as well as more than 1,400 pages of declassified material relating to Hitler from the archives of the Office of Strategic Services (the precursor to the CIA). The complete transcript of Eichmann's trial for war crimes is posted, along with photographs and other documents relating to him. People: From A to Z also addresses British historian David Irving's libel suit against Deborah Lipstadt; in 2000, a British high court found in Lipstadt's favor, essentially sustaining her charge that Irving was guilty of Holocaust revisionism and denial.

Two other sections of The Nizkor Project merit the attention of researchers. The complete, 22-volume transcript of the Nuremberg Trials is posted to the site, although researchers may find it easier to access the same information via the Avalon Project (see below). Finally, a section entitled Special Features includes Techniques of Holocaust Denial and frequently asked questions about the Holocaust.

CONTENT   ★ ★ ★ ★
AESTHETICS   ★ ★ ★ ★
NAVIGATION   ★ ★ ★

A Teacher's Guide to the Holocaust
http://fcit.coedu.usf.edu/holocaust/default.htm

Produced by the Florida Center for Instructional Technology, A Teacher's Guide to the Holocaust is a well-designed site that integrates primary documents, photographs, maps, video, movies, music, and art. A phenomenal resource, the site will appeal not only to teachers and their students but to anyone interested in a comprehensive understanding of the Holocaust.

Visitors should begin with the Timeline, an informative and thorough history of the Holocaust. Beginning with chapters entitled Rise of the Nazi Party and Nazification, the Timeline continues with The Ghettoes, The Camps, Resistance, Rescue and Liberation, and Aftermath. Each chapter includes links to audio clips and external sites.

Serving as a vivid reminder that individuals other than the victims and their tormentors played a role in the Holocaust, the People section has separate pages entitled Victims, Perpetrators, Bystanders, Resisters, Rescuers, Liberators, Survivors, and Children. The chapter on survivors includes numerous videos of survivor testimony and extensive links to similar recollections on other web sites. A unique section on the arts presents art and music from the ghettos and camps, art considered "degenerate" by the Nazis, and musical selections preferred by Nazi leaders.

Teacher's Resources alone makes A Teacher's Guide to the Holocaust a must visit. Well organized and easily navigable, this section includes primary documents, photographs, maps, and movies. Among the documents, teachers and researchers will find key proclamations and orders from Nazi leaders; Robert Jackson's opening address at the Nuremberg Trials, in which he lays out Nazi activities and war crimes; and extensive excerpts from *Nazi Conspiracy and Aggression*, which was prepared by the Nuremberg prosecution. The several thousand photographs and drawings available in Galleries can be searched easily. Movies show survivor testimony, reveal life in the camps and ghettos, and provide coverage of events such as Kristallnacht. In addition, Teacher's Resources contains an excellent collection of maps of Europe's political boundaries, the Warsaw and other ghettos, and the location of and blueprints for various camps, as well as graphic representations of expulsions and deportations. Given this plethora of resources, A Teacher's Guide to the Holocaust wisely offers teachers a series of suggested activities appropriate for elementary, middle school, and high school students.

CONTENT ★ ★ ★ ★
AESTHETICS ★ ★ ★ ★
NAVIGATION ★ ★ ★

United States Holocaust Memorial Museum
http://www.ushmm.org

The United States Holocaust Memorial Museum in Washington, DC, is the nation's most important repository of material relating to the Holocaust. The museum's archival holdings include more than 13 million pages of documentation, 7,000 oral histories, and thousands of photographs. Unfortunately, only a fraction of this material is available online. Nevertheless, this aesthetically pleasing and well-designed site remains a must visit and an ideal starting point, especially for students of Holocaust-related studies.

From the site's home page, visitors should enter the History section to reach the Learning Center for a terrific overview of the Nazi's rise to power, their persecution of European Jewry, and the Holocaust. Individual pages cover such topics as refugees, the camp system, forced labor, the ghettos, the Third Reich, anti-Semitism, the Final Solution, and the extermination camps. Each page includes a textual overview, photos, links to related topics and events, and, in some cases, film footage.

From the History page, visitors can also access a collection of personal histories, which includes excerpts of text and video from the museum's vast holdings. Snippets from these oral histories have also been incorporated into the Online Exhibitions section, which can be reached through the History page. Teachers and educators will find Online Exhibitions particularly suited for their students. Topics include the 1936 Olympics, Kristallnacht, and the doomed voyage of the *St. Louis*, a ship laden with Jewish refugees who were denied sanctuary in the United States and numerous other countries in 1939.

The site's vast array of photographs can be accessed by following the Research link on the home page to Collections to Photographs. Covering the period from just after World War I into the 1950s, thousands of images depict Jewish life in Europe before the Holocaust; the rise of the Nazis to power; the deportation of Jews; and life in the ghettos, concentration camps, and killing centers. A search of the photographic archive produces brief captions and thumbnail sketches of all results. By clicking the thumbnail sketch, visitors can view a larger image, a more extensive description of the image, and a link to other photographs related to the subject and keyword of the search.

CONTENT   ★ ★ ★ ★
AESTHETICS   ★ ★ ★ ★
NAVIGATION   ★ ★ ★

SURVIVOR ORAL HISTORIES

Poland's Holocaust: A Family Chronicle of Soviet and Nazi Terror
http://www.geocities.com/CapitolHill/Parliament/6764/intro.html

Created by Christopher Gladun, a Canadian journalist and teacher, Poland's Holocaust began as a *Toronto Star* article that soon developed into an excellent history of one family's wartime experience. More than a family history, however, this aesthetically beautiful site provides a wrenching account of the tragic consequences of the 1939 Nazi-Soviet Non-Aggression Pact. Millions of Poles died not only as the result of Nazism and the Holocaust but also from the horrors of Stalinism and communism. Researchers and educators will marvel at the richness of the primary materials that make this site a must visit.

Gladun's mother, Janina Silkowska, grew up in Krzemieniec, a city in eastern Poland. Less than three weeks after Germany invaded Poland on September 1, 1939, residents of the city awoke to the astonishing realization that Hitler and Stalin had agreed to divide Poland. As the Red Army rolled into Krzemieniec, Silkowska joined the underground movement to resist the Soviets and Nazis, was captured by the Soviet secret police, and sent to the Gulag. Gladun's father,

Leon, was one of fewer than five hundred survivors of the Katyn Massacre, in which Stalin ordered the slaughter of 27,000 Polish Army officers. He later fought in Italy against the Germans but was unable to return to Poland.

The wartime memoirs of Janina Silkowska (previously published in Polish) and the diaries of Leon Gurden form the heart of this exceptional site. Extensive excerpts from both documents are interspersed with an excellent collection of photographs. Christopher Gladun has added additional accounts to supplement his parents' words; for instance, after reading Janina's discussion of the Nazi invasion, researchers can read a related dispatch from the American ambassador to Poland.

A series of wartime letters written to and from various family members accentuates an already rich site. A World War II timeline, with an emphasis on the Polish experience, helps place the memoirs, diary entries, and letters in a broader context.

CONTENT   ★ ★ ★ ★
AESTHETICS   ★ ★ ★ ★
NAVIGATION   ★ ★ ★

Voice Vision: Holocaust Survivor Oral Histories
http://holocaust.umd.umich.edu

Over the past two decades, Dr. Sid Bolkosky has interviewed more than 150 Holocaust survivors. A historian on the faculty of the University of Michigan at Dearborn, Bolkosky has created a rich archive of quality interviews that reflect his professional training. Audio and video tapes of the interviews, along with full transcripts, are housed in the university's Mardigan Library. Although only thirteen of these interviews are currently available online, the library is in the process of adding to the web page. Furthermore, the quality of the available interviews makes Voice Vision an absolute must visit for researchers interested in firsthand accounts of the Holocaust.

From the home page, visitors can select Interviews Online or scroll down The Survivor Interviews. The managers of the web site have provided a brief but helpful description of each interview subject. These men and women grew up all over Europe—Poland, Romania, Hungary, Czechoslovakia, and the Netherlands—but share a past of deportation, confinement, and the murder of loved ones. Somehow, they survived, a testament to their courage and determination, and now live as witnesses to man's capacity for evil.

Organized into as many as thirty chapters, each interview comes with a sensibly organized and easily navigable table of contents. Such topics as family, religion, politics, life before the war, deportation, forced labor, ghetto life, camp life, resistance, and liberation are covered. Researchers may also listen to the interviews.

CONTENT   ★ ★ ★ ★ ★
AESTHETICS   ★ ★ ★ ★
NAVIGATION   ★ ★ ★ ★

Women and the Holocaust
http://www.interlog.com/~mighty/home.html

Edited by Judy Cohen, a Holocaust witness/survivor, this site is dedicated to the understanding, study, and remembrance of the particular experiences of women during the Holocaust. Women and the Holocaust contains poetry written by female survivors as well as extensive reviews of books on all aspects of women and the Holocaust. In addition, the site includes numerous scholarly articles and essays from a variety of publications that consider the various roles played by women during the Holocaust—mothers, partisans, resistance fighters, fugitives in the forest, and, of course, survivors.

While the articles and essays have been published elsewhere, the site also includes a section entitled Fragments and Personal Reflections; visitors will find firsthand accounts from more than a dozen women, including Cohen, who spent portions of the war in hiding, in camps, and in ghettos. Fifteen at the time the Nazis occupied her native Hungary in the spring of 1944, Cohen movingly describes the awful series of events that began with her family being forced into a ghetto, their deportation on a cattle car, and their arrival at Auschwitz-Birkenau. Separated from her parents, a sister-in-law, and a niece, who were sent to the gas chambers, Cohen and her three sisters endured never ending hunger and humiliation as they fought to survive. Eventually separated from her sisters, who thought she had been gassed, Cohen survived the war only to discover that two of her three sisters did not.

Cohen's account, like the other personal reflections on Women and the Holocaust, provides a vivid reminder of the horrific evil perpetuated by the Nazis. Researchers, educators, and students who want to understand the extreme suffering of women during the Holocaust would do well to hear these voices.

CONTENT   ★ ★ ★ ★
AESTHETICS   ★ ★ ★ ★
NAVIGATION   ★ ★ ★ ★

WAR CRIMES

The Avalon Project: The Nuremberg War Crimes Trials
http://www.yale.edu/lawweb/avalon/imt/imt.htm

A part of The Avalon Project: World War II Documents (see Chapter 1), the Nuremberg War Crimes Trials collection is an unsurpassed resource. Beautiful graphics, easy navigation, and substantive content make this the best web site of its kind.

The centerpiece of The Avalon Project: The Nuremberg War Crimes Trials is the *Trial of the Major War Criminals Before the International Military Tribunal*, the 22-volume official history of the proceedings, which is presented unedited. Literally every word of the proceedings is available online. All motions, orders, testimonies, and rulings are included. A search engine allows one to access sections of the proceedings relevant to a particular topic or individual. In addition, four of the eight volumes of *Nazi Conspiracy and Aggression* (Washington, DC, 1946) are also available online. Each volume contains English translations of important letters, decrees, and orders issued by Nazi leaders.

Visitors also will find the full text of such key documents as the Wannsee Protocol, which laid out plans for the Final Solution, and the four-count indictment against Hermann Göring, Rudolf Hess, and their fellow defendants. Appendices attached to the indictment outline the "Statement of Individual Responsibility of Crimes" as well as the crimes charged to Nazi groups and organizations. Additional source materials document the road to World War II from the Versailles Treaty, to the Munich Pact, to the Nazi-Soviet Non-Aggression Pact.

CONTENT   ★ ★ ★ ★
AESTHETICS   ★ ★ ★ ★
NAVIGATION   ★ ★ ★ ★

SUGGESTED READINGS

Browning, Christopher. *Nazi Policy, Jewish Workers, German Killers* (New York, 2000).

Chang, Iris. *The Rape of Nanking: The Forgotten Holocaust of World War II* (New York, 1998).

Dawidowicz, Lucy. *The War against the Jews, 1933–1945* (New York, 1986).

The Encyclopedia of Jewish Life Before and During the Holocaust (New York, 2001).

Gilbert, Martin. *Never Again: The History of the Holocaust* (New York, 2000).

Goldhagen, Daniel Joseph. *Hitler's Willing Executioners: Ordinary Germans and the Holocaust* (New York, 1997).

Greene, Joshua M., and Shiva Kumar, eds. *Witness: Voices from the Holocaust* (New York, 2000).

Johnson, Eric A. *Nazi Terror: The Gestapo, Jews, and Ordinary Germans* (New York, 2000).

Klemperer, Victor. *I Will Bear Witness: A Diary of the Nazi Years 1942–1945* (New York, 2001).

Kremer, S. Lillian, ed. *Holocaust Literature: An Encyclopedia of Writers and Their Work* (New York, 2002).

Laqueur, Walter. *Generation Exodus: The Fate of Young Jewish Refugees from Nazi Germany* (Hanover, NH, 2001).

Laqueur, Walter, and Judith Tydor Baumel, eds. *The Holocaust Encyclopedia* (New Haven, CT, 2001).

Lewy, Guenter. *The Nazi Persecution of the Gypsies* (New York, 2001).

Lipstadt, Deborah E. *Beyond Belief: The American Press and the Coming of the Holocaust, 1933–1945* (New York, 1993).

———. *Denying the Holocaust* (New York, 1994).

Neufeld, Michael J., and Michael Berenbaum. *The Bombing of Auschwitz: Should the Allies Have Attempted It?* (New York, 2000).

Newton, Verne W., ed. *FDR and the Holocaust* (New York, 1996).

Novick, Peter. *The Holocaust in American Life* (New York, 1999).

Pritchard, R. John. "War Crimes, International Criminal Law, and the Postwar Trials in Europe and Asia." In *World War II in Asia and the Pacific and the War's Aftermath, with General Themes,* edited by Loyd E. Lee (Westport, CT, 1998).

Roseman, Mark. *A Past in Hiding: Memory and Survival in Nazi Germany* (New York, 2001).

Schindler's List (DVD and VHS, 1993).

Shermer, Michael, and Alex Grobman. *Denying History: Who Says the Holocaust Never Happened and Why Do They Say It?* (Berkeley, CA, 2000).

Siedlecki, Janusz Nel, et al. *We Were in Auschwitz* (New York, 2000).

Szpilman, Wladyslaw. *The Pianist* (New York, 2000).

Weisel, Elie. *Night* (Austin, TX, 1999).

Wyman, David. *The Abandonment of the Jews: America and the Holocaust, 1941–1945* (New York, 1984).

Yamamoto, Masahiro. *Nanking: Anatomy of an Atrocity* (Westport, CT, 2000).

CHAPTER 9

UNIT
HISTORIES

The National Archives and Records Administration (NARA) holds the army's official unit records from World War II, including after action reports, lessons learned, and daily journals. These records are contained in Record Group 407 (Records of the Adjutant General's Office, 1917–) and are available at the National Archives at College Park, 8601 Adelphi Road, College Park, MD 20740-6001 (telephone, 301-713-6800). Non-textual records such as motion pictures, photographs, maps, aerial photos, and video and audio tapes are also located at NARA.

For a solid scholarly study of a particular unit see Stephen E. Ambrose, *Band of Brothers: E Company, 506th Regiment, 101st Airborne from Normandy to Hitler's Eagle's Nest* (2001), a bestseller with its own HBO miniseries (the web site for the show, http://www.hbo.com/band/landing/currahee.html, is reviewed in Chapter 3). Divisions were complicated operations; to understand their organization, researchers and students should read "Component (Organic) Elements of U.S. Army Divisions in World War II" at http://www.army.mil/cmh-pg/lineage/cc/comp.htm and the army's Order of Battle—organization, commanders, statistics, and casualties—for every division in Europe at http://www.army.mil/cmh-pg/documents/ETO-OB/ETOOB-TOC.htm. A good regimental history of the 36th Division, including material on its activities in North Africa, Italy, and France at can be found online at http://www.kwanah.com/txmilmus/gallery/36div.htm.

Three out of four soldiers in the American army served behind the lines in a long "tail"; about one-fourth served as teeth in combat units. The long tail was necessary in part because of the vast logistics problem of combat so far from home. The challenge for Pentagon planners was determining how many combat divisions would be needed. In 1941 the plan was to raise 213 divisions of about 15,000 soldiers each. By 1943 the decision was made to concentrate on industrial production and field an army of only 100 divisions. In the end the country gambled that it could win with only 90 army divisions (plus six marine divisions.) The United States used significantly fewer divisions than Germany or the Soviet Union, but each American division was far better armed and supplied as a result of the long tail. "The 90-Division Gamble" is an important scholarly article by Maurice Matloff available at http://www.army.mil/cmh-pg/books/70-7_15.htm

Capsule histories of most infantry divisions can be found at http://grunts.net/army/infantry1.html and http://grunts.net/army/infantry2.html (see review of Grunts.net below). On the training of soldiers, there are several full-length official histories online. Amphibious training is covered at http://www.army.mil/cmh-pg/books/agf/agf22/amphib-fm.htm and training for mountain warfare at http://www.army.mil/cmh-pg/books/agf/agf23.htm. For a good army study of its small unit combat operations in Italy and France in 1944, see http://www.army.mil/cmh-pg/books/wwii/smallunit/smallunit-fm.htm. The experiences of parachute troops on D-Day are depicted in many movies and in an official study at http://www.army.mil/cmh-pg/documents/WWII/506-Nor/506-nor.htm. The army had numerous Special Operations units, whose achievements are well covered at http://www.army.mil/cmh-pg/books/wwii/70-42/70-42c.htm. There are good stories told by tankers in armored units at http://www.tankbooks.com/tanksfor/tanks.htm and http://www.tankbooks.com/youngkid/Default.htm (see review of Tankbooks.com in Chapter 5).

The medical service department of the army has a very good multivolume history available in larger libraries. One overview volume is online at http://www.armymedicine.army.mil/history/booksdocs/wwii/orgadmin/. For other online research studies see the Army Nurse Corps short official history at http://www.army.mil/cmh-pg/books/wwii/72-14/72-14.htm (see review of Women in the United States Army in Chapter 7).

There are surprisingly few good studies of the ordinary life of sailors, so researchers must rely on memoirs for information. Many ships have web sites, such as the battleship BB56 USS *Washington* at http://www.usswashington.com/ and Battleship *North Carolina* (see review below). Researchers also should be sure to visit the navy reunions listed at http://www.warships1.com/.

Visuals of the major aircraft used by the army air force are available by searching ebay.com for "B-29," "B-17," "B-24," "P-47," or "P-51." On the workhorse fighter the P-47 ("P" stands for Pursuit), see http://www.p47pilots.com/, and for images of the B-24 heavy bombers see http://www.486th.org/. A fascinating oral history of a bombing raid appears at http://www.tankbooks.com/Ninelives/contents.htm.

The great majority of POWs were captured not as individuals but as entire units, which surrendered formally and were marched off to prison camps for the duration of the war. The great movie *The Bridge on the River Kwai* provides a horrific—but accurate—account of the POW camps run by the Japanese. For an American memoir of life in Japanese camps see http://www.qmmuseum.lee.army.mil/WWII/qm_prisoner.htm, and for the history of the Philippine Division captured at Bataan, including two accounts by POWs, see http://grunts.net/army/phillipine.html.

The 106th Division formed late in the war, and many of its members were college students whose deferments had run out. The 106th had been in Europe only fifteen days when the Germans made a massive attack and began the Battle of the Bulge. The division was placed in a "quiet" sector for orientation, and on average had the youngest (the average age was twenty-two) and most inexperienced troops involved in the battle. After five days in its new position—with no inkling whatever of imminent action—the 106th had spread out over a front line that was three times the normal distance and, thus, three times harder to defend. For some American and German memories of this young division's participation in the Battle of the Bulge, see http://www.mm.com/user/jpk/wardiary.htm. The German Stalag camps were fairly well run as far as American and British prisoners were concerned; they were not mistreated, including Jews and blacks. For a fascinating German site (in English) about Stalag VII-A, see http://www.moosburg.org/info/stalag/indeng.html, and for an American view see http://www.merkki.com/.

WEB SITE REVIEWS

GENERAL

Grunts.net
http://www.grunts.net

Although a commercial site with more than the usual number of annoying advertisements, Grunts.net provides an exhaustive array of division and unit histories for all branches of the military. The histories are by no means limited to World War II, but excellent organization and easy movement throughout the site allow visitors to find what they are looking for. To cite one example, the entries for the United States Army, which far outnumber the material related to other service branches, are divided into infantry divisions, airborne divisions, armored and cavalry divisions, and the rangers. A click on the icon for the 3d Infantry Division, for instance, takes visitors to separate chapters on World War I, World War II, Korea, Vietnam, the Cold War, and even Desert Storm. The chapter on World War II includes a history of the division's activities as well as links to separate biographies of each of the divisions' recipients of the Medal of Honor. Furthermore, the main page for each service branch contains additional information on key World War II battles, such as Guadalcanal, Iwo Jima, and Midway.

In addition to the division and unit histories, Grunts.net has special features on African Americans in the military, including links to the web pages of all-black units such as the Buffalo Soldiers and Tuskegee Airmen. The site also has photographs from Pearl Harbor and of the marines on Iwo Jima. Visitors to Grunts.net should not expect to find an archive of primary documents, but they will find basic unit histories that provide a good launching point for more serious investigation.

CONTENT   ★ ★ ★ ★
AESTHETICS   ★ ★ ★
NAVIGATION   ★ ★ ★ ★

EUROPEAN THEATER

Super Sixth: The Story of Patton's 6th Armored Division in WWII
http://members.aol.com/super6th

Maintained by the son of a veteran of Patton's Sixth Army, this site follows the Sixth Army from its landing on the beaches of Normandy in July 1944 (six weeks after D-Day) to its participation in the battles of northern France, Ardennes-Alsace, the Rhineland, and central Europe. Webmaster Bruce Frederick has created a site that includes excerpts from out-of-print official histories of the division and its accompanying battalions, lists and citations of medal of honor recipients, oral histories, maps, and photographs.

Frederick makes an excellent case for the importance of oral histories when he remarks in his introduction to Personal Stories that "official histories don't convey the experience of the men in the fox holes, gun turrets, artillery positions, or supply truck driver's seats. A paragraph in an after-action report might describe an encounter as 'light resistance.' However, for the GI targeted by the gunfire or mortar shell, that 'light resistance' might represent the most terrifying event of his life." Researchers will benefit if Frederick can add eventually to the handful of oral histories currently on the site.

Perhaps the most interesting feature on Super Sixth is a collection of original maps and accompanying text that detail the movements of Patton's Army throughout 1944–45. Researchers will need a fast modem and plenty of time to download the JPEG files, but their patience will be rewarded.

The one drawback to this site is its navigability. From the opening page, visitors have to scroll through a lengthy series of items before finally coming to On This Web Site. From this point, navigation becomes easier, but a more user-friendly opening page would help. On a related note, the opening page contains a wonderful collage of photographs; the table of contents, however, lists no additional photographs on the site.

CONTENT   ★ ★ ★
AESTHETICS   ★ ★ ★
NAVIGATION   ★ ★ ★

Trigger Time: 101st Airborne WW2
http://www.101airborneWW2.com

Among those who parachuted behind enemy lines on D-Day, the 101st Airborne played a crucial role in the subsequent Allied advance across northern France, Holland, Belgium, and central Europe. The 101st, nicknamed the Screaming Eagles, is perhaps most famous for successfully defending Bastogne, a critical rail center, during the Battle of the Bulge. Completely surrounded for a week by portions of eight German divisions that had severed the link between the 101st and the 82nd Airborne, the Screaming Eagles nonetheless stalled the last great German offensive of the war. Created by webmaster Mark Bando, who began interviewing World War II veterans of the 101st Airborne in the late 1960s, Trigger Time provides an informed, although ultimately disappointing, look at one of the most celebrated divisions in the United States Army.

Researchers should begin with the Unit Histories section, which combines a synopsis of the division's history with separate histories for the 501st, 502nd, and 506th Parachute Infantry Regiments (the men of the 506th's "Easy" Company are the subject of the recent HBO miniseries *Band of Brothers* as well as the book of the same name). The regimental histories are particularly helpful, although researchers should not expect to find detailed official histories or after action reports. War Stories offers several firsthand accounts. Each of these provides a welcome perspective, but it is unfortunate that Trigger Time includes so few oral histories given that Bando has interviewed more than nine hundred veterans of the 101st.

Trigger Time has additional pages on divisional and regimental commanders, equipment, uniforms, and insignia (including an interesting section on the numerous versions of the "screaming eagle"). Given the enormous attention showered on the men of the 506th's "Easy" Company, visitors will want to read

Bando's thoughts on *Band of Brothers*. Perhaps the most interesting revelation on Trigger Time appears in the section entitled Troop Carrier, in which Bando discusses a lawsuit that pilots of the 101st's troop carriers have considered filing against Stephen Ambrose for his portrayal of them as incompetent and cowardly. The pilots charge that in an attempt to portray the paratroopers in the best possible light, Ambrose denigrated the troop carriers' performances, despite his admission that he did not interview a single troop carrier pilot during the course of his research.

CONTENT   ★ ★ ★
AESTHETICS ★ ★ ★
NAVIGATION ★ ★ ★ ★

70th Infantry Division "Trailblazers"
http://www.trailblazersww2.org

Attached to the Seventh Army and thrust into the front lines in late December 1944, the 70th Infantry Division spent eighty-six consecutive days in combat. By the end of the war in Europe, the Trailblazers had seen action in the campaigns of Ardennes/Alsace, the Rhineland, and central Europe. Among the better sites devoted to a specific unit, this official division site includes a thorough history of the division's activities, complete with an array of supporting documents such as maps and reports of operations. One of the maps is particularly useful in that it is referenced in many of the reports. In addition, visitors will find letters written to and from the front as well as a brief but fascinating account from a German soldier who fought the Trailblazers in the Ardennes Forest.

The site also contains casualty lists, profiles of commanding officers, and photographs. Separate pages on individual regiments and supporting units contain additional histories and supporting documents that complement an already worthwhile site. Although not available online, the site includes a list of 70th Division holdings in the archives of the CMH. One final feature is worth noting: the site has a search mechanism to aid researchers and other visitors interested in locating information on relatives or other individuals who served in World War II. Attractive graphics and logical organization make this an easy site to navigate.

CONTENT   ★ ★ ★ ★
AESTHETICS ★ ★ ★ ★
NAVIGATION ★ ★ ★ ★

104th Infantry Division

http://www.104infdiv.org/index.htm

Maintained by the National Timberwolf Association, this site traces the exploits of
the 34,000 men who wore the Timberwolf, the insignia of the 104th Infantry
Division. Activated in September 1942, the 104th engaged in 195 consecutive
days of battle from October 1944 until the end of the European war in May
1945. A straightforward and easy-to-navigate site index takes researchers to separate chapters on a variety of topics, including the division's history, commanders, casualties, and decorations. One of the most useful chapters is a series
of battle maps that allows researchers to follow the 104th across Europe, from
the campaigns of northern France, to the Battle of the Bulge and the Rhineland,
to the final battles of central Europe.

Told primarily through first-person accounts, the site includes an intense description of the events of April 11–12, 1945, when members of the 104th stumbled
upon the Nordhausen concentration camp. Soldiers with the 104th discovered
5,000 corpses among the 6,000 inmates, who were barely alive. Visitors will find
the account deeply disturbing, but it is an important reminder of the totality
of the horror of World War II.

The most outstanding feature of this site is a section entitled War Stories. The
nearly one hundred oral histories vary in terms of length, depth, and overall
quality, but, taken together, they encapsulate the collective experiences of the
division. The stories are neatly indexed and searchable by author, unit within
the division, and place where the story is set—for example, Belgium, England,
France, Holland, or Germany. Reflecting the division's activity, most of the stories are set in Germany and Holland. A handful of miscellaneous stories include
the point of view of a GI's wife. The only obvious omission from an otherwise
excellent site is photographs.

CONTENT   ★ ★ ★ ★
AESTHETICS   ★ ★ ★ ★
NAVIGATION   ★ ★ ★ ★

225th AAA Searchlight Battalion

http://www.skylighters.org

Webmaster Larry Belmont has put together an exceptional resource in an attempt
to preserve the history and contributions of a frequently overlooked group of
American soldiers. Trained to point spotlights into the sky so that gunners
could shoot down German planes, skylighters have never received the attention accorded the infantry and aviators.

The 225th Searchlight Battalion earned four battle stars in World War II for its participation in Normandy and the battles in northern France, the Rhineland, and central Europe. This site documents the battalion's efforts in each of these engagements through a comprehensive collection of official unit histories, oral histories, photographs, primary documents, radio addresses, and more. Well organized and easily navigable, the site includes an archive of hundreds of photographs in twenty-five separate collections, each taken by a different member of the battalion. Extensive documentation accompanies the unit histories. Special reports provide information on other searchlight battalions in World War II as well as a fascinating look at barrage balloons and other forms of anti-aircraft weaponry. Additional features, including a look at the importance of cigarettes to men in the foxholes and the use of spotlights and radar prior to World War II, enhance an already worthwhile collection.

CONTENT   ★ ★ ★ ★ ★
AESTHETICS ★ ★ ★ ★
NAVIGATION ★ ★ ★ ★

461st Bomb Group: The Liberaiders
http://www.461st.org

A terrific collection of archival material awaits visitors to the official site of the 461st Bomb Group. Stationed at Torretta Field outside Cerignola, Italy, the 461st flew missions into the heart of central Europe in Hungary, Czechoslovakia, and Yugoslavia. The creators of this site have gathered together a complete set of the bomb group's official histories, which are organized by month and can be read online or downloaded as PDF files. A separate section, also organized by month, provides details on every one of the 461st's missions. Although tedious at times, such reports are invaluable for researchers.

The creators have successfully balanced such official reports with more personalized accounts of unit activities. A collection of interviews provides a fascinating look at everything from assembling a crew to being shot down and captured. Visitors should be aware, however, that these interviews are accessible only via RealPlayer; no transcripts exist at this time. The site includes a particularly interesting section entitled Kriegsgefangenen (German for POW). Although still in the early stages of development, the section lists all members of the 461st who were shot down and captured. The list is supplemented with firsthand accounts of some POWs, and over time more of these stories will be added.

Detailed information on the design, including the nose art, of the planes flown by the men of the 461st can be found in the Aircraft section. A number of wonderful photographs are sprinkled throughout most sections of the site. In addition to images of the planes, the airfield, the town of Cerignola, and even selected targets, an entire section on crews has photos of many of the 461st's flight crews, arranged according to the name of the pilot. It is the goal of the creators of the site to eventually post a photograph of every flight crew in the group. Still in development and at times slow to load, 461st Bomb Group is nonetheless well organized and easy to navigate.

CONTENT   ★ ★ ★ ★
AESTHETICS   ★ ★ ★ ★
NAVIGATION   ★ ★ ★ ★

The 504th Parachute Infantry Regiment
http://www.geocities.com/pentagon/5340

Part of the famed 82nd Airborne commanded by Matthew Ridgeway, the 504th's first combat experience proved disastrous when friendly fire shot down twenty-three planes carrying American paratroopers as they prepared to jump into Sicily in July 1943. The regiment recovered and amassed a spectacular record in the battles of Sicily, Naples-Foggia, Anzio, the Rhineland, Ardennes-Alsace, and central Europe. Had their numbers not been depleted by losses in Italy, the 504th more than likely would have participated in the Normandy invasion as well. The regiment's fierce determination led a German officer to refer to the men as "Devils in Baggy Pants," a nickname that stuck throughout the duration of the war.

This site provides an excellent overview of the regiment's history as well as separate histories on each of the major battles in which the 504th fought. Researchers will appreciate an additional section that places the 504th within the larger context of the 82nd Airborne and includes separate links to other parachute and glider regiments and battalions in the 82nd. The Memories section provides a handful of excellent oral histories, including one account of the 82nd's role in burying the mother of Marlene Dietrich in Berlin at the war's end. Although not extensive, a section entitled Pictures includes some nice images, while Troopers contains head and shoulder shots of several dozen members of the 504th. Although slow to load at times, the site is nonetheless well organized.

CONTENT   ★ ★ ★ ★
AESTHETICS   ★ ★ ★ ★
NAVIGATION   ★ ★ ★

PACIFIC THEATER

Battleship North Carolina
http://www.battleshipnc.com

Now a memorial in Wilmington, North Carolina, the USS *North Carolina* took part in every major naval battle in the Pacific during World War II. In the process, the *North Carolina* earned fifteen battle stars, more than any other battleship. From the home page of the battleship's official web site, researchers should begin with the site map, which is divided into six separate units. One unit contains information for visitors to the memorial, while another offers an online tour of the ship, its decks, and its armaments. Another section of the site provides rosters of the 7000 officers and crew who served on the ship during World War II and in subsequent decades.

Researchers undoubtedly will be most interested in the section entitled Heritage. In addition to a history of the ship from its commissioning in 1941, Heritage contains an extended unit on World War II. A section on battles follows the USS *North Carolina* through major engagements from Guadalcanal to Okinawa. A list of the ship's battle stars includes a helpful chronological account of the *North Carolina*'s whereabouts throughout the war. Daily Life in Stories and Pictures provides firsthand accounts from the ship's crew about the more mundane aspects of life on a ship; the daily routine, general quarters, clothing, holidays, and even romance are discussed. The stories include wonderful tidbits of information not usually found in general texts. For instance, visitors will discover why seamen dyed their hats blue and wore bell-bottom pants.

The one drawback to the site is its rather clumsy navigation. A visitor always has the option of returning to the site map by clicking a link at the bottom of every page. Unfortunately, however, the side bar does not provide a thorough list of options; for instance, it requires several steps to get from the entry on Guadalcanal to that on Okinawa.

CONTENT   ★ ★ ★ ★
AESTHETICS   ★ ★ ★ ★
NAVIGATION   ★ ★ ★

SUGGESTED READINGS

There are literally thousands of books that highlight the activities of particular units during World War II. A number of these titles have been incorporated into the Suggested Readings for Chapters 3, 4, and 5.

Ambrose, Stephen E. *Band of Brothers: E Company, 506th Regiment, 101st Airborne from Normandy to Hitler's Eagle's Nest* (New York, 2001).

———. *The Wild Blue: The Men and Boys Who Flew the B-24s over Germany* (New York, 2001).

Astor, Gerald. *The Mighty Eighth: The Air War in Europe as Told by the Men Who Fought It* (New York, 1998).

Bowman, Martin W. *B-17 Flying Fortress Units of the Eighth Air Force* (Sparkford, UK, 2000).

Brown, John Sloan. *Draftee Division: The 88th Infantry Division in World War II* (Lexington, KY, 1986).

Caldwell, Donald L. *JG 26: Top Guns of the Luftwaffe* (New York, 1993).

Craven, Wesley Frank, and J. L. Cate. *The Army Air Forces in World War II*, 7 vols. (Chicago, 1948–1958).

Franks, Kenny A. *Citizen Soldiers: Oklahoma's National Guard* (Norman, OK, 1984).

Lee, Loyd E. "Unit Histories and the Experience of Combat," in *World War II in Asia and the Pacific and the War's Aftermath, with General Themes* (Westport, CT, 1998).

Neill, George W. *Infantry Soldier: Holding the Line at the Battle of the Bulge* (Norman, OK, 2000).

O'Donnell, Patrick K. *Beyond Valor: World War II's Ranger and Airborne Veterans Reveal the Heart of Combat* (New York, 2001).

Perret, Geoffrey. *There's a War to Be Won: The United States Army in World War II* (New York, 1991).

Stanton, Doug. *In Harm's Way: The Sinking of the USS Indianapolis and the Extraordinary Story of Its Survivors* (New York, 2001).

Weal, John. *BF 109: Aces of the Russian Front* (New York, 2001).

CHAPTER 10

PHOTOGRAPHS, POSTERS, AND PROPAGANDA

WORLD WAR II IN PICTURES

The sites reviewed in this chapter appear elsewhere in *World War II on the Web*. In some instances, the reviews have been revised to emphasize the visual materials available on each site. For a discussion of photos, posters, and other visual media in conjunction with World War II, see the introduction to Chapter 6.

WEB SITE REVIEWS

GENERAL

African Americans in World War II
http://www.historyplace.com

Maintained by The History Place, African Americans in World War II is a small but important collection of thirty-three photographs. Unlike most of the World War II images of African Americans in the Navy Historical Center's collection, which depict blacks as mess stewards and manual laborers, the photographs posted to this web site emphasize the combat contributions of African Americans in Europe and the Pacific.

By selecting African Americans in WWII on the home page, visitors will find neatly arranged images of infantrymen firing at nests of German machine guns in Italy, a tank crew awaiting orders in Germany, a squadron preparing for the day's mission from its base in Italy, troops guarding a German prisoner, marines preparing to face the Japanese in the Pacific, and a marine patrol cautiously making its way through the jungle on a Japanese-held island. Additional images highlight the contributions of African American women, who served in the military as nurses and also as welders, machine operators, and mechanics at defense factories on the home front.

CONTENT   ★ ★ ★
AESTHETICS ★ ★ ★ ★
NAVIGATION ★ ★ ★ ★

American Memory from the Library of Congress
http://rs6.loc.gov/ammem/amhome.html

For a full review of this site, see p. 96.

American Memory, the Library of Congress's digital archive, includes more than 7 million items from more than one hundred separate collections. Among these vast holdings are several collections of visual imagery of deep relevance to researchers, educators, and students interested in the American home front during World War II.

"America from the Great Depression to World War II: Photographs from the FSA-OWI, 1935–1945" (http://memory.loc.gov/ammem/fsowhome.html) is perhaps the single most important collection of American documentary pho-tography ever assembled. In the mid- to late 1930s, the Farm Security Admin-istration (FSA) hired the nation's most accomplished documentary photographers—including Dorothea Lange, Margaret Bourke-White, and Walk-er Evans, among others—to record the experience of Americans as they strug-gled to cope with the Great Depression. With the onset of war, the corps of photographers shifted their attention to home front mobilization, producing thousands of images for the Office of War Information (OWI). All told, the FSA-OWI collection contains more than 160,000 black and white and 1,600 colored photographs.

The immense size of the collection is both its greatest strength and weakness. The corps of photographers captured every conceivable aspect of World War II mobilization. Images abound of aircraft assembly lines and female war workers. And although the collection is searchable by subject, creator, and geographic location, "World War II" does not appear in the subject index. Consequently, certain researchers, depending on what they hope to find, face a daunting task as they sift through the photographs. The much smaller collection of colored photographs provides the same search options, but it does include "World War II, 1939–1945" in the subject index.

"By the People, For the People: Posters from the WPA, 1936–1943" (http://memory.loc.gov/ammem/wpaposters/wpahome.html) contains more than 900 of the original 2,000 posters, lithographs, and woodcuts produced at the behest of the New Deal's Works Progress Administration (WPA). Hired to publicize a variety of New Deal–era health, cultural, and educational programs, the artists, like the photographers, turned their attention to the war effort in the early 1940s. The collection's subject index includes headings for war blackouts, war bonds and funds, war posters, and war work. Researchers may also search the collection by keyword or creator.

CONTENT   ★ ★ ★ ★
AESTHETICS   ★ ★ ★
NAVIGATION   ★ ★ ★

Dr. Seuss Went to War: A Catalog of Political Cartoons by Dr. Seuss
http://orpheus.ucsd.edu/speccoll/dspolitic

Theodore Geisel, better known as Dr. Seuss, earned fame and fortune as an author and illustrator of children's books. Few fans think of Dr. Seuss as a political cartoonist, but from 1941 to 1943 he was the chief editorial cartoonist for *PM*, a New York newspaper. During his tenure, Geisel produced 400 cartoons, all of which are now housed in the special collections library at the University of California at San Diego. Most of the cartoons in the collection are relevant to World War II.

Visitors to Dr. Seuss Went to War will instantly recognize Dr. Seuss's distinctive style. All of the characters in these drawings, including Roosevelt, Hitler, Stalin, and the ever-present animals, look like they would feel right at home in Dr. Seuss's more famous children's books. The site is well organized and allows visitors to search the cartoons by date or subject. The date index is subdivided by year, month, and day. The subject index is organized into four subgroups: People, Countries/Regions, War/Domestic Issues, and Battles and Battlefields. Visitors will find sketches of many important World War II political and military leaders, including more than 100 of Hitler. No major aspect of the war escaped Dr. Seuss's attention. From the isolationist American First Committee, led by Charles Lindbergh, to the attack on Pearl Harbor, to war industries and racism, Dr. Seuss covered it all. The only unfortunate aspect of this collection is that Dr. Seuss did not remain at *PM* through the end of war. One can only imagine what he might have drawn during the final two and one-half years of the war.

CONTENT   ★ ★ ★ ★
AESTHETICS   ★ ★ ★ ★
NAVIGATION   ★ ★ ★

Franklin Delano Roosevelt Library and Digital Archive
http://www.fdrlibrary.marist.edu

For a full review of this site, see p. 31.

In addition to more than 13,000 primary documents, the Franklin Delano Roosevelt Library and Digital Archive includes thousands of photographs divided into three sections: Franklin and Eleanor Roosevelt, The Great Depression and the New Deal, and World War II. Shot by photographers hired by the federal government, the photographs are in the public domain and thus available to the public without copyright restrictions. Images from World War II run the gamut from the ceremonial to the horrific. Visitors will find images of female welders on the home front, commando training, soldiers in combat, leaders such as Roosevelt and Churchill, and the gruesome juxtaposition of Christmas wreaths and a pile of dead bodies at Buchenwald.

The site offers a straightforward keyword search engine and allows visitors to browse through an extensive list of photographic descriptions, but it provides no index or table of contents for the collection of photographs. Furthermore, keyword searches produce descriptions of relevant images but no thumbnail sketches. Consequently, researchers must click on each description to see an image, a process that encumbers navigation.

CONTENT ★ ★ ★ ★ ★
AESTHETICS ★ ★ ★ ★
NAVIGATION ★ ★ ★ ★

German Propaganda Archive
http://www.calvin.edu/academic/cas/gpa

For a full review of this site, see p. 49.

The German Propaganda Archive contains a rich collection of primary source materials on Nazi propaganda. Part of a larger site devoted to exposing the use of propaganda in both Nazi Germany and the German Democratic Republic (East Germany), the archive is maintained by Randall Bytwerk, a professor of Communication Arts and Sciences at Calvin College in Michigan. Pre-1933 Nazi Propaganda includes cartoons from a Nazi magazine as well as more than forty color posters that provide visual imagery of Nazi election slogans and attacks on Jews and communists.

The bulk of the archive can be found in the six main sections organized collectively under the heading 1933–1945 Material. Visual Material contains a fascinating array of photographs, postcards, art, cartoons, posters, and even postage stamps. Photographs document Hitler's seizure of power in 1933 and a subsequent rally in Nuremberg. Booklets celebrate Hitler's "achievements." Nearly four dozen posters document important events from the election of 1933 to World War II.

The remaining sections—War Propaganda, 1939–1945, Miscellaneous Propaganda, and Material from Nazi Periodicals for Propagandists—are equally rich. A collection of leaflets from D-Day, found amidst the collection in War Propaganda, 1939–1945, attempts to demoralize American troops and lead them to question their participation in the war. One asks if the American GI can be sure of getting a job if he is lucky enough to make it home alive. Another reads: "A gravestone somewhere in France or somewhere in Europe. He was rather a nice boy, was Sam Doodle, his parents joy, beloved of all who used to know him. But he lost, first his head and then his life and became an ass and then a stiff."

The primary source materials available on the German Propaganda Archive are staggering in their richness and scope. Serious researchers will not want to miss this well indexed and easily navigable site.

CONTENT ★ ★ ★ ★ ★
AESTHETICS ★ ★ ★ ★
NAVIGATION ★ ★ ★ ★

Museum of Tolerance Online
http://motlc.wiesenthal.com

For a full review of this site, see p. 132.

Housed at Los Angeles's Simon Wiesenthal Center, the Museum of Tolerance's online archive is extraordinary in its scope, yet at times difficult to navigate on account of inconsistent organization. Designed to serve as a learning tool for students and teachers as well as an online archive for researchers, the site includes thousands of extraordinary photographs. For some inexplicable reason, however, the site includes no separate, comprehensive index of the photograph collection. Fortunately, an index is available at http://history1900s. about.com/library/holocaust/aa122299a.htm?iam+ask&terms=german+tokyo+rose. Organized alphabetically by subject, the index provided by About.com links directly to the Museum of Tolerance's online photographic archive. It remains unclear why access to the photographs in the same sensible manner is not possible directly from the Museum of Tolerance's home page.

Visitors will find images from major battles and campaigns: the Battle of Britain, the Battle of the Bulge, the Normandy invasion, and the invasion of the Philippines, just to name a few. The collection includes photographs of Roosevelt, Churchill, Stalin, Eisenhower, MacArthur, Montgomery, Hitler, Himmler, Goebbels, and other major Allied and Axis political and military leaders. Hundreds of photographs depict the human suffering in each of the concentration camps; there are more than 150 pictures from Auschwitz alone. Other pictures capture the physical destruction suffered in cities such as Berlin as well as the imprisonment of Jews in the ghettoes of Warsaw and other cities.

CONTENT   ★ ★ ★ ★
AESTHETICS   ★ ★ ★
NAVIGATION   ★ ★ ★

THE HOME FRONT

Powers of Persuasion: Poster Art From World War II
http://www.archives.gov/digital_classroom/lessons/powers_of_persuasion/powers_of_persuasion.html

Part of a larger exhibit displayed at the National Archives in the mid-1990s, Powers of Persuasion contains thirty-three posters and one sound file that represent what the site's curators refer to as a "constant battle for the hearts and minds of the American citizenry." Throughout the duration of the war, propaganda and persuasion "became a wartime industry, almost as important as the manufacturing of bullets and planes." The posters in this collection are divided into two groups: one set of posters aims to instill pride and patriotism, while the other presents a shocking, harsh view of war, in particular of the consequences of an Axis victory. These latter images, according to the exhibit, "appeal to darker impulses, fostering feelings of suspicion, fear, and even hate."

Among the posters that instill pride, patriotism, and general confidence in the American war effort, researchers will find appeals to strong men to "man the guns" and to patriotic women to "get a war job." In an attempt to minimize the effect of pervasive and overt discrimination at home, images of black and white war workers, along with a personal message from heavyweight champion Joe Louis, attempt to convey the importance of racial solidarity. Appeals to conserve gas include the admonition that "when you ride alone, you ride with Hitler." In addition, Norman Rockwell's famous prints of the Four Freedoms are included along with an excerpt from Roosevelt's speech on the same subject.

A second set of images attempt to instill fear in an American public physically removed from the war itself. Claiming that "our homes are in danger now," threatening and brutal caricatures of Hitler and a Japanese leader loom over the United States. Menacing talons imprinted with a swastika and rising sun reach for a blond American mother and her baby. Warning Americans to be alert to domestic spies while tapping into assumptions about the propensity of women to gossip, one image depicts a typical American woman on a wanted poster; her crime: "Murder: Her Careless Talk Costs Lives."

CONTENT   ★ ★ ★ ★
AESTHETICS   ★ ★ ★ ★
NAVIGATION   ★ ★ ★ ★

Produce for Victory: Posters on the American Home Front, 1941–1945

http://www.americanhistory.si.edu/victory

Organized by the Smithsonian Institution's National Museum of American History, this online companion to an exhibition of the same name includes more than forty posters issued by federal agencies, businesses, and private organizations. Intended to mobilize those on the home front to recognize war aims as their "personal mission," the posters urged workers and families to do their part to boost production in the factories and at home. The collection is organized into six groups: Every Citizen a Soldier; The Poster's Place in War Time; Retooling for Victory: The Factory Front; Efficient Workers; War Aims through Art: The U.S. Office of War Information; and Fighting for an Ideal America. Each section includes a brief but helpful introduction that considers the most prominent themes and uses of imagery. The title, original dimensions, and name of the artist or sponsoring agency accompany a thumbnail sketch of each image, which, when clicked, provides a larger version of the poster.

Major corporations such as General Motors (GM) and Oldsmobile produced posters urging their employees to work harder and more efficiently. One GM poster proclaimed "It's A Two Fisted Fight" against an image of two hands holding a rifle and a wrench. Set against a silhouette of a hand with a crochet needle, an artist hired by the New Deal's Works Progress Administration urged Americans to "Remember Pearl Harbor: Purl Harder." Another government-sponsored artist urged Americans to "Grow It Yourself: Plan a Farm Garden Now."

Idealized images of the American family pervaded World War II poster art. A series of "This Is America . . . Keep It Free" posters proclaimed the virtue of small-town, wholesome individuals and their families. The Kroger Grocery Company produced a poster of children wearing gas masks with the prayer "Dear God, Keep Them Safe" above the children. An artist hired by Oldsmobile painted an image of a mother reading to her children with the intonation "Don't Let Anything Happen to Them . . . Keep Firing."

CONTENT   ★ ★ ★ ★
AESTHETICS   ★ ★ ★ ★
NAVIGATION   ★ ★ ★ ★

U.S. Army Signal Corps Photograph Collection
http://eagle.vsla.edu/signal.corps

More than 1.5 million men and women departing for and returning from service in World War II passed through the Hampton Roads Port of Embarkation in Newport News, Virginia. Photographers with the U.S. Army's Signal Corps dutifully recorded the movements of these legions; more than 3,500 of their images are now housed in the Library of Virginia's U.S. Army Signal Corps Photograph Collection (SCC). This massive photographic archive, available online in its entirety, details "the preparation and loading of war materials, the activities of the U.S. Quartermaster Corps, U.S. military personnel arriving and departing through the ports of Hampton Roads, civilian employees, Red Cross workers, wounded personnel, entertainers, animals, and German and Italian prisoners of war."

The SCC is so extensive that first-time visitors may feel overwhelmed. The site has an excellent search engine designed for a variety of types of searches, but it lacks an index with predetermined categories that would facilitate navigation. Consequently, researchers without a clear sense of what or who they are looking for may find it difficult to navigate the site. Nevertheless, once embarking upon a search, the engine will produce a number of hits, each of which provides a thumbnail sketch of the relevant images and brief descriptions. Clicking on the number of each hit will produce a full description with all known information, and larger images can be accessed by clicking on the thumbnails. The Signal Corps photographers faithfully recorded the names of their subjects; consequently, individuals in most images are identified by name, and their names are cross-listed with the search engine. For example, visitors can search for Red Skelton and will be led to two images of Private First Class Richard "Red" Skelton. On the other hand, a visitor would have to know to search for Skelton; otherwise, one would have no chance of finding his picture but for sheer chance.

The Library of Virginia's SCC is one of the most extensive collections of World War II photographs available on the web. The variety and richness of images make this site a must visit.

CONTENT ★ ★ ★ ★ ★
AESTHETICS ★ ★ ★ ★
NAVIGATION ★ ★ ★ ★

War Relocation Authority Photographs of Japanese-American Evacuation and Resettlement, 1942–1945

http://www.oac.cdlib.org/dynaweb/ead/calher/jvac

Between 1942 and 1945, War Relocation Authority (WRA) staff photographers recorded more than 7000 images of all aspects and phases of Japanese American internment. Pictures depict Japanese American merchants closing their shops in advance of their evacuation; mounds of baggage in city centers awaiting transport to resettlement centers; and, of course, evacuees themselves boarding buses headed for assembly centers and camps. Photographers also recorded Japanese Americans at the seventeen assembly centers to which they were sent before being transported to the ten relocation camps. The bulk of the photographs in the collection, not surprisingly, portray life inside the camps. A final batch of images document the resettlement of Japanese Americans after the camps' closings.

Downloading the site's large files requires patience, but navigation is otherwise quite easy. The collection is exceedingly well organized into eighteen series. Each of the ten relocation camps has its own series, while the others depict pre-evacuation activities, assembly centers, relocation, and resettlement. Each series, in turn, is divided into numerous groups. The images in each group are identified by caption, name of the photographer, date taken, and WRA identification number. Clicking a small icon next to each caption produces the actual image.

The WRA photographs are simply staggering in their number and scope. Researchers and educators interested in visual representations of Japanese American internment will make this site their first, and perhaps last, stop on the web.

CONTENT   ★ ★ ★ ★
AESTHETICS   ★ ★ ★
NAVIGATION   ★ ★ ★

Women in World War II From the National Archives
http://www.nara.gov/nara/searchnail.html

For a full review of this site, see p. 123.

For a full review of this site, see p. 123.

This online collection from the massive holdings of the National Archives consists of 150 photographs, posters, and textual documents. Taken together, this material provides a rich record of the experience of American women in World War II. Unfortunately, the site does not have its own URL and therefore cannot be bookmarked. Researchers must first go to the above address, click on "NAIL Digital Copies Search," and then enter keywords "women" and "world war ii." Be sure that both "media" and "NARA units" are set to "all media" and "all units" respectively. A successful search should produce 150 hits. Although it is possible to refine a search, researchers will discover that there is no index and thus no alternative to scrolling through the results of a search. This process, however, is made considerably less cumbersome by choosing "display all hits," which allows access to twenty-five search results at a time, each of which includes a thumbnail sketch, title, and control number as well as easy links to a full description and larger image.

Despite such navigational difficulties, researchers will quickly appreciate the value of this site. Numerous photographs show women at work in the defense plants, manning the rivet guns and welding torches, building assault boats, and forging weapons casings. White and black women appear side by side, as do women and men. This collection includes photographs of nurses bandaging injured troops, members of the Women's Army Corps (WAC) enjoying a little rest and relaxation in North Africa, and nurses with the army air forces undergoing training exercises.

A number of posters issued by federal agencies to engender support for the war effort are also available. Trumpeting the contributions of women of all ages as nurses, industrial workers, and mothers, these posters encouraged women to join the military, get a defense job, and "harvest war crops." An entire series of posters entitled "Women's Place in War," issued by the WAC, shows women performing a variety of tasks, from repairing radios, to observing the weather, to drafting maps.

```
CONTENT      ★ ★ ★ ★ ★
AESTHETICS   ★ ★ ★ ★
NAVIGATION   ★ ★ ★
```

World War II Poster Collection

http://www.library.nwu.edu/govpub/collections/wwii-posters

The Northwestern University library has gathered together a superb collection of more than 325 posters issued by various federal agencies from 1941 through 1945. From the home page, visitors can search the collection by date, title, topic, or keyword, which will generate thumbnail pictures of the relevant posters with titles, dates, and agencies that created them. Visitors can then choose to display a more complete record as well as a larger JPEG file for the poster itself. Northwestern University does not sell reproductions of these posters, but the National Archives and Records Administration does.

Despite the various options, searching World War II Poster Collection can appear daunting simply because of the size of the archive. Visitors not looking for a particular image ought to begin with a search by topic. The designers have sensibly organized the collection into the following categories: War Bonds, Don't Talk, Victory Gardens/Save the Forest, Canning/Rationing, Defense Work, Conserve Materials for War Effort, Home Efforts, Stay Healthy, Civil Defense, Office of Price Administration.

The posters provide a terrific look at the various components of home front mobilization, from conservation and rationing, to civil defense, to warnings against gossip for fear the enemy may be lurking nearby. The art itself is worth a visit; the posters as a whole are an invaluable resource for understanding the concerns of a society at war.

```
CONTENT      ★ ★ ★ ★ ★
AESTHETICS   ★ ★ ★ ★
NAVIGATION   ★ ★ ★ ★
```

SOLDIERS/POWs

"Dad" Rarey's Sketchbook Journals

http://www.rareybird.com

In early 1942, George Rarey was drafted into the army air forces and eventually assigned to the 379th Fighter Squadron. A cartoonist and commercial artist prior to his induction, Rarey catalogued his war experience in a series of sketchbooks, producing hundreds of drawings between 1942 and his death in the skies over France just weeks after D-Day. Known as "Dad" to the rest of the squadron because, at twenty-five, he was older than most of them, Rarey also painted nose art on the planes of many of his squadron mates.

This site, run by Rarey's son, who was but a few months old when Rarey was shot down, contains many of Rarey's sketches accompanied by excerpts of letters from Rarey to his wife, her memoirs, and the recollections of members of the 379th Fighter Squadron. Visitors can follow Rarey's journey from his induction, when he drew "a quick and telling cartoon of a bewildered disheveled little civilian saying adieu to the world as he had known and loved," to flight school, to the trip across the Atlantic, and into combat. While in England training for the impending invasion of France, Rarey learned of his son's birth, an occasion that prompted him to write, "This happiness is nigh unbearable . . . what a ridiculous and worthless thing a war is in the light of such a wonderful event."

On June 21, 1944, Rarey wrote to his wife:

> Every night I crawl into my little sack and light up the last cigarette of the day and there in the dark with the wind whippin' around the tent flaps I think of you—of your hair and eyes and pretty face—of your lovely young body—of your warmth and sweetness. It isn't in the spirit of frustration but of fulfillment. I've known these things and knowing them and having them once, I have them forever. That wonderful look in your eyes when we'd meet after being apart for a few hours—or a few weeks—always the same—full of love. Ah, Betty Lou, you're the perfect girl for me—I love ya, Mama!

A sketch that accompanied the letter proved to be Rarey's last. He died several days later.

In addition to Rarey's sketchbooks, the site includes images of the nose art and numerous portraits that Rarey drew of other pilots. A brief but telling excerpt from his wife's memoir tells of their days together in New York City just prior to his induction.

CONTENT   ★ ★ ★ ★
AESTHETICS   ★ ★ ★ ★
NAVIGATION   ★ ★ ★ ★

Memoir of Sgt. William Heller
http://www.warfoto.com

A war photographer with the 3rd Infantry Division, William Heller captured the war through pictures rather than words. This site, run by his son, contains over 200 photographs that chronicle the 3rd Division's march from Casablanca in North Africa to Hitler's Eagle Nest in Berchtesgaden. Along the way, the 3rd Division took part in the invasions of Sicily, Italy, and Southern France before marching across Germany. Heller took of the photographs on this site, while other photographers assigned to the 3rd Division contributed the rest.

The photos document nearly every aspect of army life: combat, including amphibious landings and maneuvers in the Italian Alps; the United States Organizations (USO) appearances of such stars as Bob Hope, Jack Benny, and Marlene Dietrich; daily experiences of GIs, including their attendance at prayer services; and generals reviewing the troops and plotting strategy. The most graphic images include the dead on the battlefields and medics treating wounded soldiers. No pictures, however, capture the horror of World War II as clearly as do Heller's shots of dead children in Dachau. Other memorable photographs include a picture of the French Resistance shaving the head of a woman who fraternized with German soldiers and a group of war correspondents holding up Hermann Göring's pajamas after the capture of Hitler's guest house.

A logically organized table of contents allows for straightforward navigation. Although the photographs themselves are exceptional in their quality, the site's design is rather busy and somewhat distracting. Taken as a whole, however, the pictures available on Memoir of Sgt. William Heller provide a riveting look at the war.

CONTENT ★ ★ ★ ★
AESTHETICS ★ ★ ★
NAVIGATION ★ ★ ★ ★

PACIFIC THEATER

African Americans and the U.S. Navy—World War II
http://www.history.navy.mil/photos/prs-tpic/af-amer/afa-wwii.htm

Part of the Online Library of Selected Images of the U.S. Navy Historical Center (see Chapter 4), this site contains several dozen photographs, but no significant text. The navy remained the most thoroughly segregated branch of the military through World War II, and the photographs depict the narrow range of jobs available for blacks. Consequently, many of the images depict black mess stewards such as Cook Third Class Doris "Dorie" Miller who won the Navy Cross for his heroism during the attack on Pearl Harbor.

The images in the two parts of World War II Service at Pacific Bases depict black construction battalions, logistics support companies, and supply depot personnel on Guam, Okinawa and other islands. A series of images shows black enlisted men in training at various stateside facilities. So restrictive was the navy that the one image of blacks firing weapons in World War II Shipboard Service actually depicts mess attendants at play while the USS *Copahee* sailed from California to the southwest Pacific. A click of the thumbnail sketch produces a larger image that clearly shows the men horsing around.

Visitors to African Americans and the U.S. Navy—World War II should not expect a wealth of information, but they will find a site with important images of African Americans serving in the U.S. Navy. Links from the page will take visitors to the Navy Historical Center's home page.

CONTENT   ★ ★ ★
AESTHETICS   ★ ★ ★
NAVIGATION   ★ ★ ★

Pearl Harbor Photo Archive
http://www.ibiblio.org/memory

Hosted by ibiblio.org, the "public's visual archive" and the home to both Hyperwar (see p. 58) and World War II Resources (see p. 10), the Pearl Harbor Photo Archive contains 150 photographs, posters, and cartoons from the National Archives and Records Administration. Researchers will find an extensive collection of photographs taken during and soon after the surprise attack. The archive includes an eerie photograph taken from the air by a Japanese pilot; numerous images of American warships exploding, burning, and sinking; and shots of the salvage operations that began in the immediate aftermath of the attack.

The images in the archive, however, are not limited to the attack on December 7, 1941. In fact, one of the strengths of this collection is the inclusion of numerous posters and cartoons produced later in the war, which urge Americans to "Remember Pearl Harbor" and "Avenge Pearl Harbor" by purchasing war bonds, joining the Coast Guard, and lending general support to the war effort. In addition, visitors to the archive will find photographs of such luminaries as Franklin and Eleanor Roosevelt and Douglas MacArthur on visits to Pearl Harbor.

The 150 images are organized into groups of twenty-five. Unfortunately, no index is available for the site at this time; consequently, researchers must scroll through the entire collection to see what is available. Each thumbnail image is accompanied by a title, date, and National Archives control number. Clicking on the thumbnail produces a larger image of the photograph or poster. Anyone interested in visual imagery related to Pearl Harbor will consider the Pearl Harbor Photo Archive a must visit.

CONTENT   ★ ★ ★ ★
AESTHETICS   ★ ★ ★ ★
NAVIGATION   ★ ★ ★

World War II in the Pacific
http://historyplace.com/unitedstates/pacificwar/index.html

One of many World War II pages hosted by The History Place, World War II in the Pacific is a superb collection of fifty photographs, all of which come from the files of the National Archives. Although many of these images appear on multiple web sites, researchers will appreciate a chance to find such quality images, all from the war in the Pacific, assembled on one site. A thumbnail sketch and brief textual description of each image allows visitors to scroll quickly through the index; a full-size version of the photograph can be viewed by clicking on the smaller image.

Many of the images depict fierce battle scenes on Okinawa, Iwo Jima, the Solomon Islands, and other islands (including the famous image of marines raising the flag over Iwo Jima). Visitors will see Allied POWs with their hands bound behind their backs during the infamous Bataan Death March in April 1942. Other pictures depict the American surrender at Corregidor the following month and American POWs celebrating July 4, 1942, despite the threat of death from their captors.

The site includes a number of images from the decks of American ships as planes take off from aircraft carriers and gunners shoot at kamikazes. One image captures a Japanese plane being shot down, while another records the mayhem on the deck of the USS *Bunker Hill* after it was struck by two kamikazes within thirty seconds, resulting in more than six hundred casualties.

Additional photographs of note document two soldiers taking a cigarette break in their foxhole on Peleliu, a surgeon plying his trade in an underground bunker on one of the Solomon Islands, and Colonel Paul Tibbets, pilot of the Enola Gay, waving as he prepares to take off from Tinian Island to deliver the first atomic bomb.

CONTENT ★ ★ ★
AESTHETICS ★ ★ ★ ★
NAVIGATION ★ ★ ★

PART II

SITES WORTH A VISIT

A TOPICAL INDEX

A WORLD AT WAR

DOCUMENTS

American War Library: World War II Files Menu

http://members.aol.com/forcountry/ww2/ww2menu.htm

A worthy collection of speeches and primary documents relating to all phases of World War II; selections include speeches from Franklin Roosevelt and Adolf Hitler.

The Avalon Project: World War II Documents

http://www.yale.edu/lawweb/avalon/wwii/wwii.htm

Perhaps the single most important collection of World War II documents available on the Internet; part of the Yale Law School's Avalon Project, which includes documents in law, history, and diplomacy from the second century B.C. to the present.

The Center for Military History WWII Online Bookshelves

http://www.army.mil/cmh-pg/online/Bookshelves/WW2-List.htm

Primary documents, including the official U.S. Army Green Books on the Cross-Channel attack, the Battle of the Bulge, Okinawa, and Guadalcanal, as well as numerous commemorative books and brochures on key individuals and campaigns in every theater of operation; navigation is tricky, so it is best to consult the full review.

Quotes From World War II

http://www.angelfire.com/la/raeder/worldwarIIquotes.html

Includes memorable utterances from officials in France, Germany, Italy, Japan, the USSR, the United States, China, and England, organized by country.

World War II Air Power

http://www.danshistory.com/ww2/index.shtml

Marred only by the advertisements endemic to many commercial sites; primary documents, including diplomatic texts, and support chapters on campaigns, aircraft, weapons, air defense, and technology.

WWII Resources

http://www.ibiblio.org/pha

One of the most comprehensive sources of official government and diplomatic documents relating to World War II on the Internet; a 400-page chronology of events leading up to the war accompanies official American, British, French, German, and Japanese documents.

WWII Armed Forces Orders of Battle and Organization

http://www.freeport-tech.com:80/WWII/index.htm

Organized by country and theater of operation; includes assignments, attachments, commanders, and authorized troop strengths.

MAPS

Maps of World War II

http://www.onwar.com/maps/wwii/index.htm

Close to ninety maps from all theaters of combat providing operational-level information (the point of view of a general or admiral rather than that of a field commander).

World War II Maps at the University of Texas Library

http://www.lib.utexas.edu/maps/historical/history_ww2.html

Close to fifty maps, many of them high-quality color images, from the special collections of the University of Texas Library.

World War II Photos and Maps

http://baby.indstate.edu/gga/gga_cart/gecar127.htm

Confusing organization mars an otherwise terrific collection maintained by the Department of Geography at Indiana State University.

TIMELINES AND GENERAL SITES

Grolier's World War II Commemoration

http://gi.grolier.com/wwii/wwii_mainpage.html

Comprehensive series of encyclopedic style entries, with photographs, on major events, battles, and leaders; created by Encyclopedia Americana.

Home of Heroes

http://www.HomeofHeroes.com

Interesting features on various Medal of Honor recipients; confusing organization and navigation makes research difficult.

K-9 History: The Dogs of War

http://community-2.webtv.net/Hahn-50thAP-K9/K9History

A fascinating look at the role that dogs have played in warfare, including World War II.

The World at War, History of WWII, 1939-1945

http://www.euronet.nl/users/wilfried/ww2/ww2.htm

Exceptionally detailed timeline interspersed with links to individual battles, campaigns, commanders, and other items of interest.

World War II From Teacher Oz's Kingdom of History

http://www.teacheroz.com/wwii.htm

No original information, but a collection of links so extensive as to warrant a visit; school teacher Tracey Oz includes links to every imaginable topic in a well-organized and easy-to-navigate format.

World War II Medal of Honor Recipients

http://www.army.mil/cmh-pg/moh1.htm

Comprehensive list for all World War II recipients of the Medal of Honor; organized alphabetically with a separate index of African American recipients.

World War II Plus 55

http://www.usswashington.com/dl_index.htm

Comprehensive day-by-day look at the war in 1941 and 1942; provides a sense of how many different events took place simultaneously across the globe.

World War II Timeline

http://ac.acusd.edu/History/WW2Timeline/start.html

A broadly conceived timeline organized by date and topic with photographs, maps, and some primary documents; created as a class project at the University of San Diego.

EQUIPMENT

AFV News

http://www.activevr.com/afv

A comprehensive site on all aspects of Armored Fighting Vehicles; maintained by George Bradford, a long-time member of the AFV Association.

American Aircraft in WWII

http://www.ixpres.com/ag1caf/usplanes

Includes photographs and specifications on all American planes; well organized by name, manufacturer, type, and function of aircraft.

Battleship, Carriers, and Warships

http://www.warships1.com

A comprehensive collection on warships from around the world, but not specific to World War II.

Dictionary of American Naval Fighting Ships

http://www.hazegray.org/danfs

A massive compilation that includes information on over 7000 ships; no separate index for World War II.

Destroyers: DANFS Online

http://www.hazegray.org/danfs/destroy

History, specifications, and photographs of numerous destroyers, escorts, and frigates; well indexed by ship, but no separate listing for World War II.

Heavy Bombers

http://www.heavybombers.com

A highly specialized site focusing on the B-17, B-24, and B-29; links to more than 100 heavy and very heavy bombardment groups.

Planes and Pilots of WWII

http://home.att.net/~C.C.Jordan

Billed as "an online World War II aviation history magazine" by webmaster C. C. Jordan; contains numerous articles on all aspects of World War II aviation.

Tanks: Armored Warfare Prior to 1946

http://mailer.fsu.edu/~akirk/tanks

History, photographs, and specifications of all sorts of armored tracking vehicles; organized by nation.

Tanks of WWII

http://www.onwar.com/tanks

Detailed drawings and specs of hundreds of tanks; organized by nation.

World War II Vehicles.Com
http://www.wwiivehicles.com

Organized by country; extensive information on the history and specifications of Allied and Axis fighting vehicles; entries for the United States alone include light, medium, and heavy tanks, self-propelled guns, tank destroyers, and armored cars.

P OLITICAL AND MILITARY LEADERS

GENERAL

The Generals of World War II
http://www.generals.dk

A comprehensive list of generals from all nations and commands.

Phil's WWII Pages
http://www.stokesey.demon.co.uk/wwii/home.html

General reference on the key leaders of each nation; material drawn from leading secondary works.

WWII Political and Military Leaders
http://expage.com/page/gren14

A comprehensive list plus short biographies of key World War II figures.

BRADLEY, OMAR NELSON

Omar Nelson Bradley
http://www.army.mil/cmh-pg/brochures/bradley/bradley.htm

A textual biography of the last American five-star general; part of a series of commemorative brochures prepared by the Center for Military History.

CHURCHILL, WINSTON SPENCER

Churchill: The Evidence
http://www.churchill.nls.ac.uk/main.html

Posters, letters, maps, and photographs present a compelling biography of Britain's wartime leader; created by the National Library of Scotland and the Churchill Archives as a teaching resource.

Life and Times of Winston S. Churchill

http://www.winstonchurchill.org

Vast collection of speeches, quotations, and scholarly articles on all aspects of Churchill's personal and public life; maintained by the Churchill Society in Washington, DC.

EISENHOWER, DWIGHT DAVID

Dwight David Eisenhower

http://www.army.mil/cmh-pg/brochures/ike/ike.htm

A textual biography of the supreme commander of Allied Expeditionary Forces; part of a series of commemorative brochures prepared by the Center for Military History.

Eisenhower Library

http://www.eisenhower.utexas.edu

Some photographs, journal entries, and after action reports from D-Day; majority of the Eisenhower Library's holdings are not available online.

HITLER, ADOLF

Adolf Hitler

http://www.us-israel.org/jsource/Holocaust/hitlertoc.html

A good, but by no means exhaustive, collection of primary documents and secondary works that focus on Hitler's years in power; part of the Jewish Virtual Library's larger site on the Holocaust.

The History Place: Adolf Hitler

http://www.historyplace.com/worldwar2

Forty-two almost encyclopedic chapters, split evenly between Hitler's rise to power and his leadership of the Third Reich; information drawn from leading secondary sources; part of a larger site on World War II in Europe from The History Place.

MacARTHUR, DOUGLAS

Douglas MacArthur: The American Experience

http://www.pbs.org/wgbh/amex/macarthur/index.html

Full transcript, including interviews, of a PBS documentary; an interactive map allows visitors to follow America's most controversial general around the globe.

PATTON, GEORGE

Patton Historical Society

http://www.geocities.com/pattonhq/homeghq.html

A limited collection of photographs and speeches, including Patton's famous "Speech to the Third Army" on the eve of D-Day.

Patton's War

http://www.loc.gov/exhibits/treasures/trm090.html

A photograph and brief diary entry from the collections of the Library of Congress.

ROOSEVELT, FRANKLIN DELANO

Fireside Chats of Franklin D. Roosevelt

http://www.mhric.org/fdr/fdr.html

The full text of thirty-one fireside chats delivered between 1933 and 1944; the first thirteen deal almost exclusively with the Great Depression, the rest with World War II.

Franklin Delano Roosevelt Library and Digital Archive

http://www.fdrlibrary.marist.edu

More than 13,000 digitized documents and thousands of photographs from Roosevelt's presidential papers; one of the single most valuable collections of World War II primary documents available; online collection should continue to grow over time.

STALIN, JOSEPH

Joseph Stalin Reference Archive, 1879-1953

http://csf.colorado.edu/mirrors/marxists.org/reference/archive/stalin

An extensive collection of information, but unfortunately almost nothing on World War II.

J. V. Stalin Internet Library

http://www.marx2mao.org/Stalin/Index.html

Another impressive and comprehensive collection, but very little that pertains directly to World War II.

T R U M A N ,   H A R R Y   S .

Project Whistlestop: Harry S. Truman Digital Archive

http://www.trumanlibrary.org/whistlestop

A terrific collection of primary documents, photographs, and letters organized into study collections on topics such as the decision to drop the atomic bomb, the desegregation of the armed forces, and the Truman Doctrine; ideal resource for teachers.

EUROPEAN/ATLANTIC/MEDITERRANEAN THEATER OF OPERATIONS

G E N E R A L

Band of Brothers

http://www.hbo.com/band

Personal accounts, videos, and a wide range of related exhibits created in conjunction with the HBO miniseries, but not limited to chronicling the exploits of the subjects of the series; awkward organization and navigation, but exceptional graphics.

BBC Online

http://www.bbc.co.uk/education/history/wwtwo.shtml

Collection of BBC news reports and audio clips, as well as the diary of a British woman on the home front; most of the site, however, is from a contemporary perspective.

The Center for Military History WWII Online Bookshelves

http://www.army.mil/cmh-pg/online/Bookshelves/WW2-List.htm

Primary documents, including the official U.S. Army Green Books on the Cross-Channel Attack and the Battle of the Bulge, as well as numerous commemorative books and brochures on key individuals and campaigns in the European and Mediterranean theaters; navigation is tricky, so it is best to consult the full review.

Propaganda Leaflets of the Second World War

http://www.cobweb.nl/jmoonen/index.html

Although difficult to navigate, a valuable source of mostly anti-German propaganda dropped by British and Allied pilots; leaflets dropped by Germans include a warning to British soldiers that American troops stationed in England were sleeping with their wives.

ATLANTIC/MEDITERRANEAN THEATER

Convoy HX72 and U-100

http://www.canonesa.co.uk

A fascinating account of a German U-boat's pursuit of a British vessel as it sailed from Nova Scotia to the United Kingdom.

Italy and the Pacific: "The Forgotten Campaigns of World War II"

http://www.geocities.com/techbloke

Despite annoying commercial advertisements, excellent photographs and beautiful graphics make this an attractive site; in part a tribute to the webmaster's father, a Canadian who fought in Italy, and father-in-law, an American who fought in the Pacific.

The Merchant Marine in World War II

http://www.usmm.org/ww2.html#anchor252856

Includes extensive chronological and geographical lists of losses at the hands of German U-boats; separate chapters document the contribution of women and African Americans.

North African Campaign

http://www.topedge.com/panels/ww2/na/index.html

History and photographs of the battles, commanders, and tactics of the North African campaign.

The U-boat War, 1939–1945

http://www.uboat.net

Neraly 13,000 pages devoted to every German U-boat and the men who commanded them; an excellent index allows visitors to track the movements and encounters of every German submarine.

USS Savannah (CL-42)

http://www.concentric.net/~drake725

Daily diary entries and fascinating minute-by-minute accounts of battles in the Mediterranean and the invasions of Sicily and Italy.

EUROPEAN THEATER

Battle of Arnhem Archive

http://www.extraplan.demon.co.uk/index.htm

Detailed account of the 1st British Airborne Division's effort to secure a key bridge at Arnhem, the Netherlands, in the fall of 1944.

Battle of Monte Cassino

http://www.accessweb.com/users/rbereznicki/over.html-ssi

Maps, orders of battle, and day-by-day chronologies of the four separate engagements waged between January and June 1944.

Battle of the Bulge

http://users.skynet.be/bulgecriba/battlebul.htm

An impressive compilation of primary materials, including the letters and memoirs of soldiers and nurses, after action reports, combat interviews, maps, and lists of units involved in the last great German offensive of the war; the official web site of the Center of Research and Information on the Battle of the Bulge.

D-Day Museum

http://www.ddaymuseum.org

The official site of the D-Day Museum in New Orleans; online collection in the process of development.

D-Day on the Web

http://www.isidore-of-seville.com/d-day/index.html

Historical essays, photos, diaries, and personal histories; most of the material drawn from other sites, but still worth a visit.

Guts and Glory

http://www.pbs.org/wgbh/pages/amex/guts/index.html

Transcripts of PBS documentaries on D-Day and the Battle of the Bulge; includes firsthand accounts from both engagements, as well as biographies of key figures such as George Patton and Erwin Rommel.

Normandy 1944

http://www.normandy.eb.com

An extensive compilation of primary and secondary materials; a textual overview by historian John Keegan provides context for the personal histories of Allied and German troops, newsreels, radio broadcasts, and dispatches from war correspondents; also includes biographies of the major Allied and Axis military and political leaders.

World War II Analyzed

http://www.worldwar2.be

Created by a lawyer in Belgium; fairly comprehensive look at units, weapons, tactics, and personalities involved in European land-based campaigns.

World War Two in Europe

http://www.historyplace.com/worldwar2/timeline/ww2time.htm

A textual and photographic timeline of the causes of the war and other important events; maintained by The History Place.

C O D E   B R E A K I N G

Codebreaking and Secret Weapons in World War II

http://home.earthlink.net/~nbrass1/enigma.htm

Textual overview of the history of code breaking in World War II.

Codes and Ciphers in the Second World War

http://www.codesandciphers.org.uk

Exceptionally detailed explanation of the inner workings of the Enigma and other cipher systems; an online simulator with fascinating 3-D graphics allows visitors to see inside a code machine and how it works; created by Tony Sale, one of Bletchley Park's famed cryptologists.

Decoding Nazi Secrets

http://www.pbs.org/wgbh/nova/decoding

Full text of a PBS documentary, along with background on the Enigma machine, efforts to crack its code, and a detailed explanation as to how the machine worked; an interactive component allows visitors to decode a message.

German Enigma Cipher Machine

http://home.us.net/~encore/Enigma/enigma.html

Devoted to crediting Polish mathematicians with key breakthroughs in deciphering the Enigma before World War II; critical of the PBS series and other accounts that focus only on England's Bletchley Park.

Venona Project

http://www.nsa.gov/museum/venona.html

A collection of declassified National Security Agency documents pertaining to the Enigma and Venona projects; most information from the immediate postwar period.

G E R M A N   W A R   E F F O R T

Feldgrau.com

http://www.feldgrau.com

A comprehensive history of the German military from 1919 to 1945; includes primary and secondary sources, a day-by-day timeline, and interviews with veterans of the German army; maintained by amateur historian Jason Pipes.

German Propaganda Archive

http://www.calvin.edu/academic/cas/gpa

Includes speeches by Joseph Goebbels and Hitler, along with chilling posters, cartoons, photographs, and other forms of German propaganda; maintained by Randall Bytwerk, a professor at Calvin College in Grand Rapids, Michigan.

Third Reich Factbook

http://www.skalman.nu/third-reich

Created by Swede Marcus Wendel; focuses on the military history of the Third Reich and other Axis nations; Wendel overtly disclaims any association, affiliation, or sympathy with neo-Nazi organizations.

P O W s

A Raid on Munich

http://camomilesworld.com/raid/index.html

A firsthand account of a Canadian Royal Air Force pilot's capture, imprisonment, and forced participation in the infamous Lamsdorf Death March.

Stalag Luft I Online

http://www.merkki.com

Created by the family of a former prisoner; includes photos, personal accounts from prisoners and a guard, and even issues of the *POW-WOW,* the camp newspaper billed by its publishers as the "only truthful newspaper in Germany."

PACIFIC THEATER OF OPERATIONS

G E N E R A L

Bataan Death March

http://www.sfps.K12.nm.us/academy/bataan/main.html

A class project that chronicles the experiences of New Mexicans captured at Bataan; includes some firsthand accounts.

The Battle of Midway

http://www.centuryinter.net/midway/midway.html

Mostly technical information with an interesting discussion of the historiographical debate over the performance of key admirals.

Battling Bastards of Bataan

http://home.pacbell.net/fbaldie/Battling_Bastards_of_Bataan.html

Dedicated to setting straight the record of the fall of the Philippines, the Bataan Death March, and subsequent imprisonment of American and Filipino POWs; poorly designed index makes navigation difficult, but site contains useful information.

The Burma Campaign

http://www.rothwell.force9.co.uk/burmaweb

History, geography, and personalities involved in British forces' longest battle of World War II (December 1941 to August 1945); includes a summary of American participation beginning in 1943.

Cactus Air Force

http://www.ixpres.com/ag1caf/cactus

No primary documentation, but an informative, albeit not very balanced, secondary treatment of the pilots who flew over Guadalcanal from August to November 1942.

The Center for Military History WWII Online Bookshelves

http://www.army.mil/cmh-pg/online/Bookshelves/WW2-List.htm

Primary documents, including the official U.S. Army Green Books on Okinawa and Guadalcanal, as well as numerous commemorative books and brochures on key individuals and campaigns of the Pacific theater; navigation is tricky, so it is best to consult the full review.

Full Fathom Five: U.S. Submarine War Against Japan

http://www.geocities.com/Pentagon/1592

Features cutaways of different classes of submarines along with patrol reports of several vessels; still under development, but accessible.

Hyperwar: A Hypertext History of the Second World War

http://www.ibiblio.org/hyperwar

A vast collection of primary documents that focus on the history of the American military in World War II, including policy statements, treaties, and official army, navy, and marine corps reports; will eventually include more extensive coverage of the European and China-India-Burma theaters, but for the present emphasizes the war in the Pacific.

Iwo Jima

http://www.iwojima.com/index.cfm

General treatment of the battle for Iwo Jima, including excellent photographs; most interesting feature examines the lives of the six marines featured in Joe Rosenthal's now famous flag-raising photograph.

Kilroy Was Here

http://www.kilroywashere.org

A fascinating look at the origins of one of World War II's most enduring myths: the legend of a super-GI who left his calling card, "Kilroy Was Here," all over the Pacific.

The Merchant Marine in World War II

http://www.usmm.org/ww2.html#anchor252856

Includes accounts of involvement in the invasion of Okinawa and other major engagements in the Pacific; separate chapters document the contribution of women and African Americans.

Navajo Code Talkers Dictionary

http://www.history.navy.mil/faqs/faq12-1.htm

A fascinating glossary of the Navajo alphabet and vocabulary, plus code words for countries, people, ships, and other words and phrases.

Naval Air War in the Pacific

http://www.ixpres.com/ag1caf/navalwar

A collection of photographs and paintings, many from the Navy Historical Center.

Navy Historical Center: World War II

http://www.history.navy.mil/wars/index.html#anchor12058

Information on a wide variety of topics, from the major naval battles of the Pacific, to an emergency appendectomy on board a submarine; includes a smattering of oral histories and some excellent photographs, but few official reports or other primary documents.

The Pacific War: The United States Navy

http://www.microworks.net/pacific

Not an extensive collection of primary documents, but a good overview of the battles, equipment, and personalities who waged war in the Pacific.

World War II in the Pacific

http://www.historyplace.com/unitedstates/pacificwar/index.html

Collection of fifty outstanding photographs, all from the National Archives.

PEARL HARBOR

Pearl Harbor Photo Archive

http://www.ibiblio.org/memory

A must-see collection of 150 photographs and posters from the National Archives that document the attack on Pearl Harbor and the immediate aftermath; includes an image taken during the attack from the cockpit of a Japanese plane.

Pearl Harbor-Radio Broadcasts

http://www.umkc.edu/lib/spec-col/ww2/pearlharbor/ph.htm

Audio versions of broadcasts from a variety of radio stations in the immediate aftermath of the attack at Pearl Harbor; a joint project of the University of Missouri at Kansas City and the Truman Presidential Library.

Pearl Harbor Remembered

http://www.execpc.com/~dschaaf/mainmenu.html

Maps, timelines, video clips, and remembrances from survivors of the attack.

WWII Resources: The Pearl Harbor Attack Hearings

http://www.ibiblio.org/pha/pha/index.html

A portion of one of the most important collections of World War II documents available on the Internet; full text of every congressional hearing and investigation, along with photographs, posters, and related materials.

THE U.S. AND JAPANESE NAVIES

D. L. James' Naval, Maritime, and Aviation Pages

http://www.odyssey.dircon.co.uk/nm.htm

Secondary accounts of the major Pacific engagements; drawn primarily from Samuel Eliot Morison's *History of United States Naval Operations in World War Two*.

Imperial Japanese Navy Page

http://www.combinedfleet.com

A comprehensive collection of maps, images, data, and biographies pertaining to the Japanese navy, the men who commanded it, and the battles waged in the Pacific.

Warships in WW2 Pacific

http://www.cr.nps.gov/history/online_books/butowsky1/index.htm

Not a comprehensive look at every ship in the American Pacific fleet, but useful descriptions of a few ships in each class, including submarines and PTs; from an online book from the National Park Service.

THE ATOMIC BOMB

The A-bomb WWW Museum

http://www.csi.ad.jp/ABOMB/

Created by professors at Hiroshima City University to encourage the pursuit of peace; exhibits include personal accounts of survivors and the experiences of children.

Atomic Bomb: Decision

http://www.dannen.com/decision

Documents on the decision to drop the atomic bomb with an emphasis on the efforts of Leo Szilard and other Manhattan Project scientists to prevent its use; material drawn primarily from the National Archives.

The Decision to Drop the Atomic Bomb

http://www.trumanlibrary.org/whistlestop/study_collections/bomb/large/bomb.htm

Collection of primary documents drawn from the Truman Presidential Library; designed as a teaching tool for advanced high school students.

THE SOLDIERS' STORIES

GENERAL ORAL HISTORY

The Drop Zone Virtual Museum

http://www.thedropzone.org

An extensive collection of oral histories with World War II rangers and airborne personnel, including several German paratroopers; most interviewees saw action in Europe and the Mediterranean and a few fought in the Pacific.

The Rutgers Oral History Archives of World War II

http://fas-history.rutgers.edu/oralhistory/orlhom.htm

The most significant collection of World War II oral histories available on the Internet; more than 200 in-depth, high-quality interviews with prewar and postwar graduates of Rutgers College and the New Jersey College for Women that shed light on virtually every aspect of American life in the 1930s and 1940s, from the Great Depression, to the home front, to battles in Europe and the Pacific.

Tankbooks.com

http://www.tankbooks.com

An archive of more than fifty oral histories and 125 stories; webmaster Aaron Elson began collecting the firsthand accounts after attending a reunion of the 712th Tank Battalion, his late father's unit.

Wartime Memories

http://www.wartimememories.co.uk

Recollections of air raids and evacuations from residents of the United Kingdom; provides a perspective to the war different from that of most Americans.

EUROPEAN/ATLANTIC/MEDITERRANEAN THEATER

"Dad" Rarey's Sketchbook Journals

http://www.rareybird.com

A cartoonist and commercial artist prior to the war, George Rarey documented the exploits of the 379th Fighter Squadron until his death in combat soon after D-Day.

Dad's War: Finding and Telling Your Father's WWII Story

http://members.aol.com/dadswar/index.htm

Created by Wesley Johnson as a tribute to his father, a veteran of the Battle of the Bulge and other European engagements; provides details of Johnson's father's wartime experience and offers recommendations to others interested in their own fathers' histories.

D-Day Account of Chaplain John Burkhalter

http://www.highrock.com/JohnGBurkhalter/D-day.html

One revealing letter written by a chaplain to his wife in which he discusses his belief in God's presence on the beaches of Normandy.

Diaries and Photos of Two German Soldiers

http://www.geipelnet.com

The experiences of two German brothers, one of whom served in the Luftwaffe, the other on the eastern front in a Panzer battalion; provides an interesting juxtaposition with firsthand American accounts of the war.

Interview with an American/Jewish POW in Hitler's Germany

http://militaryhistory.about.com/homework/militaryhistory/library/weekly/aao21301a.htm

A navigator with the 398th Bomb Group of the 8th Air Force, Lt. Aaron Kuptsow was shot down in November 1944 and spent the rest of the war as a POW at Stalag Luft I.

Memoir of James J. Ryan

http://www.geocities.com/Pentagon/Base/2036

An excellent collection of photographs, diary entries, and other accounts of Ryan and the 467th Bomb Group of the 777th Bomb Squadron of the 15th Air Force; shot down in August 1944, Ryan was imprisoned at Stalag Luft III, scene of the "Great Escape" in March 1944.

Memoir of James Waldrop

http://www.geocities.com/Pentagon/Quarters/5173

Another excellent archive of photographs and personal accounts of a member of the 467th Bomb Group of the 777th Bomb Squadron of the 15th Air Force; detailed mission reports enhance an already fine site.

Memoir of Sgt. Albert Panebianco

http://home.nc.rr.com/alpanebianco

A member of the 45th Infantry Division, Panebianco took part in the invasions of Sicily and Italy and helped liberate Dachau.

Memoir of Sgt. William Heller

http://www.warfoto.com

More than 200 outstanding photographs by Heller, who served with the 3rd Infantry Division in North Africa, Sicily, Italy, Southern France, and Germany; combat, the USO, daily life of the soldiers, and generals are all depicted.

Mud and Guts

http://mariposa.yosemite.net/mudnguts/index.htm

Intensely moving letters written from the front, along with the personnel recollections, recorded immediately after the war by Arthur Clayton, who served in Europe with the 103rd Infantry Division.

My Dad Goes To War

http://www.thejucketts.com/ww2.htm

A well-designed account of the activities of Lynn Juckett, who served with the 78th Infantry Division Headquarters in Europe; beautiful graphics and excellent photographs enhance the textual description of Juckett's experiences.

Private Art

http://www.private-art.com

A terrific archive of letters written to and from Private Arthur Pranger of the 86th Chemical Mortar Battalion; correspondents include Pranger's parents, sister, brother, and a friend, all of whom shed light on the conditions on the home front.

A World War II Experience: The Story of Colonel William M. Slayden II at the Battle of the Bulge

http://www.grunts.net/wars/20thcentury/wwii/slayden/slayden.html

A staff officer with the VIII Corps of the U.S. First Army, Slayden provides a calm and measured, yet nonetheless riveting, account of the Battle of the Bulge, including the chaos, death, and destruction at the outset of the German attack in the Ardennes Forest.

PACIFIC THEATER

Frankel-y Speaking About World War II in the South Pacific

http://www.frankel-y.com

An elegantly written online book drawn from the thousands of letters that Stanley Frankel wrote to his future wife and others, including a literary agent, from the South Pacific; with an eye toward future publication, Frankel approached the war as both a participant and observer, completely unprepared for the horrors of war, yet forced to adjust rapidly.

"Highlights of My Army Career": Memoirs of Myron J. Nelson

http://www.geocities.com/Pentagon/Quarters/4667

Short but thoughtful account of daily life in the China-Burma-India theater.

In Hell There Is a Place Called Death's Railway

http://www.angelstation.com/swillner

Text of speech delivered at West Point in 1976 by Stanley Willner, a merchant mariner captured by the Germans, turned over to the Japanese, and imprisoned at the Death's Railway POW camp in Thailand.

A Marine Diary: My Experiences on Guadalcanal

http://www.gnt.net/~jrube/intro.html

A 20-year-old corporal with the 1st Marine Division, J. R. Garrett kept a diary that provides a sense of palpable fear; includes photographs of airplanes, ships, and combat.

To Hell and Back: A Guadalcanal Journal

http://users.erols.com/jd55/guadalcanal.html

An intensely emotive account that draws upon the diary of Private James Donahue of the 1st Marine Division; includes an essay written by his daughter.

Twelve Hundred Days

http://home.attbi.com/~rgrokett/POW/index.html

Russell Grokett was captured at Bataan, forced on the infamous Bataan Death March, and remained a POW for 1,200 days, most of them in a labor camp in Manchuria.

When Victory Is Ours: Letters Home From the South Pacific, 1943–1945

http://www.topshot.com/dh/Victory.html

Letters, photographs, and diary entries written during the war but discovered fifty years later; tells the story of Morris Coppersmith, the commander of a small transport ship.

A World War II Diary in the Pacific

http://www.sinclair.edu/sec/his103/103d01.htm

Contains diary entries kept in 1944–45 by Jack "Weary" McKnight, a sailor on the aircraft carrier USS *Essex;* accompanying film footage shows a kamikaze penetrate the deck of the *Essex* in November 1944.

THE HOME FRONT

GENERAL

American Memory from the Library of Congress

http://rs6.loc.gov/ammem/amhome.html

The most important visual archive of the United States during the Great Depression and World War II; more than 150,000 photographs, 900 of the original 2,000 Works Progress Administration posters, and numerous other items; the sheer size makes navigation difficult, so it is best to consult the full review.

Defense of Americas

http://www.army.mil/cmh-pg/brochures/doa/doa.htm

A 20-page commemorative brochure from the Center for Military History that highlights efforts to defend the home front.

A Long Way Home

http://www.culturalbridge.com/jpyam.htm

Memoir of two Japanese American sisters visiting Japan at the outbreak of the war and unable to return to the United States until the end of the conflict.

A People at War

http://www.archives.gov/exhibit_hall/a_people_at_war/a_people_at_war.html

Textual excerpts, and a few photos, from a National Archives exhibit that highlights the contributions of both civilians and military personnel to the war effort; brief excerpts highlight the roles played by women and minorities, including the Navajo Codetalkers.

The Rutgers Oral History Archives of World War II

http://fas-history.rutgers.edu/oralhistory/orlhom.htm

The most significant collection of World War II oral histories available on the Internet; more than 200 in-depth, high-quality interviews with prewar and postwar graduates of Rutgers College and the New Jersey College for Women shed light on virtually every aspect of American life in the 1930s and 1940s, from the Great Depression, to the home front, to battles in Europe and the Pacific.

U.S. Army Signal Corps Photograph Collection

http://eagle.vsla.edu/signal.corps

More than 3,500 photographs document the arrival and departure of some of the 1.5 million men and women who passed through the embarkation point at Hampton Roads, Virginia; maintained by the Library of Virginia in Richmond.

World War II: The Home Front

http://library.thinkquest.org/15511/index.html

A student project that simulates the lives of five American families from September 1943 to June 1944; a terrific example of creative teaching and learning.

Wright Museum of American Enterprise

http://www.wrightmuseum.org

Great resource of the most popular songs, movies, plays, books, and fads from 1939 to 1945.

INTERNMENT ON THE HOME FRONT — JAPANESE AMERICANS AND POWS

Children of the Camps

http://www.pbs.org/childofcamp/index.html

Transcript of a PBS documentary supplemented with extensive photographs, maps, and other original documents; an excellent introduction to the topic.

Confinement and Ethnicity: An Overview of World War II Japanese-American Relocation Sites

http://www.cr.nps.gov/history/books/gnrlpub.htm

An online book published by the National Park Service; provides extensive information on all ten internment camps as well as a helpful history of key events.

Conscience and the Constitution

http://www.pbs.org/conscience

Letters, photographs, and other original materials document the refusal of a group of young Japanese American men to being drafted into the U.S. Army, the only way out of the internment camps for most of them; includes the full transcript of a PBS documentary.

Documents and Photographs Related to Japanese Relocation During World War II

http://www.archives.gov/research_room/alic/reference_desk/military_resources/japanese_internment.html

A handful of key documents and about twenty photographs designed by the National Archives for classroom use.

Evacuation and Internment of San Francisco Japanese

http://www.sfmuseum.org/1906/ww2.html

Timeline of events surrounding the evacuation of Japanese Americans from the city with a complete set of newspaper articles and a number of photographs.

Japanese American Exhibit and Access Project

http://www.lib.washington.edu/exhibits/harmony/default.htm

A beautifully designed site with a comprehensive overview of the experiences of detainees at Camp Harmony; contains original documents, photographs, drawings, and laws and regulations, as well as children's classroom materials.

Japanese American Internment Camps During World War II

http://www.lib.utah.edu/spc/photo/9066/9066.htm

Collection of photographs drawn from the library at the University of Utah; emphasis on the Tule and Topaz internment camps.

Japanese American National Museum

http://www.janm.org/main.htm

Detailed information, including maps, on each of the ten internment camps; helpful chronology situates World War II and internment within the broader context of the Japanese American experience.

Kriegsgefangen: The German Prisoners of World War II

http://www.kriegsgefangen.de

Translated into occasionally broken English; pictures and text describe life of German POWs held in Camp Farragut, Idaho.

Masumi Hayashi Photography

http://www.csuohio.edu/art_photos

Personally developed by a professor at Cleveland State University; includes internment camp photos, a map, and a unique "family album" section with survivors' personal photos and text describing their experiences.

Race, Racism and the Law

http://www.udayton.edu/~race/02rights/intern01.htm

Limited selection of photos and documents on Japanese internment available on web sites; focus on court cases and legal issues.

The University of Arizona Library

http://www.library.arizona.edu/images/jpamer/wraintro.html

Nicely organized, brief overview of the Poston and Butte internment camps in Arizona.

War Relocation Authority Photographs of Japanese-American Evacuation and Resettlement, 1942–1945

http://www.oac.cdlib.org/dynaweb/ead/calher/jvac

A phenomenal and well-organized archive of more than 7000 photographs from the resettlement and internment camps; taken by War Relocation Authority photographers.

LETTERS FROM THE HOME FRONT

Private Art

http://www.private-art.com

A terrific archive of letters written to and from Private Arthur Pranger of the 86th Chemical Mortar Battalion; correspondents include Pranger's parents, sister, brother, and a friend, all of whom shed light on the conditions on the home front.

PUBLICATIONS AND POSTERS

Dr. Seuss Went To War: A Catalog of Cartoons by Dr. Seuss

http://orpheus.ucsd.edu/speccoll/dspolitic

A stunning archive of 400 war-related editorial cartoons drawn by Theodore Geisel; visitors will immediately recognize the style that later defined Dr. Seuss.

Government Publications from World War II

http://www2.smu.edu/cul/ww2/title.htm

Full text of more than forty official reports concerning conditions on the home front; specific topics include women laborers in war industries, GI Bill benefits, and the return of military personnel to civilian life.

Powers of Persuasion: Poster Art From World War II

http://www.archives.gov/digital_classroom/lessons/powers_of_persuasion/
powers_of_persuasion.html

Thirty-three posters that were part of a National Archives exhibit; topics include the contributions of women and the need for racial solidarity.

Produce For Victory: Posters on the American Home Front, 1941–1945

http://www.americanhistory.si.edu/victory

More than forty prints drawn from a Smithsonian Institution exhibit.

Propaganda Posters

http://www.openstore.com/posters/index.html

Approximately thirty posters drawn primarily from the much larger collection housed at Northwestern University (see World War II Poster Collection).

World War II Poster Collection

http://www.library.nwu.edu/govpub/collections/wwii-posters

Collection of more than three hundred posters issued by an array of U.S. government agencies; easily searchable by date, title, topic, and keyword; housed at the Northwestern University Library.

NEW OPPORTUNITIES—WOMEN AND AFRICAN AMERICANS IN WORLD WAR II

GENERAL

The Rutgers Oral History Archives of World War II

http://fas-history.rutgers.edu/oralhistory/orlhom.htm

The most significant collection of World War II oral histories available on the Internet; more than twenty in-depth, high-quality interviews with prewar and postwar graduates of the New Jersey College for Women provide insight into the experiences of women in the 1930s and 1940s, from the Great Depression to the war.

U.S. Army Signal Corps Photograph Collection

http://eagle.vsla.edu/signal.corps

More than 3,500 photographs document the arrival and departure of some of the 1.5 million men and women who passed through the embarkation point at Hampton Roads, Virginia; maintained by the Library of Virginia in Richmond.

AFRICAN AMERICANS

92nd Infantry Division

http://www.indianamilitary.org/92ndinfdiv/History.htm

A very brief history of the all-black Buffalo Soldiers who fought in Italy.

6888th Postal Battalion

http://www.grunts.net/afamerican/6888th.html

A very brief history of the only unit of black women in the Women's Army Corps; the 6888th delivered mail, drove vehicles, and manned supply rooms in the European theater.

African Americans and the U.S. Navy—World War II

http://www.history.navy.mil/photos/prs-tpic/af-amer/afa-wwii.htm

Several dozen photographs, but no significant text, of blacks at work in the most segregated branch of the military; as a result of limited opportunities, most photographs depict black cooks and mess stewards.

African Americans in World War II

http://www.historyplace.com

A collection of thirty-three photographs depicting all aspects of African American involvement in WWII.

Integration of the Armed Forces

http://www.redstone.army.mil/history/integrate/welcome.html

An extensive chronology of African American participation in World War II, as well as World War II–era film footage that depicts blacks in both positive and negative lights.

Integration of the Armed Forces, 1940–1965

http://www.army.mil/cmh-pg/books/integration/IAF-fm.htm

A massive online book by Morris J. MacGregor; three chapters specifically address the role of blacks in the army, navy, and marines during World War II.

Lest We Forget: African Americans in World War II

http://www.coax.net/people/lwf/ww2.htm

Articles, documents, and general information on the African American experience in World War II, some of it drawn from other sites.

The Men of Montford Point

http://members.aol.com/nubiansong/montford.html

A daughter created this personal web site as a tribute to her father and his segregated company, the first black marines.

The Triple Nickles: The 555th Parachute Infantry Battalion

http://www.triplenickle.com/index.html

The first African American parachute infantry battalion; it was prepared for combat in Europe in 1944 but was sent instead to jump into forest fires in the Pacific Northwest in search of Japanese balloon bombs; later saw combat in Korea; some photos and documents.

The Triple Nickels from the Drop Zone Scrapbook

http://www.thedropzone.org/scrapbook/555photo.html

Small but unique collection of photographs from the 555th Parachute Infantry Division.

Tuskegee Airmen

http://www.coax.net/people/lwf/tus_air.htm

The most celebrated unit of all-black aviators.

WOMEN AT HOME, AT WORK, AND AT WAR

The American War Bride Experience, 1939–1949

http://www.geocities.com/Heartland/Meadows/9710/WarBrides.html

A fairly limited but interesting look at both American-born and foreign-born war brides.

American Women and the Military

http://www.gendergap.com/military/USmil.htm

Short biographies of nurses, several of whom were captured and imprisoned as POWs.

American Women's History: A Research Guide

http://www.mtsu.edu/~kmiddlet/history/women.html

Created by a librarian, this online resource guide contains bibliographies and links to many related sites; excellent resource for teachers and students.

The Coast Guard and the Women's Reserve in World War II

http://www.uscg.mil/hq/g-cp/history/h_wmnres.html

Online article provides good overview of the women known as SPARs (from the Coast Guard motto, Semper Paratus, meaning "Always Ready").

A People at War: Women Who Served

http://www.archives.gov/exhibit_hall/a_people_at_war/a_people_at_war.html

Brief overview from the National Archives of women who served in non-combat missions.

Postergirls of WWII

http://www.geocities.com/queenknuckles/postergirls.htm

Propaganda and recruiting posters aimed at women; primarily from the United States and Great Britain, along with a few from Canada, Germany, and the Soviet Union.

Rosie the Riveter and Other Heroes

http://www.u.arizona.edu/~kari/rosie.htm

Class-assignment that offers an overview on Rosie the Riveter, with some pictures.

United States Air Force Museum: Women Pilots in WWII

http://www.wpafb.af.mil/museum/history/wasp/wasp.htm

Official overview of the Women's Auxiliary Ferrying Squadron (WAFS) and Women Airforce Service Pilots (WASP) programs, plus lists of the women who served and details of their experiences.

United States Merchant Marine

http://www.usmm.org

Brief overview of female merchant mariners.

WASP on the Web

http://www.wasp-wwii.org/wasp/home.htm

Songs, photographs, cartoons, posters, speeches, and interviews that document the experience of more than 2000 Women Airforce Service Pilots (WASP), the first women in American history trained to fly military aircraft.

What Did You Do in the War, Grandma?

http://www.stg.brown.edu/projects/WWII_Women/tocCS.html

More than two dozen excellent interviews with female residents of Rhode Island; begun as a class project at South Kingstown High School.

Women at War: Redstone's WWII Female "Production Soldiers"

http://www.redstone.army.mil/history/women/welcome.html

Photographs and an online article detailing the working experience of white and black women at the Redstone Arsenal in Alabama.

Women Come to the Front

http://www.loc.gov/exhibits/wcf/wcf0001.html

A limited, but worthwhile look at eight female journalists, photographers, and broadcasters; drawn from an exhibit at the Library of Congress.

Women in the United States Army: The Army Nurse Corps

http://www.army.mil/cmh-pg/books/wwii/72-14/72-14.htm

A brief history of the more than 59,000 women who served in the Army Nurse Corps in all theaters of operation and often in the line of fire; published by the Center for Military History.

Women in the United States Army: The Women's Army Corps

http://www.army.mil/cmh-pg/brochures/wac/wac.htm

A brief history of the more than 150,000 women who served in the Women's Army Corps (WAC); not originally considered a part of the army, the women eventually won full benefits, including protections accorded prisoners of war.

Women in the U.S. Navy

http://www.history.navy.mil/faqs/faq48-1.htm

An extensive bibliography of materials relating to women in the navy, along with a handful of oral histories and fifty recruiting posters encouraging women to join Women Accepted for Voluntary Emergency Service (WAVES).

Women in World War II From the National Archives

http://www.nara.gov/nara/searchnail.html

More than 150 photographs, posters, and primary documents from the holdings of the National Archives; see the full review for instructions on navigation, which can be difficult.

THE HOLOCAUST AND WAR CRIMES

THE HOLOCAUST

An Auschwitz Alphabet

http://www.spectacle.org/695/ausch.html

Author Jonathan Wallace uses the alphabet to describe concentration camp experiences; good resource for K–12 classrooms.

Center for Holocaust and Genocide Studies at the University of Minnesota

http://www.chgs/umn.edu

Selection of original photographs, personal recollections, cartoons, posters, and press reports on the Czech ghetto, Theresienstadt, from 1943 to 1945; includes additional material on other aspects of the Holocaust and WWII.

Cybrary

http://www.remember.org

A sprawling site, often difficult to navigate, but nice collection of interviews, photographs, and primary and secondary sources.

Ghetto Fighters' House

http://www.gfh.org/il

A museum site and excellent photographic archive; well sourced and catalogued.

The Holocaust from the Jewish Virtual Library

http://www.us-israel.org/jsource/index.html

Part of a comprehensive site on Jewish history, the chapters on the Holocaust and World War II include photographs, newspaper articles, and government documents as well as secondary information; maintained by the American-Israeli Cooperative Enterprise.

The Holocaust History Project

http://www.holocaust-history.org

A privately run collection of documents, recordings, essays, and some photographs established to combat Holocaust deniers.

Mauthausen Memorial

http://www.mauthausen-memorial.gv.at/engl/index.html

Photographs, maps, and text discuss the history, daily life, and architecture of the only Stage III concentration camp; available in both English and German.

Memorial and Museum of Auschwitz-Birkenau

http://www.auschwitz-muzeum.oswiecim.pl

A textual overview with photographs, maps, and building plans of the camp.

Museum of Tolerance Online

http://www.wiesenthal.com/mot/index.cfm

Contains a massive collection of primary documents, photographs, and other materials relating to the Holocaust and World War II housed at the Simon Wiesenthal Center in Los Angeles; best to consult full review because of difficult-to-navigate organization; index of online archive of photographs located at: http://history1900s.about.com/library/holocaust/aa122299a.htm?iam+ask&terms=german+tokyo+rose.

The Nizkor Project

http://www.nizkor.org

Articles, essays, books, and various primary sources devoted to combating Holocaust denial; affiliated with the League for Human Rights of B'nai Brith Canada.

A Teacher's Guide to the Holocaust

http://fcit.coedu.usf.edu/holocaust/default.htm

A beautifully designed site that incorporates primary documents, photographs, maps, video, music, art, and film; developed by the Florida Center for Instructional Technology.

United States Holocaust Memorial Museum

http://www.ushmm.org

An extensive online archive of text, photographs, personal histories, and audio and video clips that document the history of the Third Reich and the Holocaust.

Yad Vashem Holocaust Memorial Museum

http://www.Yad-vashem.org.il

Excellent photograph collection and curricular units for classroom use; created by Yad Vashem, the official Holocaust Martyrs' and Heroes' Remembrance Authority in Israel.

THE NANKING MASSACRE

Nanking Massacre

http://www.cnd.org/njmassacre

Graphic photographs and primary documents relating to the Nanjing Massacre and other "atrocities committed by the Japanese Army in China during WWII"; maintained by the China News Daily.

The Nanking Massacre

http://www.gotrain.com/dan/nanking1.htm

A brief overview of the Nanjing Massacre and Tokyo War Crimes Trials, with a few photographs; includes bibliography but no primary documents.

SURVIVOR ORAL HISTORIES

Poland's Holocaust: A Family Chronicle of Soviet and Nazi Terror

http://www.geocities.com/CapitolHill/Parliament/6764/intro.html

Letters, memoirs, and personal accounts document one family's fight against Nazi and Soviet terror in eastern Poland.

To Save A Life: Stories of Holocaust Rescue

http://www.humboldt.edu/~rescuers/

Book of interviews with rescuers and the rescued; includes photographs.

Voice Vision: Holocaust Survivor Oral Histories

http://holocaust.umd.umich.edu

Thirteen interviews with Holocaust survivors conducted by Sid Bolkosky of the University of Michigan at Dearborn; more of his 150 interviews are scheduled to appear online soon.

Women and the Holocaust

http://www.interlog.com/~mighty/home.html

Dedicated to the understanding, study, and remembrance of the particular experience of women during the Holocaust; includes a dozen oral histories.

WAR CRIMES

The Avalon Project: The Nuremberg War Crimes Trial

http://www.yale.edu/lawweb/avalon/imt/imt.htm

The complete record of the Nuremberg War Crimes Trial; well organized and beautifully presented.

UNIT HISTORIES

In general, most unit web sites are similar in their sponsorship and types of content. Most sites have been created by veterans, or their children, in conjunction with the unit's veterans' organization. They contain a historical overview of activities during World War II, as well as some combination of photographs, maps, letters, diary entries, personal recollections, unit rosters, and previously published accounts of unit activities. Because these sites tend to be similar, individual descriptions have not been provided in most cases; exceptions have been made where additional information appeared appropriate, such as in identifying segregated units.

GENERAL

Chemical Mortar Battalions

http://www.4point2.org

Individual pages on a number of units; some served in Europe, others in the Pacific.

Grunts.net

http://www.grunts.net

An exhaustive collection of unit histories for all branches of the military; not limited to World War II.

EUROPEAN THEATER

B-24 Liberators
http://users.rlc.net/catfish/liberatorcrew/default.html

Dakota Squadron
http://aztec.asu.edu/dakota/home.html

Darby Rangers
http://www.DarbyRangers.com

"I Am An American": The Story of the Nisei Warriors
http://www.homeofheroes.com/moh/nisei/index.html

A segregated unit of Japanese Americans; enlistment was one of the only means of being released from the internment camps; the most decorated unit in World War II.

Super Sixth: The Story of Patton's 6th Armored Division in WWII
http://members.aol.com/super6th

Trigger Time: 101st Airborne in WW2
http://www.101airborneWW2.com

Tuskegee Airmen
http://www.coax.net/people/lwf/tus_air.htm

The most celebrated unit of all-black aviators.

2nd Armored "Hell on Wheels" Division
http://2ndarmoredhellonwheels.com

7th Engineer Battalion
http://www.7thengineers.org

10th Mountain Division
http://10thMtnDivDesc.org

63rd Infantry Division
http://www.63rdinfdivassn.com

69th Infantry Division
http://www.69th-infantry-division.com

70th Infantry Division: "Trailblazers"
http://www.trailblazersww2.org

92nd Infantry Division
http://www.indianamilitary.org/92ndinfdiv/History.htm

A very brief history of the all-black Buffalo Soldiers who fought in Italy.

104th Infantry Division
http://www.104infdiv.org/index.htm

106th Infantry Division
http://www.mm.com/user/jpk/mindex.htm

225th AAA Searchlight Battalion
http://www.skylighters.org

353rd Fighter Group
http://geocities.com/slybird353

419th Field Artillery Battalion
http://www.419th.com

461st Bomb Group: The Liberaiders
http://www.461st.org

504th Parachute Infantry Regiment
http://www.geocities.com/pentagon/5340

746th Tank Battalion

http://ro.com/~blan

PACIFIC THEATER

Alamo Scouts

http://www.alamoscouts.org

Annals of the Flying Tigers

http://www.danford.net/avg.htm

Legendary aviator Pappy Boyington and the American Volunteer Group flew for the Chinese Air Force in the months prior to Pearl Harbor.

Battleship North Carolina

http://www.battleshipnc.com

The Men of Montford Point

http://members.aol.com/nubiansong/montford.html

Daughter created this personal web site as a tribute to her father and his segregated company, the first black marines.

USS Guam CB2

http://www.ussguam.com

USS Washington

http://www.usswashington.com/index.htm

7th Bomb Group

http://7thbg.org/index.html

504th Bomb Group

http://www.geocities.com/Pentagon/Quarters/3109

SUBMARINES

USS Bowfin

http://www.bowfin.org

USS Cod
http://www.usscod.org

USS Pampanito
http://www.maritime.org/pamphome.shtml

USS Silversides
http://www.sos.state.mi.us/history/preserve/phissite/silversi.html

ABOUT THE AUTHORS

J. Douglas Smith teaches twentieth-century American political and social history at Occidental College in Los Angeles, California. He is the author of *Managing White Supremacy: Race, Politics, and Citizenship in Jim-Crow Virginia* (Chapel Hill, NC, 2002). His work has appeared in *The Washington Post*, the *Virginia Magazine of History and Biography*, and the *Journal of Southern History*.

Richard Jensen is professor emeritus of history at the University of Illinois at Chicago and Research Associate at the National Center for Supercomputer Applications. In 1992 he founded H-Net, the groundbreaking and highly successful web-based book review, information, and scholarly discussion source for the academic community. He has written extensively on using the web for historical research and has conducted computer research training programs all over the world. In addition, he has written a number of articles on World War II. Jensen is a recognized authority on reviewing military history web sites.

ABOUT THE CD

The CD version of *World War II on the Web,* **WWII.pdf,** can be viewed only with **Adobe Acrobat Reader,** which is provided on this CD.

OPENING WWII.PDF IF ACROBAT READER IS INSTALLED ON YOUR COMPUTER

Macintosh: WWII.pdf will open immediately upon placing the CD in your drive.

Windows: There are several ways to open a file on a CD:

1. From the desktop: double click on the hard-drive icon (My Computer), double click on the CD-drive icon, double click on the file named WWII.pdf. Acrobat Reader will launch and the file will open.
2. From the Menu Bar: Go to Start—Find and type in the file name WWII.pdf. Hit Enter when the file is located on the CD drive.
3. From Acrobat Reader: Launch Acrobat Reader. Click on File in the menu bar and select Open. Then locate the file WWII.pdf on the CD in the drive and hit Enter.

OPENING WWII.PDF IF ACROBAT READER IS NOT INSTALLED ON YOUR COMPUTER

Macintosh: double click on the Acrobat Reader Installer icon on the CD and follow the setup instructions.

Windows: There are several ways to install a program from a CD:

1. From the desktop: double click on the hard-drive icon (My Computer), double click on the CD-drive icon, double click on the file named "ar505enu.exe"—this is the Acrobat Installer. The program will launch, and then simply follow the setup instructions.
2. From the Menu Bar: Go to Start—Run—Browse and highlight the CD drive in the drop-down window. The file named "ar505enu.exe" will appear. Double click on the file and proceed as in (1) above.

Acrobat Reader is provided free of charge by Adobe (http://www.adobe.com) and can also be downloaded from their web site at: http://www.adobe.com/products/acrobat/readstep2.html or http://www.adobe.com/products/acrobat/alternate.html

README.PDF

Provided in text, rtf, and pdf formats, this document lists system requirements for using Arobat Reader, describes the interactive features of WWII.pdf, and provides important information for users new to Acrobat Reader. The text and rtf versions can be viewed in WordPad or NotePad (Windows), in SimpleText (Mac), or in your word-processing software. The pdf version can be viewed only in Acrobat Reader.
